Usborne

The
Very Best
Baking Book
for Children

Usborne

The
Very Best
Baking Book
for Children

Fiona Patchett & Abigail Wheatley

Designed by Helen Edmonds, Anna Gould & Mike Olley

Illustrated by Francesca Carabelli, Jessie Eckel, Non Figg,
Nancy Leschnikoff, Mark Ruffle & Molly Sage

Photography by Howard Allman

Recipes & food preparation by Catherine Atkinson, Dagmar Vesely & Maud Eden

Contents

Using this book

This book is full of delicious recipes that anyone can bake. Everything is explained in a clear and simple way, with pictures to show you what you need to do. Once you've got to grips with a few baking basics, you can get cooking!

At the front of the book are pages like this, with basic baking tips and advice about equipment.

Read these pages before you start baking.

The main part of the book is divided into sections, each featuring a different type of recipe.

At the start of each section there's a list of all the recipes in that section.

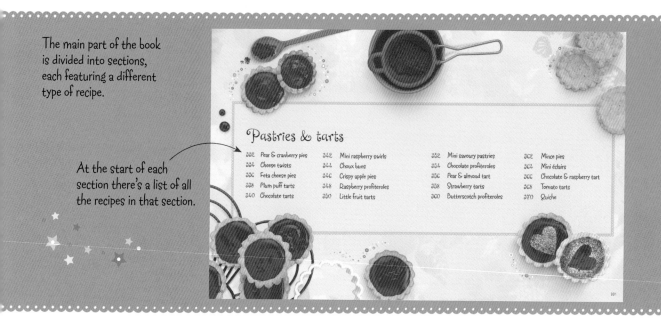

Recipe pages look like this. This dot tells you if there are nuts in a recipe.

The introduction tells you more about the recipe. Sometimes there's allergy information here too.

Boxes like this have ideas for ways to adapt the recipe.

The ingredients and equipment you need are listed here. You can also find out how much the recipe makes.

These steps show you what to do at each stage of the recipe.

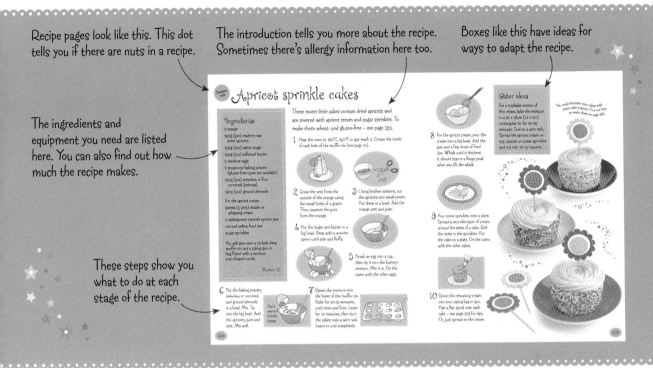

Pages like this at the end of the book tell you more about baking and decorating.

The instructions help you with specific techniques featured in some of the recipes.

Right at the back of the book you'll find allergy advice, which will help you find out which recipes are suitable for those with food allergies, and which recipes can be adapted to make them suitable. There's also an index of all the recipes in the book.

Getting started

The tips on this page will help you to get to grips with some baking basics. It's a good idea to read them before you start cooking.

Before you start

Before you start cooking, read the recipe carefully and check you've got all the ingredients and equipment you need. Then, wash your hands.

Follow the recipe

When you're baking, it's important to do exactly what the recipe says, or it might not turn out quite right. Always measure ingredients accurately and use the size of cake tin the recipe tells you to.

Your oven

All ovens are different – yours may cook things more quickly or slowly than the recipe says. If you're using a fan oven, shorten the cooking time or lower the temperature – the oven manual will help you with this.

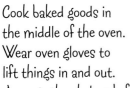

Cook baked goods in the middle of the oven. Wear oven gloves to lift things in and out.
Arrange the shelves before you turn the oven on. Only open the oven door when the cooking time is up, or if you think something is burning.

Butter & margarine

When a recipe says to use softened butter, leave it at room temperature for an hour before you start cooking. Only use margarines that say they are suitable for baking, and avoid 'low fat' types.

Food allergies

If you're cooking for someone with a food allergy or intolerance, this book will help you. Recipes that contain nuts are clearly marked. The ingredients lists show where allergy-free alternatives can be substituted. And on pages 388-393 you can find out which recipes are suitable for those with food allergies.

Weighing and measuring

The recipes show two different types of weights. Use either, but don't swap between them.

Measure small amounts with measuring spoons.

For some ingredients, you only need a pinch – the amount you can pick up between your thumb and first finger.

Baking basics

Greasing & lining tins & trays

For greasing, dip a paper towel into softened butter or cooking oil. Rub it over the inside of the tin or tray.

To line a tin or tray, put it on some baking parchment. Draw around it. Cut out the shape. Put it in the tin or on the tray.

Beating butter & sugar

1 Put the sugar and butter in a big bowl. Stir them together with a wooden spoon.

2 Beat very quickly with the spoon, until the mixture is pale and fluffy.

3 If it's hard to beat, pour hot water into a fresh bowl. Pour it out, dry the bowl, then transfer the mixture to it and try again.

Sifting

1 Put the ingredients in a sieve. Hold it over a bowl. Tap the sieve, so the ingredients fall through.

2 If there are lumps left in the sieve, squash them through with the back of a spoon.

Breaking eggs

Crack the egg sharply on the edge of a cup or bowl. Pull the shell apart, so the white and yolk slide into the cup or bowl. Pick out any bits of shell.

Beating eggs

Beat the yolk and white with a fork, to mix them together well.

Separating eggs

1 Break the egg (see above), but let the white and yolk slide onto a small plate.

2 Cover the yolk with an egg cup. Hold the egg cup. Hold the plate over a bowl. Tip, so the white slides in.

Mixing gently, or 'folding'

1 Use a spatula or a big metal spoon. Move it gently through the mixture, making the shape of a number 8.

2 Stop as soon as everything is mixed together.

Beating egg whites

1 Beat the egg white very quickly with a whisk, until it becomes very thick and foamy.

2 Lift up the whisk. If the foam stays in a floppy point, you have whisked enough. Keep on whisking until it does.

Biscuits & cookies

Tiny pink cookies

Ingredients:

50g (2oz) softened butter

25g (1oz) icing sugar

¼ teaspoon pink or red food dye

1 teaspoon milk

¼ teaspoon vanilla essence

75g (3oz) plain flour

You will also need 2 baking trays and some tiny star and heart cookie cutters.

Makes around 65

These miniature pink cookies are cut out using tiny heart and star cookie cutters – though you could use whatever shape of tiny cutter you like. You could also use another shade of food dye, if you prefer.

1 Heat the oven to 180°C, 350°F or gas mark 4. Use a paper towel to wipe the baking trays with a little cooking oil.

2 Put the butter into a bowl and stir it until it is smooth. Sift the icing sugar into the bowl and stir it in until the mixture is smooth.

3 Add the food dye to the mixture and stir it in until the mixture is pink. Then, add the milk and the vanilla essence.

Cut the shapes close together.

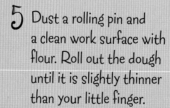

4 Sift the flour into the bowl and stir everything together. Then, use your hands to squeeze the mixture until it comes together in a ball of dough.

5 Dust a rolling pin and a clean work surface with flour. Roll out the dough until it is slightly thinner than your little finger.

6 Use the cutters to cut lots of shapes from the dough. Then, use a spatula to lift the shapes onto the baking trays.

 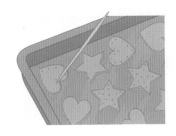 

7 Squeeze the scraps of dough together to make a ball. Roll out the dough again and cut more shapes. Put them onto the trays.

8 Make patterns on some of the cookies by pushing the end of a cocktail stick into them. Don't worry if it goes all the way through.

9 Bake the cookies for 6-8 minutes. Then, take them out of the oven and leave them on the trays until they are cool.

Some of these cookies were dusted with icing sugar when they were cool.

You could put some cookies into a gift box to give as a present.

15

Oat & raisin cookies

1 orange

75g (3oz) raisins

75g (3oz) plain flour

75g (3oz) porridge oats

½ teaspoon of baking powder

50g (2oz) chilled butter

75g (3oz) soft light brown sugar

1 medium egg

You will also need 2 baking trays.

Makes around 20

These sweet oat cookies look rough and chunky, but in fact they're deliciously moist and chewy. This is because the raisins are soaked in orange juice to plump them up, before they're mixed into the cookie dough.

1 Heat the oven to 180°C, 350°F or gas mark 4. Use a paper towel to wipe a little cooking oil over the baking trays.

2 Grate the zest from the outside of the orange, using the small holes of a grater. Put the zest in a small bowl.

3 Cut the orange in half and squeeze the juice from one half. Add 1 tablespoon of the juice to the zest. Put the raisins in too.

4 Put the flour, oats and baking powder in a large bowl. Cut the butter into chunks and put them in too. Rub the butter into the flour (see page 375). Stop when it looks like small breadcrumbs.

5 Add the sugar to the flour mixture and stir it in. Break the egg into a cup and beat it with a fork. Pour the egg, raisins, zest and juice into the large bowl.

These cookies taste delicious eaten while they're still warm, with a glass of cold milk.

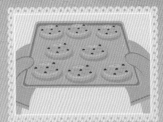

6 Stir everything together. Take heaped teaspoonfuls of the mixture and drop them onto the baking trays, spacing them well apart. Put the trays in the oven.

7 Bake for 12-15 minutes, until the cookies are golden-brown. Take them out of the oven and leave them for a few minutes. Then put them on a wire rack to cool.

Other flavours

For oat and seed cookies, use just 50g (2oz) raisins and add 25g (1oz) sesame and 25g (1oz) sunflower seeds to the cookie mixture in step 5. Seeds may not be suitable for those with nut allergies.

For oat, lemon and white chocolate cookies, replace the orange with 1 lemon and leave out the raisins. In step 5, add 75g (3oz) white chocolate chips.

Chocolate-dipped shortbread

Ingredients:

150g (5oz) plain flour

25g (1oz) ground rice or rice flour

100g (4oz) butter

50g (2oz) caster sugar

100g (4oz) white chocolate

You will also need a 20cm (8in) round cake tin and a heatproof bowl that fits snugly in a saucepan.

Makes 8 wedges

This recipe is for plain shortbread baked in a round tin and cut into traditional, wedge-shaped pieces. The pieces are then dipped in melted white chocolate – but you could use plain or milk chocolate, if you prefer.

1 Heat the oven to 150°C, 300°F or gas mark 2. Grease and line the tin (see page 10). Mix the flour and ground rice in a large bowl.

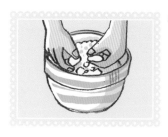

2 Cut the butter into chunks. Rub it into the flour until the mixture looks like fine breadcrumbs. Stir in the sugar.

3 Squeeze the mixture into a ball. The heat from your hands makes the dough stick together.

4 Press the mixture into the tin with your fingers. Use the back of a spoon to smooth the top and make it level.

5 Use the pointed end of a fork to press a pattern of dots all around the edge. Then, cut across the mixture to make 8 equal pieces.

6 Bake for 30 minutes until golden. Leave in the tin for 5 minutes. Then cut across it again and put the pieces on a wire rack to cool.

7 Break up the chocolate and put it in the heatproof bowl. Fill the pan a quarter full with water and heat it until the water bubbles. Take the pan off the heat.

8 Wearing oven gloves, lower the bowl into the pan. Stir until the chocolate melts. Wearing oven gloves, lift the bowl out of the pan.

9 Dip the shortbread into the chocolate, then put it onto a sheet of baking parchment on a plate. Refrigerate for 20 minutes, or until the chocolate has set.

For a festive look, decorate your shortbread with bought sugar stars.

Sparkly star biscuits

Ingredients:

3 tablespoons caster sugar

pink food dye

75g (3oz) softened butter

1 small lemon

25g (1oz) soft light brown sugar

3 tablespoons runny honey

1 medium egg

175g (6oz) plain flour

You will also need 2 baking trays and medium and small star cutters.

Makes 20

These pretty star-shaped biscuits have cut-out middles and a sparkly finish, made by sprinkling them with pink-tinted caster sugar before you put them in the oven.

1 Use a paper towel to wipe a little cooking oil over the baking trays.

2 Put the caster sugar into a bowl, then add a few drops of food dye. Stir the sugar until it is pink. Then, spread it on a plate to dry.

3 Put the butter into a large bowl and stir it until it is fluffy. Grate the zest from the outside of the lemon. Put the zest in the bowl, too.

Use the small holes of a grater.

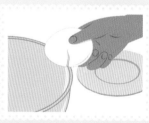

Keep the egg white for later.

4 Put the brown sugar and honey in the bowl. Stir everything well with a wooden spoon, until the mixture is smooth.

5 Carefully break the egg on the edge of a bowl. Pour the egg carefully onto a saucer, so the yolk doesn't break.

6 Put an egg cup over the yolk. Tip the saucer so that the egg white dribbles into a bowl. Then, stir the yolk into the butter mixture.

7 Sift the flour over the butter mixture. Stir it in, then squeeze the mixture into a flattened ball. Wrap it in plastic food wrap.

8 Put the dough in a fridge for 30 minutes. Meanwhile, heat the oven to 180°C, 350°F or gas mark 4. Then, dust a clean work surface and a rolling pin with a little flour.

Cut the stars close together.

9 Roll out the dough until it is slightly thinner than your little finger. Then, use the medium cutter to cut out lots of shapes.

10 Use the small cutter to cut a star from the middle of each biscuit. Press the scraps into a ball, roll it out and cut out more stars.

11 Brush a little egg white over each star and sprinkle some of the pink sugar on top. Use a spatula to lift the stars onto the baking trays.

12 Bake the biscuits for 8-10 minutes, until they are golden. Leave them on the trays for 2 minutes, then lift them onto a wire rack to cool.

Stripey biscuits

Ingredients:

For the vanilla dough:

25g (1oz) icing sugar

50g (2oz) softened butter

3 rounded tablespoons plain flour

1 teaspoon milk

1 teaspoon vanilla essence

For the chocolate dough:

25g (1oz) icing sugar

1 tablespoon cocoa powder

50g (2oz) softened butter

3 rounded tablespoons plain flour

2 teaspoons milk

For the mint dough:

25g (1oz) icing sugar

50g (2oz) softened butter

1 teaspoon peppermint essence

¼ teaspoon green food dye

3 rounded tablespoons plain flour

½ teaspoon milk

You will also need 2 baking trays.

Makes around 25

These little square biscuits have stripes made from vanilla, chocolate and mint dough. You roll out the dough and then stack and slice it to make the stripes.

1 For the vanilla dough, sift the icing sugar into a bowl. Add the butter. Beat until smooth. Sift on the flour and add the milk and vanilla. Mix.

2 For the chocolate dough, sift the icing sugar and cocoa into a bowl. Add the butter. Beat until smooth. Sift on the flour, add the milk and mix.

3 For the mint dough, sift the icing sugar into a bowl. Add the butter, peppermint essence and food dye. Beat until smooth. Sift on the flour and add the milk. Mix.

4 Use your hands to pat, squeeze and roll each of the mixtures into a log shape around 8cm (3in) long. Wrap them in plastic food wrap. Put them in the fridge for 30 minutes.

5 Sprinkle flour on a clean work surface and a rolling pin. Roll the rolling pin over one of the logs, to make a rectangle around 8cm (3in) wide and 15cm (6in) long.

6 Roll out the other two logs in the same way. Brush a little water over one strip of dough. Lift another strip on top. Brush it with water, then lift on the third strip.

7 Cut off any wavy edges. Cut the stack in half lengthways, like this. Brush the top of one stack with water. Lift the other stack on top and pat it gently so it sticks on.

8 Very gently, wrap the dough in plastic food wrap and put it on a tray. Put it in the fridge to chill for 30 minutes.

9 Heat the oven to 180°C, 350°F or gas mark 4. Grease the baking trays (see page 10).

10 Unwrap the dough. Using a sharp knife, cut it into ½cm (¼in) slices. Put the slices on the baking trays.

11 Bake for 12-15 minutes. Leave the biscuits for 2 minutes to cool a little, then use a spatula to move them to a wire rack, to cool completely.

Chocolate & cherry cookies

Ingredients:

75g (3oz) softened butter
75g (3oz) caster sugar
75g (3oz) soft light brown sugar
1 medium egg
1 teaspoon vanilla essence
175g (6oz) plain flour
½ teaspoon baking powder
50g (2oz) dried cherries
100g (4oz) milk chocolate chips

You will also need 2 baking trays.

Makes around 24

These soft cookies are made from vanilla cookie dough flavoured with dried cherries and milk chocolate chips. It's a delicious combination, but you could try other flavours such as white chocolate chips with dried cranberries, or plain chocolate chips with chopped, ready-to-eat dried apricots.

1 Heat the oven to 180°C, 350°F or gas mark 4. Use a paper towel to wipe a little oil over the baking trays.

2 Put the butter and both types of sugar into a large mixing bowl. Stir until the mixture is smooth. Break the egg into a small bowl and beat it well with a fork.

3 Add the vanilla essence to the egg and mix it in. Then, add the egg mixture to the large bowl, a little at a time, stirring well each time.

4 Sift the flour and baking powder into the bowl. Stir the mixture until it is smooth. Cut the cherries in half and add them to the mixture too.

Space the spoonfuls out well.

5 Add roughly half the chocolate chips to the mixture and stir them in well. Then, put heaped teaspoonfuls of the mixture onto the baking trays.

24

6 Carry on until all the mixture is used up. Flatten each cookie with the back of a fork and sprinkle them with the remaining chocolate chips.

7 Bake the cookies for 10 minutes until golden-brown. Leave on the trays for a few minutes. Use a spatula to lift them onto a wire rack to cool.

Bright flower biscuits

Ingredients:

50g (2oz) softened butter or margarine

50g (2oz) caster sugar

1 medium egg

2 teaspoons milk or water

125g (4½oz) plain flour

15g (½oz) cornflour

around 12 see-through boiled sweets

You will also need a baking tray, medium-sized flower cutters and small round or flower cutters. If you're planning to hang up your biscuits, you will also need a wide drinking straw and some ribbon.

Makes around 12

These flower-shaped biscuits have see-through middles made from bright boiled sweets. You can hang them up for special occasions or parties.

Use the white in the recipes on pages 148-165.

1 Heat the oven to 180°C, 350°F or gas mark 4. Line the baking tray (page 10). Put the butter or margarine and sugar in a big bowl. Beat until smooth.

2 Separate the egg, following the instructions on page 11. Mix the yolk into the butter and sugar mixture.

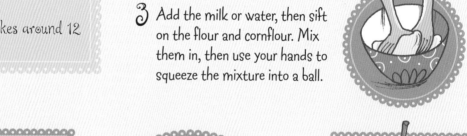

3 Add the milk or water, then sift on the flour and cornflour. Mix them in, then use your hands to squeeze the mixture into a ball.

4 Dust a clean work surface and rolling pin with a little flour. Roll out the dough until it's as thick as your little finger.

5 Use the medium-sized cutters to cut out lots of shapes. Use a spatula to lift the shapes onto the tray.

6 If you want to hang up your biscuits, make a hole near the edge of each shape by pressing the straw through it, like this.

You could decorate your biscuits with writing icing.

7 Use the small cutters to cut a hole in the middle of each shape. Squeeze the scraps together, roll them out again and make more biscuits.

If you hang up your biscuits, don't eat them afterwards, as they might be dirty.

8 Take a sweet. Leave it in its wrapper. Put it on a board. Cover it with a tea towel. Hit it with the rolling pin, to crush it into pieces. Take off the tea towel. Remove the wrapper.

9 Put some pieces of sweet in the hole in the middle of a biscuit. Fill it to the top. Crush more sweets, one at a time, and put the pieces in the holes, until all the biscuits are full.

10 Bake for 12 minutes. Leave on the tray until completely cold. To hang them up, push a loop of ribbon through a hole. Push the ends of the ribbon through the loop and pull.

Orange shortbread stars

These shortbread biscuits are flavoured with orange zest, although you could leave this out if you want to make plain shortbread. If you don't have a star cutter, use any other shape of large cutter instead.

1 Heat the oven to 170°C, 325°F or gas mark 3. Grease the baking trays (see page 10). Sift the flour into a big bowl.

2 Sift the semolina or ground rice into the bowl too. Cut the butter into chunks and put them in the bowl. Stir with a wooden spoon, to coat the butter with flour.

3 Rub the butter and flour between your fingertips and thumbs, following the instructions on page 375. Carry on until the mixture looks like fine breadcrumbs.

4 Grate the zest from the outside of the orange, using the small holes of a grater. Add the zest and the sugar to the mixture in the bowl.

5 Cut the orange in half and squeeze the juice from one half. Sprinkle 2 teaspoons of the juice into the bowl, then stir everything together.

6 Holding the bowl in one hand, use your other hand to squeeze the dough into a ball. The heat from your hand will make the dough stick together.

7 Sprinkle some flour onto a clean work surface and onto a rolling pin. Put the dough onto the work surface and roll it out until it is half as thick as your little finger.

To make dots like these, poke a cocktail stick into the biscuits before you bake them.

8 Use the cutter to cut out lots of star shapes. Use a spatula to lift them onto the baking trays. Squeeze the scraps into a ball.

9 Roll out the dough and cut out more stars. Bake for 12-15 minutes. Leave for 2 minutes, then lift the biscuits onto a wire rack to cool.

Mini chocolate chip cookies

Ingredients:

1 large lemon

75g (3oz) softened butter or margarine

75g (3oz) caster sugar

75g (3oz) soft light brown sugar

1 medium egg

175g (6oz) plain flour

½ teaspoon baking powder

150g (5oz) white chocolate chips

For decorating:

100g (4oz) white chocolate

You will also need 2 baking trays.

Makes around 40

These little cookies have lemon dough and white chocolate chips, but you can make classic chocolate chip and other flavours – see the opposite page.

Use the small holes.

1 Heat the oven to 180°C, 350°F or gas mark 4. Grease the baking trays (see page 10). Grate the zest from the outside of the lemon. Then, squeeze the juice from half the lemon.

2 Put the lemon zest, butter or margarine, caster sugar and soft light brown sugar in a big bowl. Beat them until the mixture is smooth.

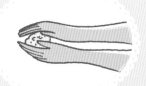

3 Break the egg into a small bowl. Beat with a fork. Add it to the big bowl a little at a time, beating well each time. Add 1 teaspoon of lemon juice and mix that in, too.

4 Sift the flour and baking powder into the bowl. Stir the mixture until it is smooth. Add the white chocolate chips and stir them in.

5 Take a half teaspoon of the mixture and use your hands to roll it into a ball. Put the ball of dough on a tray and flatten it slightly.

6 Make more cookies in the same way with the rest of the mixture. Bake for 10 minutes, until golden. Leave the cookies on the trays for a few minutes.

7 Use a spatula to lift the cookies onto a wire rack to cool. When they have cooled, melt the white chocolate and drizzle it over them (see page 381).

Other flavours

For classic chocolate chip cookies, leave out the lemon and use plain or milk chocolate chips. At step 3, add 1 teaspoon vanilla essence instead of the lemon juice.

Instead of the lemon, you could use 1 orange or 2 limes.

For chocolate cookie dough, use just 150g (5oz) flour, then sift in 4 tablespoons cocoa powder with the flour in step 4.

Contains nuts

Chocolate florentines

Ingredients:

8 glacé cherries

25g (1oz) butter

25g (1oz) demerara sugar

25g (1oz) golden syrup

25g (1oz) plain flour

40g (1½oz) mixed candied peel

40g (1½oz) flaked almonds

75g (3oz) plain chocolate

You will also need 2 baking trays and a heatproof bowl that fits snugly in a saucepan.

Makes around 12

These biscuits can be varied by using different fruits and nuts. You could use different coloured glacé cherries or tropical glacé fruits, but keep the total weight of the fruit and nuts the same.

1 Heat the oven to 180°C, 350°F or gas mark 4. Grease and line the baking trays (see page 10). Put the cherries on a chopping board. Cut them into quarters.

2 Put the butter, sugar and syrup in a pan. Gently heat the ingredients until everything has just melted. Take the pan off the heat.

Space the spoonfuls out well.

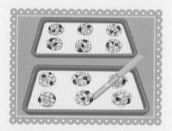

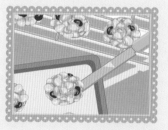

3 Add the flour, cherries, candied peel and almonds to the pan. Mix well. Spoon teaspoonfuls of the mixture onto the baking trays.

4 Bake for 10 minutes until deep golden. Use a blunt knife to push in any wavy edges. Leave to cool for 2 minutes.

5 Lift the florentines onto a cooling rack. Then, fill a pan around a quarter full with water. Heat until the water bubbles. Take the pan off the heat.

Wear oven gloves.

6 Break up the chocolate. Put it in the heatproof bowl. Carefully put the bowl in the pan. Stir the chocolate until it has melted. Take the bowl out of the pan.

7 Use a teaspoon to spread melted chocolate over the flat base of each florentine. Then, use a fork to make zig-zag patterns in the chocolate.

Space them out well.

8 Cover a board or plate with baking parchment. Arrange the florentines on it, with the chocolate side up. Wait until the chocolate sets before you eat them.

Cinnamon shortbread fingers

Ingredients:

175g (6oz) plain flour

50g (2oz) rice flour or ground rice

1 teaspoon ground cinnamon

1 pinch ground nutmeg

125g (4½oz) butter

65g (2½oz) caster sugar

For the topping:

1 tablespoon caster sugar

100g (4oz) plain, milk or
white chocolate

You will also need a 20cm (8in)
square cake tin and a tray.

Makes 24

These chocolate-drizzled shortbread fingers are gently spiced with cinnamon and nutmeg. If you prefer plain shortbread, just leave out the spices.

1 Heat the oven to 150°C, 300°F or gas mark 2. Grease and line the tin (see page 10).

2 Sift the flour, rice flour, cinnamon and nutmeg into a big bowl. Cut the butter into chunks. Stir them into the flour mixture, to coat them with flour.

3 Use the tips of your fingers and thumbs to rub the butte into the flour, following the instructions on page 375. Sto when the mixture looks like small breadcrumbs.

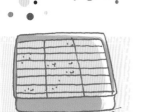

4 Stir in the sugar. Then, use your hands to squeeze the dough, so it sticks together. Don't worry if there are a few loose crumbs.

5 Tip all the mixture into the cake tin. Use your fingers to push it into the corners and press it all down firmly. Level the top with the back of a spoon.

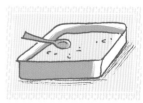

6 Mark 2 lines across the shortbread. Mark 7 lines in the other direction, to make 24 fingers. Bake for 35 minutes, until golden. Scatter over the caster sugar for the topping.

7 Leave in the tin for 5 minutes. Then cut the shortbread into 24 fingers, following the marks you made earlier. Cool for 5 more minutes, then move the fingers carefully to a wire rack to cool.

8 Line a tray with baking parchment (see page 10). When the fingers are cold, melt the chocolate (see page 380). Wearing oven gloves, take the bowl out of the pan.

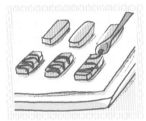

9 Arrange the shortbread fingers on the tray, spacing them out well. Drizzle over the chocolate, following the instructions on page 381.

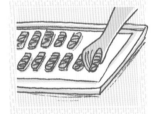

10 Put the tray in the fridge for 15 minutes. The chocolate will set firm. Then, peel the fingers off the parchment.

Other flavours and ideas

To make lemon shortbread, leave out the spices. Add the finely grated zest of 1 lemon with the sugar in step 4.

For gluten-free shortbread, simply replace the flour with gluten-free flour.

Crunchy peanut cookies

Ingredients:

1 medium egg

100g (4oz) softened, unsalted butter

100g (4oz) soft light brown sugar

100g (4oz) crunchy peanut butter

150g (5oz) self-raising flour

½ teaspoon baking powder

50g (2oz) crispy rice cereal

You will also need 2 baking trays.

Makes around 20

These sweet and nutty cookies are made from peanut butter and crispy rice cereal. They are delicious eaten with a cup of hot chocolate.

1 Heat the oven to 190°C, 375°F or gas mark 5. Use a paper towel to wipe a little oil over two baking trays. Break the egg into a small bowl and beat it well with a fork.

2 Put the butter and sugar into a bowl. Beat them until they are creamy. Add the egg a little at a time. Beat the mixture after each addition, to stop it getting lumpy.

3 Add the peanut butter to the mixture and beat it until it is well mixed in. Then, sift the flour and baking powder over the mixture. Stir everything together.

4 Put the crispy rice cereal on a plate. Scoop up a heaped teaspoon of the mixture. Roll it into a ball with your hands. Put it on the cereal.

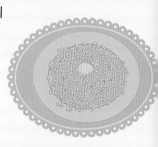

Space the balls of mixture out well.

5 Roll the mixture in the cereal to cover it. Flatten it slightly and put it on one of the baking trays. Make more balls and put them on the trays.

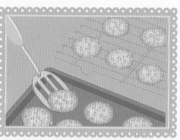

6 Bake the cookies for 20 minutes. Leave them on the baking trays for 5 minutes. Then, use a spatula to lift them onto a wire rack to cool.

Hot chocolate

To make 4 cups of hot chocolate, put 450ml (¾ pint) milk in a saucepan. Add 100g (4oz) plain chocolate, broken into pieces. Heat gently, stirring, until the chocolate melts into the milk.

You could put your cookies in a pretty box to give as a present.

You could top your hot chocolate with a little whipped cream.

37

Chocolate orange cookies

Ingredients:

1 orange

75g (3oz) softened butter or margarine

75g (3oz) caster sugar

75g (3oz) soft light brown sugar

1 medium egg

1 teaspoon vanilla essence

150g (5oz) plain flour

½ teaspoon baking powder

4 tablespoons cocoa powder

150g (5oz) plain, milk or white chocolate chips

You will also need 2 baking trays.

Makes around 24

These chocolate cookies are flavoured with orange zest and packed with chocolate chips – or you could use orange sugar-coated chocolate beans.

1 Heat the oven to 180°C, 350°F or gas mark 4. Grease the baking trays (see page 10). Grate the zest from the outside of the orange, using the small holes of a grater.

2 Put the butter or margarine, both types of sugar and the orange zest in a big bowl. Beat them until the mixture is smooth.

3 Break the egg into a small bowl. Add the vanilla and beat with a fork. Add it to the big bowl a little at a time, beating well each time.

4 Sift the flour, baking powder and cocoa powder into the bowl. Stir the mixture until it is smooth. Add 100g (4oz) of the chocolate chips and stir them in.

5 Take a heaped teaspoon of the mixture and use your hands to roll it into a ball.

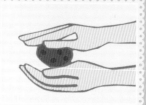

6 Put the ball of dough on the tray and flatten it slightly. Make more cookies with the rest of the mixture. Scatter the rest of the chocolate chips over the cookies and press them on, gently.

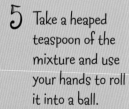

7 Bake for 10 minutes. Leave the cookies on the trays for a few minutes, then use a spatula to lift them onto a wire rack to cool.

Other flavours

Replace the chocolate chips with orange chocolate chunks, made by breaking 150g (5oz) orange chocolate into pieces, then cutting them into small chunks with a sharp knife.

For plain choc chip cookies, just leave out the orange zest.

For lemon or lime chocolate cookies, use 1 large lemon or 2 limes instead of the orange.

Lebkuchen

Contains nuts

Ingredients:

65g (2½oz) plain flour

½ teaspoon baking powder

½ teaspoon cinnamon

1 teaspoon ground mixed spice

75g (3oz) soft light brown sugar

50g (2oz) ground almonds

2 medium eggs

3 soft dates

50g (2oz) marzipan

3 tablespoons smooth apricot jam

50g (2oz) chopped mixed peel

100g (4oz) whole blanched almonds

For the icing:

25g (1oz) icing sugar

You will also need 2 baking trays.

Makes around 12

Lebkuchen are biscuits that originated in Germany. They have a soft, chewy texture and a spicy flavour. These lebkuchen are topped with almonds and a sugar glaze that's so thin you can hardly see it.

1 Put the flour, baking powder, cinnamon and mixed spice in a large bowl. Stir in the sugar and ground almonds.

2 Break the eggs into a cup or a small bowl and beat them with a fork. Cut the dates in half. Take out the stones, if there are any.

3 Put the dates in another large bowl and mash them with a fork. Mix 1 tablespoon of egg into the dates.

4 Crumble the marzipan into the date mixture. Add the jam and mash everything together.

5 Stir in the rest of the beaten egg, a little at a time. Add the mixed peel and the flour mixture. Mix everything together well.

6 Cover the bowl with plastic food wrap and put it in the fridge for 30 minutes. Heat the oven to 160°C, 325°F or gas mark 3.

Space them well apart.

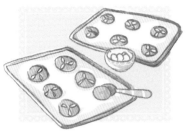

7 Line the baking trays (see page 10).
Use a dessertspoon to drop round
blobs of the mixture onto the trays.
Arrange 3 almonds on top of each blob.

8 Bake for 15 minutes, or until
lightly browned. Leave on the trays
for 5 minutes, then put on a wire
rack to cool.

9 For the icing, sift the icing
sugar into a bowl. Stir in 2
teaspoons of water. Brush the
mixture over the biscuits.

Other flavours

Instead of the icing glaze, you
could drizzle your lebkuchen with
25g (1oz) melted plain chocolate –
see page 380.

Lemon spiral biscuits

To make these pretty, lemony biscuits, you roll together a layer of pink dough and a layer of white dough. Then, you cut the roll into slices to make biscuits with a spiral pattern.

1 Grease the baking trays (see page 10). Then, sift the icing sugar into a large bowl. Add the butter and mix it in until the mixture is smooth.

2 Grate the zest from the outside of a lemon. Put the zest in the bowl. Sift the flour over the mixture and stir it in. Stir in the milk, too.

Use the small holes.

3 Put half the mixture into another bowl. Drop a few drops of pink food dye into one of the bowls. Mix it in until the mixture is completely pink.

4 Squeeze each mixture to make two balls of dough. Flatten each one a little and wrap them in plastic food wrap. Put the dough in the fridge for 30 minutes to chill.

5 Sprinkle a little flour onto a clean work surface and a rolling pin. Roll out the plain dough until it is around 25 x 15cm (10 x 6in) wide and 5mm (¼in) thick.

6 Roll out the pink dough until it is around the same size. Brush the plain dough with a little water. Carefully lift the pink dough onto the plain dough.

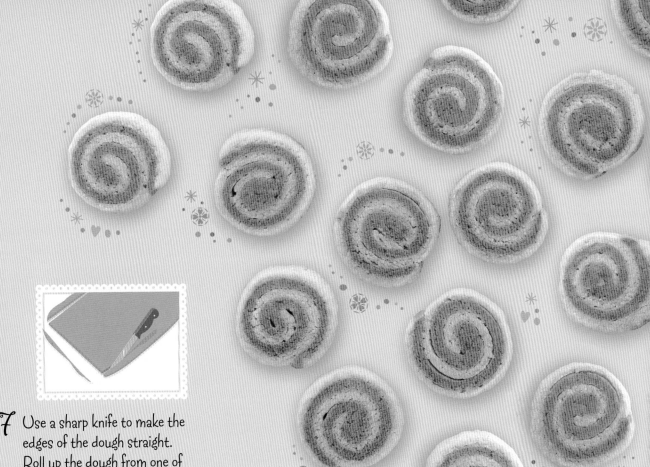

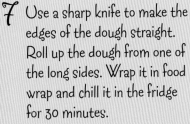

7 Use a sharp knife to make the edges of the dough straight. Roll up the dough from one of the long sides. Wrap it in food wrap and chill it in the fridge for 30 minutes.

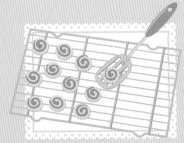

8 Heat the oven to 180°C, 350°F or gas mark 4. Take the dough out of the fridge. Then, cut the dough into 5mm (¼in) slices and put them on the baking trays.

9 Bake the biscuits for 12-15 minutes. Leave them on the baking trays for two minutes. Then, use a spatula to lift them onto a wire rack to cool.

Other flavours

Instead of the lemon zest, you could use the zest of 1 orange or 2 limes. If you prefer, you can use other shades of food dye – orange would be good for biscuits made with orange zest.

Iced biscuits & cookies

Cookie Jar

Daisy biscuits

Ingredients:

75g (3oz) icing sugar
150g (5oz) softened butter
1 lemon
225g (8oz) plain flour

For decorating:
writing icing
small sweets

You will also need 2 baking trays and
a small flower-shaped cutter.

Makes around 30

This recipe is for little lemony biscuits cut into flower
shapes and decorated with writing icing and sweets.
If you'd prefer to make your biscuits orange or lime
flavoured instead, simply use 1 orange or 2 limes
instead of the lemon.

1 Use a paper towel to wipe a little cooking oil over the baking trays

2 Sift the icing sugar into
a large bowl. Add the
butter and mix everything
together with a spoon until
the mixture is smooth.

3 Grate the zest from the
outside of the lemon using
the small holes of a grater.
Put the zest in the bowl and
mix everything together.

4 Cut the lemon in half and
squeeze the juice from it. Then,
stir 1 tablespoon of the lemon
juice into the mixture in the bowl.

5 Sift the flour into the bowl. Mix
until everything comes together
in a ball. Flatten the ball slightly.
Wrap it in plastic food wrap.

6 Put the dough in a fridge for
30 minutes to chill. Then,
sprinkle some flour onto a clean
work surface and a rolling pin.

7 Heat the oven to 180°C, 350°F or gas mark 4. Then, roll out the dough until it is half as thick as your little finger. Cut out lots of flower shapes, using the cutter.

8 Put the flower shapes onto the baking sheets. Squeeze the scraps into a ball, then roll it out again and cut out more shapes.

9 Bake for 15 minutes, until the biscuits are lightly browned. Leave them on the trays for 2 minutes, then put them on a wire rack to cool.

10 When the biscuits are cold, decorate them with icing. Draw lines, swirls and dots. Press sweets into the middle of the icing.

Festive cookies

Ingredients:

125g (4½oz) softened butter or margarine

50g (2oz) icing sugar

1 medium egg

1 teaspoon vanilla essence

225g (8oz) plain flour

For decorating:

225g (8oz) icing sugar

sugar sprinkles

You will also need 2 baking trays and some shaped cutters.

Makes around 35

These spinkle-covered vanilla cookies look festive if you make them using wintery cookie cutters, but you could use any other shape of cookie cutter you like.

1 Grease the baking trays (see page 10). Put the butter or margarine in a big bowl. Beat it until it is smooth. Sift in the icing sugar. Beat again.

2 Break the egg into a small bowl. Add the vanilla extract and beat them together well with a fork.

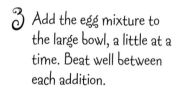

3 Add the egg mixture to the large bowl, a little at a time. Beat well between each addition.

4 Add the flour and stir the mixture until it starts to come together. Then, use your hands to squeeze it into a ball. Flatten the ball slightly.

5 Wrap the dough in plastic food wrap and put it in the fridge for 30 minutes. Heat the oven to 180°C, 350°F or gas mark 4.

6 Dust a surface and a rolling pin with flour. Unwrap the dough and put it on the surface. Roll it out until it is just thinner than your little finger. Use the cutters to cut out lots of shapes.

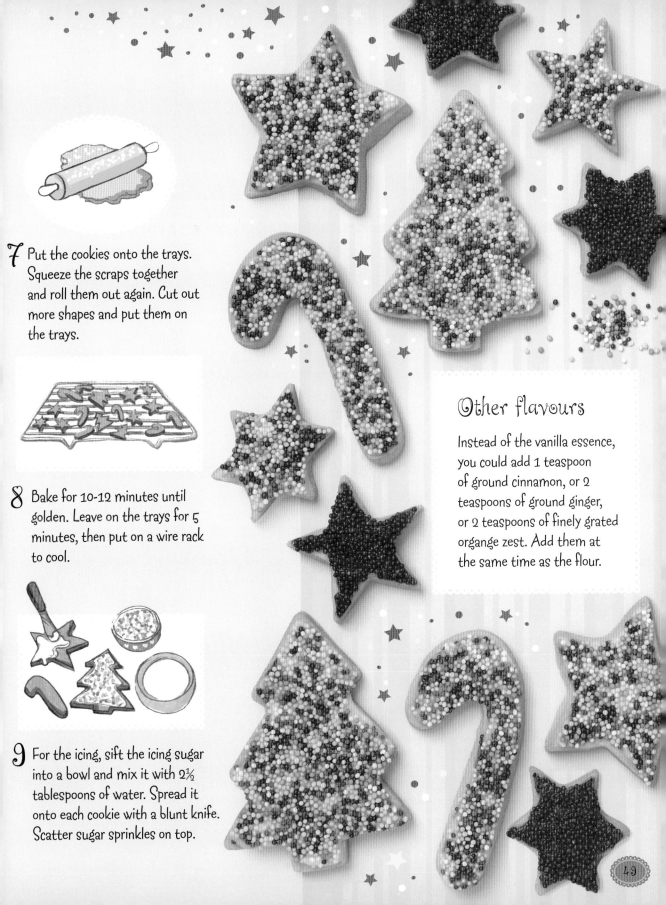

7 Put the cookies onto the trays. Squeeze the scraps together and roll them out again. Cut out more shapes and put them on the trays.

8 Bake for 10-12 minutes until golden. Leave on the trays for 5 minutes, then put on a wire rack to cool.

9 For the icing, sift the icing sugar into a bowl and mix it with 2½ tablespoons of water. Spread it onto each cookie with a blunt knife. Scatter sugar sprinkles on top.

Other flavours

Instead of the vanilla essence, you could add 1 teaspoon of ground cinnamon, or 2 teaspoons of ground ginger, or 2 teaspoons of finely grated organge zest. Add them at the same time as the flour.

49

Iced lemon biscuits

These lemon biscuits have a crisp, buttery texture. You could cover them with lemon icing and decorate them with yellow and white writing icing and sweets.

Ingredients:

For the biscuits:

1 medium lemon

125g (4½oz) plain flour

50g (2oz) icing sugar

1 medium egg

100g (4oz) softened butter

For the lemon icing:

200g (7oz) icing sugar

3 tablespoons lemon juice

yellow food dye

For decorating:

white and yellow writing icing

white and yellow sweets

You will also need a 4cm (1⅛in) round cutter and 2 baking trays.

Makes around 30

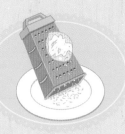

1 Grease the baking trays (see page 10). Grate the zest from the outside of the lemon, using the small holes of a grater.

2 Sift the flour and icing sugar into a big bowl and stir in the lemon zest. Cut the lemon in half and squeeze the juice into a small bowl.

You don't need the egg white –
use it in the recipes on pages 148-165.

3 Break the egg onto a plate. Hold an egg cup over the yolk and tip the saucer over a bowl, so the egg white slides off. Add the yolk to the mixture in the big bowl.

4 Add the butter and 1 tablespoon of lemon juice. Stir until you have a smooth mixture. Scoop the mixture into a ball with your hands and flatten it slightly.

5 Wrap the dough in plastic food wrap and put it in the fridge to chill for 30 minutes. While the dough is chilling, heat the oven to 190°C, 375°F or gas mark 5.

6 Dust a clean work surface and a rolling pin with flour. Unwrap the dough. Roll out the dough until it is half as thick as your little finger.

7 Use the cutter to cut out lots of circles, then lift the circles onto the baking trays. Squeeze the scraps of dough into a ball and roll it out again.

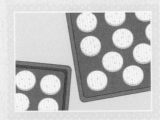

8 Cut out more circles and put them on the trays. Bake for 8-10 minutes until the biscuits are golden. Then, take them out of the oven.

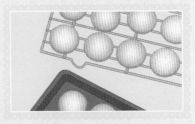

9 Leave the biscuits on the baking trays for 5 minutes, then lift them onto a wire rack. To make the lemon icing, sift the icing sugar into a small bowl.

10 Stir in 3 tablespoons of lemon juice. Put half the mixture in another bowl. Mix a few drops of yellow food dye into one bowl of icing.

11 Use a teaspoon to spread a little icing on top of the biscuits. Ice half the biscuits with white icing and half with yellow icing. Leave to dry.

12 Then, decorate the biscuits with white and yellow writing icing and sweets. You can find out how to pipe icing patterns onto biscuits on page 379.

Cinnamon cookies

Ingredients:

215g (7½oz) self-raising flour

4 teaspoons ground cinnamon

¼ teaspoon ground black pepper (optional)

50g (2oz) butter

50g (2oz) soft dark brown sugar

3 rounded tablespoons golden syrup or runny honey

For decorating:

writing icing

You will also need 2 baking trays and some cookie cutters.

Makes around 30

These crisp cookies taste deliciously of cinnamon. A little black pepper gives them a hint of spicy warmth, but doesn't actually make them taste peppery. Decorate your cookies with pretty colours of writing icing.

1 Heat the oven to 180°C, 350°F or gas mark 4. Grease and line the baking trays (see page 10).

2 Sift the flour, cinnamon and pepper into a large bowl. Put the butter, sugar and syrup or honey in a pan. Put the pan over a gentle heat, stirring now and then, until the butter has melted.

3 Take the pan off the heat, add the flour and mix until it clings together. Put a lid on the pan and leave for about 5 minutes, to let the mixture cool.

4 Sprinkle a surface and rolling pin with flour. Put the dough on the surface. Pat and squash it gently, until it you have a smooth ball of dough.

5 Put half back in the pan, with the lid on. Roll out the other piece of dough, until it is half as thick as your little finger.

6 Cut out lots of shapes using the cutters. Put the shapes on the trays. Roll out the other half of the dough. Cut more shapes.

7 Squeeze any scraps of dough together and roll them out again. Cut more shapes. Do this until all the dough is used up.

Other flavours

For plain vanilla cookies, replace the dark brown sugar with caster sugar and replace the cinnamon and black pepper with 1 teaspoon vanilla essence.

8 Bake for 8-10 minutes, until the cookies are slightly browned at the edges. Leave on the trays for a few minutes, then move them to a wire rack to cool.

9 When the cookies are completely cold, decorate them with writing icing.

Lollipop cookies

Ingredients:

1 orange

50g (2oz) caster sugar

50g (2oz) softened butter or margarine

1 medium egg

125g (4½oz) plain flour

15g (½oz) cornflour

For the icing:

100g (4oz) icing sugar

different shades of food dye

You will also need 2 baking trays, a round cookie cutter around 4cm (1⅛in) across and around 12-15 wooden skewers.

Makes around 12-15

These chunky orange cookies are baked on sticks, then decorated with bright shades of icing, to look like old-fashioned lollipops.

1 Heat the oven to 180°C, 350°F or gas mark 4. Line the baking trays with parchment (see page 10).

2 Grate the zest from the outside of the orange using the small holes of a grater. Squeeze the juice from half the orange. Put the zest in a big bowl.

3 Add the sugar and butter or margarine. Beat until they're pale and fluffy.

4 Break the egg into a cup. Beat it with a fork. Pour half of it into the big bowl and mix it in. Save the rest for later.

5 Sift on the flour and cornflour and mix them in. Then, use your hands to squeeze the mixture into a ball.

6 Dust a clean work surface and a rolling pin with flour. Roll out the dough (see page 372) until it is half as thick as your little finger.

7 Use the round cutter to cut out lots of circles. Squeeze the scraps together, roll them out again and cut more circles, until the dough is used up.

8 Use a spatula to move half the circles onto the trays. Space them well apart, to leave room for the skewers.

9 Brush egg all over the circles on the tray. Put a skewer on each one. Lay another dough circle over each of the circles on the tray. Press them on gently.

10 Bake the cookies for 12-15 minutes, until they are golden. Leave them for 10 minutes, then move them carefully to a wire rack to cool.

This cookie was flat iced, then decorated with a piped spiral.

This one was feather iced in yellow and pink.

Lollipop cookies

These spots were piped with writing icing.

You could pipe decorations onto a cookie without flat icing it first.

These cookies were made using 2 sizes of cutter.

11 To make the icing, sift the icing sugar into a bowl. Mix in 1 tablespoon of the orange juice you squeezed earlier. Divide the icing between 3 or more small bowls.

12 Mix a few drops of food dye into each bowl of icing. Then, ice the cookies, following the instructions on pages 378-379 for flat icing, piping lines and dots, or feather icing.

Iced star biscuits

Ingredients:

350g (12oz) plain flour

2 teaspoons ground ginger

1 teaspoon bicarbonate of soda

100g (4oz) butter

175g (6oz) soft light brown sugar

1 medium egg

4 tablespoons golden syrup

For decorating:

writing icing

small sweets

You will also need 2 baking trays and a large star-shaped cutter.

Makes around 25

These sweet biscuits are cut into stars, but you could make yours in any shape you like.

1 Heat the to 190°C, 375°F or gas mark 5. Grease and line the baking trays (see page 10).

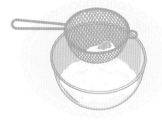 

2 Sift the flour into a large bowl. Then, sift the ginger and bicarbonate of soda into the bowl, too.

3 Cut the butter into chunks with a blunt knife. Put them in the bowl. Stir them in with a spoon, to coat them in flour.

4 Rub the butter into the flour, following the instructions on page 375. Stop when the mixture is like fine breadcrumbs. Stir in the sugar.

5 Break the egg into a small bowl, then add the syrup. Beat them together well with a fork, then stir the mixture into the flour.

6 Mix everything together until you make a dough. Then, sprinkle a clean work surface with flour and put the dough onto it.

7 Using your hands, push the dough away from you and fold it over. Do this again and again until the dough is smooth.

8 Sprinkle a little more flour onto the work surface, then roll out the dough until it is half as thick as your little finger. Use the cutter to cut out stars.

9 Lift the stars onto the baking trays. Squeeze the scraps into a ball, then roll them out again and cut out more stars.

10 Bake for 12-15 minutes, until golden-brown. Take them out of the oven. Leave them on the trays for 5 minutes.

Stick on a sweet with a dot of icing.

11 Put the biscuits onto a wire rack to cool. When they are cold, decorate them with writing icing and small sweets.

Little gem biscuits

Ingredients:

20g (¾oz) icing sugar

40g (1½oz) softened butter,
  preferably unsalted

1 lemon

50g (2oz) plain flour

For the lemon buttercream:

25g (1oz) softened butter

50g (2oz) icing sugar

1 lemon

red and blue food dye

You will also need a baking tray
and a piping gun or bag with a
star- or flower-shaped nozzle.

Makes around 30

These tiny, gem-like lemon biscuits are topped
with piped swirls of tangy lemon buttercream
in bright, jewel colours.

1 Sift the icing sugar into a big
bowl. Add the butter. Beat until
you have a smooth mixture.

2 Grate the zest from the
outside of half the lemon, on
the small holes of a grater.
Cut the lemon in half and
squeeze out the juice.

3 Add the lemon zest to
the mixture. Sift over the
flour. Stir it in. Add 1½
teaspoons of the lemon
juice and mix. Squeeze the
mixture into a ball.

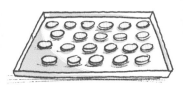

4 Put the ball on a lightly floured surface. Roll it with your hands to make a log around 2½cm (1in) across. Wrap it in plastic food wrap and put it in the fridge for 30 minutes.

5 Heat the oven to 180°C, 350°F or gas mark 4. Grease the baking tray (page 10). Unwrap the log. Use a sharp knife to cut it into ½cm (¼in) slices.

6 Arrange the slices on the baking tray. Bake for 8-10 minutes, until they are turning golden. Leave the biscuits on the tray to cool completely.

7 To make the lemon buttercream, follow the instructions for citrus buttercream on page 376. Divide the buttercream into 3 equal parts. Spoon 2 parts into separate bowls.

8 Put a few drops of red and blue food dye in two of the bowls. Mix it in. Follow the instructions on page 379 to pipe small swirls of buttercream onto the biscuits.

9 Each time you change to a new shade of buttercream, wash the piping bag or gun (or use a fresh one) to keep the colours separate.

To make white buttercream like this, use the palest butter you can find.

You can make edible star and ball decorations like these using ready-to-roll icing – find out how on page 382.

Jewelled crown biscuits

Ingredients:

50g (2oz) butter

3 tablespoons golden syrup

175g (6oz) self-raising flour

½ teaspoon ground cinnamon

½ teaspoon bicarbonate of soda

1 tablespoon light soft brown sugar

2 tablespoons milk

For decorating:

writing icing and sweets

You will also need 2 baking trays.

Makes around 16

You cut these biscuits into the shape of crowns before you bake them. When they're cool you can decorate them with different colours of writing icing and stick on sweets to look like jewels.

1 Use a paper towel to wipe a little cooking oil over the baking trays.

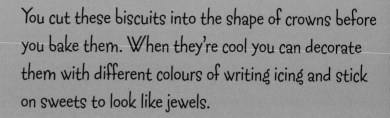

2 Cut the butter into cubes and put them into a small pan. Add the golden syrup, then heat the pan over a low heat.

3 Stir the mixture every now and then, until it has just melted. Then, take the pan off the heat and let it cool for 3 minutes.

Flatten the dough a little before you wrap it.

4 Sift the flour, cinnamon and bicarbonate of soda into a bowl and stir in the brown sugar. Make a hollow in the middle with a spoon.

5 Carefully pour the butter and syrup mixture into the hollow. Add the milk and stir until it comes together in a ball of dough.

6 Wrap the dough in plastic food wrap and put it in the fridge for 15 minutes. While the dough is chilling, heat the oven to 180°C, 350°F or gas mark 4.

7 Dust a rolling pin and a clean work surface with some flour. Roll out the dough until it is half as thick as your little finger.

8 Cut off the wobbly edges of the dough with a sharp knife, to make a square. Then, cut the square into four pieces, like this.

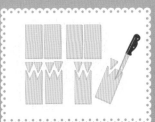

9 Cut each piece in half, to make 8 rectangles. Then, make each rectangle into a crown by cutting out two small triangles at the top.

10 Squeeze the scraps into a ball and roll it out. Cut out more crowns, then put all of the crowns onto the baking trays.

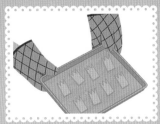

11 Bake the crowns for 8-10 minutes. Carefully lift them out of the oven and leave them on the baking trays for 5 minutes.

Stick on sweets with dots of icing.

12 Lift the crowns onto a wire rack with a spatula, and let them cool. Then, decorate them with writing icing and sweets for jewels.

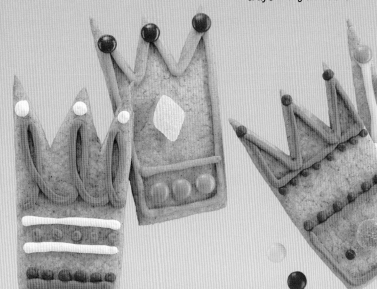

Lemon cinnamon stars

These delicious, chewy biscuits are flavoured with cinnamon and lemon. Because they are made using ground almonds instead of flour, they don't contain any wheat or gluten.

Ingredients:

2 lemons

250g (9oz) icing sugar

400g (14oz) ground almonds

2 teaspoons ground cinnamon

2 medium eggs

For the lemon icing:

125g (4½oz) icing sugar

You will also need a baking tray and a small star cutter.

Makes around 40

Use the small holes.

1 Heat the oven to 200°C, 400°F or gas mark 6. Line the baking tray (see page 10). Grate the zest from the lemons. Squeeze the juice from one of the lemons.

2 Sift the icing sugar into a large bowl. Mix in the lemon zest, ground almonds and cinnamon.

You don't need the yolks – use them in the recipe on page 26.

3 Separate the eggs (see page 11). Put the whites in a big bowl. Whisk until they form a thick foam that stays in a stiff point when you lift up the whisk.

Move the spoon in the... ...shape of a number 8.

4 Use a spatula or a big metal spoon to fold the almond mixture gently into the egg whites. It should form a dough you can roll out. If it's too sticky, mix in an extra spoon of ground almonds.

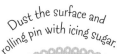
Dust the surface and rolling pin with icing sugar.

5 Put the dough onto a work surface and roll it out until it is as thick as your little finger.

6 Use the cutter to cut out star shapes and put them on the baking tray.

You could decorate these biscuits with extra lemon zest. To get long curls of zest, use a tool called a zester.

7 Bake for 5-6 minutes. Leave the stars on the tray for a few minutes, then put them on a wire rack to cool.

8 Sift the icing sugar into a bowl. Add 1½ tablespoons of the lemon juice. Mix to a smooth paste. Spread it onto the stars.

Chocolate cobweb cookies

Ingredients:

160g (5½oz) plain flour
2 tablespoons cocoa powder
100g (4oz) butter
50g (2oz) caster sugar
2 tablespoons milk
white writing icing

You will also need 2 baking trays, a big round cutter and a cocktail stick.

Makes around 18

These chocolate cookies are decorated with icing cobwebs. They would make tasty treats for Hallowe'en, or for a spooky party.

1 Grease and line the baking trays (see page 10).

2 Sift the flour and cocoa into a large bowl. Cut the butter into chunks and put them in the bowl, then rub it in with your fingers (see page 375).

3 When the mixture looks like fine breadcrumbs, stir in the sugar. Then, sprinkle the milk over the mixture and stir it in with a fork.

4 Keep on stirring until everything starts to stick together. Then, squeeze it with your hands to make a flattened ball.

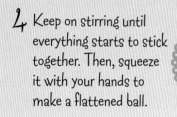

5 Wrap it in plastic food wrap. Put in a fridge for 20 minutes. Meanwhile, heat the oven to 180°C, 350°F or gas mark 4.

6 Sprinkle a clean work surface and a rolling pin with some flour. Roll out the dough until it is half as thick as your little finger.

7 Use the cutter to cut out lots of circles and carefully lift them onto the baking trays. Then, squeeze the scraps into a ball.

8 Roll out the ball and cut out more circles. Bake for 10-12 minutes, then carefully lift them out of the oven.

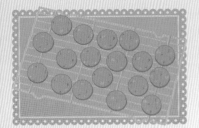

9 Leave the cookies on the baking trays for around 5 minutes. Then, lift them onto a wire rack and leave them to cool.

11 Using the cocktail stick, drag the icing from the middle to make a web. Ice the other cookies, then leave the icing to set.

10 When the cookies are cold, draw a spiral of white writing icing on each one, starting in the middle.

Other ideas

If you don't want to decorate these cookies with cobwebs, you could use lines, zig-zags or dots instead. See pages 378-379 for different icing ideas.

65

Ginger snap biscuits

Ingredients:

50g (2oz) butter

50g (2oz) soft dark brown sugar

4 tablespoons golden syrup
   or runny honey

215g (7½oz) self-raising flour

3 teaspoons ground ginger

1 teaspoon ground cinnamon

¼ teaspoon allspice (optional)

For the icing:

100g (4oz) icing sugar

different shades of food dye
   (optional)

You will also need 2 baking
trays and some small or medium
heart-shaped cutters.

Makes around 40

These crisp ginger biscuits are cut into hearts, but you could cut yours into any shape you like. They're decorated with pastel shades of glacé icing.

1 Heat the oven to 180°C, 350°F or gas mark 4. Line the baking trays with baking parchment (see page 10).

2 Put the butter, sugar and syrup or honey in a pan. Put it over a low heat until the butter melts. Take it off the heat.

3 Sift the flour, ginger, cinnamon and allspice into the pan. Stir well, to mix everything together. Put a lid on the pan and leave it to cool for 15 minutes.

4 Dust a clean surface and a rolling pin with flour. Take half the dough from the pan. Put it on the surface and roll it out (see page 372) until it's half as thick as your little finger.

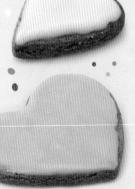

5 Use the cutters to cut out lots of shapes and put them on the trays. Squeeze the scraps together, roll them out and cut more shapes.

6 Roll out the other piece of dough and cut it into shapes in the same way, too. Bake the biscuits for 8-10 minutes, until they're golden-brown.

7 Leave them on the trays for 5 minutes. Then, move them to a wire rack. Leave them to cool completely.

8 To make the icing, sift the icing sugar into a bowl. Mix in 2 teaspoons of water, to make a smooth paste. Spoon some into two or more small bowls.

9 Put a few drops of food dye in each bowl. Mix well. Then, use a blunt knife to spread it onto the biscuits.

Cook biscuits of the same size on the same baking tray. Smaller biscuits will cook in around 8 minutes, larger ones in around 10.

67

Little gingerbread houses

Ingredients:

350g (12oz) plain flour

1½ teaspoons ground ginger

½ teaspoon ground cinnamon

1 teaspoon bicarbonate of soda

100g (4oz) butter

175g (6oz) light muscovado sugar

1 medium egg

2 tablespoons golden syrup

For decorating:

writing icing, sweets and sprinkles

You will also need 2 baking trays.

Makes around 10

Half the fun of this recipe is decorating your gingerbread houses after you've baked them. You could keep your piping simple, go for ornate designs, or try out a different decoration on each biscuit. Use any type of writing icing, sweets or sprinkles you like.

1 Heat the oven to 180°C, 350°F or gas mark 4. Line the baking trays (see page 10). Mix the flour, ginger, cinnamon and bicarbonate of soda in a large bowl.

2 Cut the butter into chunks. Rub it into the flour (see page 375). Stop when the mixture looks like fine breadcrumbs. Stir in the sugar.

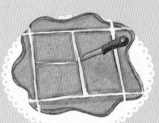

3 Break the egg into a small bowl and mix in the syrup. Add it to the flour. Stir everything together, then squeeze it into a ball.

4 Dust a clean surface and a rolling pin with a little flour. Roll out the dough, until it is as thick as your little finger.

5 Cut off the wobbly edges with a sharp knife, to make a square. Then, cut the square into four pieces, like this.

6 Cut each piece in half, to make 8 rectangles. Then, cut a triangle from the top corners of each rectangle, to make house shapes.

7 Squeeze the scraps into a ball, roll it out and cut more houses. Put them onto the trays. Bake for 12-15 minutes until dark golden.

8 Leave the houses on the trays for a few minutes, then put on a wire rack to cool. Then, decorate with writing icing and press on sweets and sprinkles.

This biscuit was flat-iced (page 378) with glacé icing (page 377) before the designs were piped on.

Confetti cookies

Ingredients:

50g (2oz) softened butter

75g (3oz) caster sugar

1 medium egg

1 teaspoon runny honey

1 teaspoon vanilla essence

2 teaspoons milk

100g (4oz) plain flour

25g (1oz) cornflour

For the icing:

150g (5oz) icing sugar

pink food dye

You will also need 2 baking trays and some tiny cutters.

Makes around 100

These cookies are so small, they look like confetti. They are cut into shapes using tiny cookie cutters and spread with pink and white icing.

1 Use a paper towel to wipe a little cooking oil over the baking trays. Heat the oven to 180°C, 350°F or gas mark 4.

You don't need the white – use it in the recipes on pages 148-165.

2 Put the butter and sugar into a large bowl. Beat until smooth. Separate the egg (see page 11). Put the yolk in the bowl and mix it in.

3 Stir in the honey, vanilla and milk. Sift the flour and cornflour into the bowl, then start to mix everything with a spoon.

4 Then, use your hands to squeeze the mixture until you make a ball of dough. If the mixture is a little dry, add a drop or two of milk.

5 Sprinkle a work surface with flour, then roll out the dough until it is half as thick as your little finger. Use the cutters to cut out shapes.

6 Put the shapes onto the baking trays. Then, squeeze the scraps into a ball, roll them out again and cut out more shapes.

7 Bake for 6-8 minutes, until they are golden-brown. Take them out of the oven. Leave them on the trays to cool.

8 For the icing, sift the icing sugar into a bowl and mix in 2 tablespoons of water. Then, spoon half the icing into another bowl.

9 Cover one bowl with food wrap to stop it drying out. Then, mix two drops of food dye into the icing in the other bowl.

Use a blunt knife.

10 Spread half the cookies with white icing. Then, spread the others with pink icing. Leave the icing to set.

Gingerbread flowers

Ingredients:

350g (12oz) plain flour

1½ teaspoons ground ginger

½ teaspoon ground cinnamon

1 teaspoon bicarbonate of soda

100g (4oz) butter or margarine

175g (6oz) light muscovado sugar

1 medium egg

2 tablespoons golden syrup

For decorating:

writing icing

You will also need 2 baking trays and a medium flower cutter.

Makes around 25

You can make these soft gingerbread flowers look really pretty by decorating them with different shades of icing. If you like really gingery cookies, add ½ teaspoon extra ginger instead of the cinnamon.

1 Heat the oven to 180°C, 350°F or gas mark 4. Use a paper towel to wipe a little oil over the baking trays. Sift the flour, ginger, cinnamon and bicarbonate of soda into a big bowl.

2 Cut the butter or margarine into chunks and put them in the bowl. Stir the mixture with a spoon, so the chunks become coated with flour.

3 Use your fingers and thumbs to rub the butter or margarine into the flour (see page 375). Stop when the mixture looks like fine breadcrumbs. Then, stir in the sugar.

4 Break the egg into a small bowl and beat it with a fork. Mix the syrup into the beaten egg. Add the egg mixture to the flour, then mix everything together.

5 Holding the bowl in one hand, use your other hand to squeeze the mixture together until you have a smooth ball of dough. Use a blunt knife to cut the dough in half.

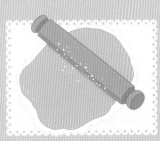

6 Sprinkle a little flour onto a clean work surface and a rolling pin. Roll out one piece of dough until it is slightly thinner than your little finger.

7 Use a flower-shaped cookie cutter to cut out lots of flower shapes from the dough. Use a spatula to lift the shapes onto the baking trays.

8 Roll out the other half of the dough and cut more flower shapes from it. Squeeze the scraps of dough together to make a ball. Roll it out and cut more shapes.

9 Bake the biscuits for 12-15 minutes, until they are dark golden. Leave the biscuits on the trays for 5 minutes to cool.

10 Use a spatula to lift the biscuits onto a wire rack. When they are cold, draw patterns on them with writing icing, or make your own icing to pipe on (see page 377).

Snowflake biscuits

Ingredients:

75g (3oz) softened butter

25g (1oz) icing sugar

115g (4oz) plain flour

For decorating:
white writing icing

You will also need 2 baking trays and a large round cutter.

Makes around 14

These biscuits are decorated with white snowflakes, but you could ice other patterns onto them using different colours of writing icing if you prefer.

1 Use a paper towel to wipe a little cooking oil over the baking trays.

2 Put the butter in a large bowl. Stir it until it is fluffy. Sift the icing sugar into the bowl and stir it in, until the mixture is smooth.

3 Sift on the flour and stir it in. Then, using your hands, squeeze the mixture into a ball. Press, to flatten it slightly.

4 Wrap the dough in plastic food wrap and put it in the fridge for 30 minutes. Meanwhile, heat the oven to 180°C, 350°F or gas mark 4.

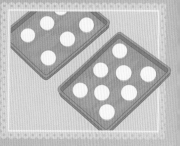

5 Dust a rolling pin and a clean work surface with flour. Roll out the dough until it is slightly thinner than your little finger.

6 Cut out lots of circles with the cutter. Then, squeeze the scraps into a ball and roll it out. Cut out more circles.

7 When you have used all the dough, put the circles onto the baking trays. Then, bake the biscuits for 10-12 minutes.

You could ice different patterns on some biscuits. See page 373 for piping ideas.

Some of these biscuits are decorated with sparkly writing icing, as well as white icing.

8 Leave the biscuits on the baking trays for 2 minutes. Then, move them onto a wire rack with a spatula and let them cool.

9 Draw a line down the middle of one biscuit with white writing icing. Draw two more lines crossing over the first one, like this.

10 Make a snowflake by adding small lines of writing icing across the ends of the lines. Then, decorate all the other biscuits, too.

Filled biscuits & cookies

Viennese biscuits

Ingredients:

175g (6oz) softened butter, preferably unsalted

40g (1½oz) icing sugar

1 teaspoon vanilla essence

175g (6oz) plain flour

40g (1½oz) cornflour

For the ganache:

75g (3oz) plain or milk chocolate

4 tablespoons double cream

You will also need 2 baking trays and a heatproof bowl that fits snugly into a saucepan.

Makes around 12

Biscuits like these are thought to have originated in Vienna. These crisp, buttery little biscuits are sandwiched together with a filling known as ganache. The ganache is made from plain chocolate, but you could use milk or white chocolate instead.

1 Heat the oven to 190°C, 375°F or gas mark 5. Grease and line the baking trays (see page 10). Put the butter in a bowl. Sift on the icing sugar. Beat until smooth.

2 Stir in the vanilla essence. Sift the flour and cornflour over the mixture. Stir them in until smooth. Put a teaspoon of the mixture onto one of the trays.

 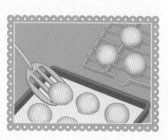 

3 Put more teaspoons of mixture onto the trays, leaving spaces between them. Flatten each blob slightly with the back of a teaspoon.

4 Bake the biscuits for 12-14 minutes, until they are pale golden-brown. Leave them on their trays for 5 minutes, then put them on a wire rack to cool.

5 For the ganache, break up the chocolate and put it in the heatproof bowl. Add the cream. Fill the saucepan a quarter full with water.

Heat the water until it bubbles, then take the pan off the heat. Wearing oven gloves, put the bowl in the pan. Stir until the chocolate has melted.

7 Wearing oven gloves, lift the bowl out of the pan. Leave to cool for a few minutes. Then, put it in the fridge for about an hour, stirring it every now and then, as it thickens.

8 When the ganache is like soft butter, take it out of the fridge. Use a blunt knife to spread some onto the flat side of a biscuit. Press another biscuit on top.

9 Sandwich the biscuits together in pairs until all the ganache and biscuits are used up. Eat them straight away, or keep them in an airtight container in the fridge.

Jam dimple biscuits

Contains coconut

Ingredients:

100g (4oz) softened butter

1 teaspoon vanilla essence

50g (2oz) icing sugar

100g (4oz) plain flour

25g (1oz) cornflour

25g (1oz) desiccated coconut

around 2 tablespoons of smooth jam such as raspberry

You will also need 2 baking trays.

Makes around 20

To make these biscuits, you roll balls of dough and make a dimple in each one with your finger. When the biscuits are cooked, you fill the dimples with jam.

Before you start, grease the baking trays (see page 10). Heat the oven to 180°C, 350°F or gas mark 4.

1 Put the butter into a large bowl and stir it until it is smooth. Then, add the vanilla essence and stir it in.

2 Sift the icing sugar into the bowl. Then, beat the mixture well with a wooden spoon until it is smooth.

3 Sift the flour and the cornflour into the bowl. Then, add the coconut. Stir everything well to make a soft dough.

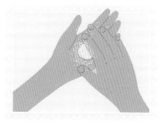 

4 Rub some flour on your hands. Then, scoop up a little of the dough with a teaspoon and roll it into a smooth ball.

5 Make more balls and put them on the greased baking trays. Leave spaces between the balls, because they spread as they cook.

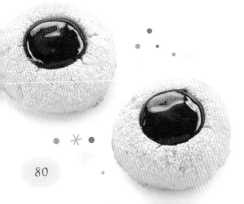

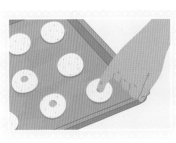

6 Push your little finger into the middle of each ball, to make a dimple. Push it in up to the first knuckle, like this.

7 Bake the biscuits for 12-14 minutes. Carefully lift them out of the oven, then leave them to cool on the trays.

8 When the biscuits have cooled, sift a little icing sugar over them. Then, use a teaspoon to fill the holes with jam.

These biscuits were filled with raspberry jam, but you could use any flavour you like.

Hidden marzipan biscuits

Ingredients:

100g (4oz) self-raising flour

25g (1oz) cocoa powder

75g (3oz) butter

50g (2oz) caster sugar

1 medium egg

100g (4oz) marzipan

For decorating:

1 teaspoon icing sugar

½ teaspoon cocoa powder

You will also need a baking tray and a medium and a small heart-shaped cutter.

Makes 12

These may look like ordinary chocolate biscuits, but when you bite into them, you'll discover a delicious marzipan middle.

1 Grease the baking tray (see page 10). Sift the flour and cocoa powder into a large bowl. Cut the butter into chunks and add them to the mixture.

2 Stir, to coat the butter in flour. Then, rub the butter into the flour following the instructions on page 375. Stop when it looks like fine breadcrumbs. Stir in the sugar.

Use the egg white in...

...the recipes on pages 148-165.

3 Break the egg onto a plate. Hold an egg cup over the yolk and tip the plate over a bowl, so the egg white slides off. Add the yolk to the mixture.

4 Stir the mixture. Then, use your hands to squeeze it into a flattened ball. Wrap it in plastic food wrap and put it in the fridge to chill for 30 minutes.

5 Sprinkle some icing sugar onto a clean work surface and a rolling pin. Roll out the marzipan until it is half as thick as your little finger. Cut out hearts with the smaller cutter.

6 Squeeze the scraps of marzipan together into a ball. Roll it out again and cut out more hearts until you have 12. Then, heat the oven to 200°C, 400°F or gas mark 6.

You may need to press hard to squash the dough together.

7 Sprinkle some flour onto a clean work surface and a rolling pin. Roll out the dough until it is half as thick as your little finger. Use the larger cutter to cut out 24 hearts.

8 Put half the chocolate hearts on the baking tray. Put a marzipan heart on each one. Put a second chocolate heart on top. Press the edges of each biscuit together.

9 Bake the biscuits for 10 minutes. When they are ready, sift a little icing sugar over them, then sift a little cocoa powder over that. Lift them onto a wire rack to cool.

Jammy cut-out biscuits

Ingredients:

100g (4oz) softened butter

50g (2oz) caster sugar

1 orange

1 medium egg

2 tablespoons ground almonds (optional)

200g (7oz) plain flour

1 tablespoon cornflour

8 tablespoons smooth jam

You will also need 2 baking trays, a 5cm (2in) round cutter and some tiny shaped cutters.

Makes around 10

These biscuits have cut-out shapes on top, so you can see the jam filling. You could try this recipe with different flavours of jam and cut out the holes in the middle with any shape of cutter you like.

1 Heat the oven to 180°C, 350°F or gas mark 4. Grease the baking trays (see page 10). Put the butter and sugar into a large bowl. Beat them until the mixture is smooth.

2 Grate the zest from the outside of the orange, using the small holes of a grater. Put the zest in the bowl and stir it in.

3 Break the egg into a cup. Beat it with a fork, then add a little to the mixture in the bowl. Mix it in well, then add some more and mix that in.

4 Carry on until you have added all the egg. Put the ground almonds in the bowl, if you are using them. Sift in the flour and cornflour.

5 Mix everything together with your hands. Pat it into a flattened ball. Wrap it in plastic food wrap and put it in the fridge for 30 minutes.

7 Using the round cutter, cut out lots of circles. Then, use the shaped cutters to cut holes in the middle of half the circles. Squeeze the scraps into a ball.

6 Sprinkle some flour onto a clean work surface and a rolling pin. Then, use the rolling pin to roll out the dough until it is around half as thick as your little finger.

8 Roll out the ball and cut more circles. Put all the circles on the baking trays. Bake the biscuits for 15 minutes. Leave them on the baking trays for 2 minutes.

9 Lift the biscuits onto a wire rack to cool. When they're cold, spread jam on the whole biscuits, as far as the edge. Place a cut-out biscuit on each one and press it down gently.

Soft-centre cookies

Ingredients:

65g (2½oz) plain chocolate

15g (½oz) butter

1 medium egg

½ teaspoon vanilla essence

40g (1½oz) caster sugar

50g (2oz) self-raising flour

15g (½oz) cocoa powder

50g (2oz) icing sugar

For the filling:

10 squares of plain, milk or
    white chocolate

You will also need a baking tray
and a heatproof bowl that fits
snugly in a saucepan.

Makes 10

When you bite into these cookies, you'll discover a surprise chocolate filling. If you eat them when they're still warm, the chocolate filling will be soft and gooey.

1 Fill a pan a quarter full of water and put it over a low heat. When it bubbles, turn off the heat. Put the chocolate in a heatproof bowl. Cut the butter into chunks and add it too.

2 Wearing oven gloves, put the bowl in the pan. Leave for 2 minutes. Stir until the chocolate and butter melt.

3 Break the egg into a small bowl. Add the vanilla and beat them together. Stir into the chocolate mixture.

As the cookies bake, cracks form on top.

4 Add the caster sugar and stir for a minute, so the sugar starts to dissolve. Wearing oven gloves, lift the bowl out of the pan and leave the mixture to cool.

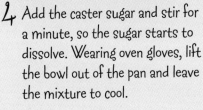

5 Sift the flour and cocoa over the mixture. Stir them in. Cover the bowl with plastic food wrap and put it in the fridge for 1 hour.

6 Heat the oven to 170°C, 325°F or gas mark 3. Line a baking tray with parchment (see page 10). Sift the icing sugar onto a plate.

7 Use a tablespoon to scoop up some mixture. Roll it into a ball with your hands. Make 9 more balls in the same way. Put one on a clean surface and press your thumb into the middle to make a hollow.

8 Press a square of chocolate into the hollow. Use your fingers to pull the dough over the chocolate, to cover it. Shape the cookie into a flattened ball.

9 Roll the cookie in the icing sugar and put it on the tray. Make the other cookies in the same way.

10 Bake for 10-12 minutes. Leave for a few minutes, then put on a wire rack to cool.

Chocolate peanut bites

These little biscuits are made with peanut butter. Each one has a dimple filled with chocolate and topped with a peanut – or you could use other nuts.

Ingredients:

50g (2oz) salted, roasted peanuts

100g (4oz) softened butter

100g (4oz) caster sugar

50g (2oz) soft light brown sugar

100g (4oz) smooth peanut butter

½ teaspoon vanilla essence

1 medium egg

150g (5oz) plain flour

50g (2oz) plain, milk or white chocolate

You will also need 2 baking trays, some kitchen foil and a heatproof bowl that fits snugly into a saucepan.

Makes around 35

1 Heat the oven to 180°C, 350°F or gas mark 4. Line the baking trays (see page 10). Put the peanuts in a sieve. Rinse under a cold tap to remove the salt. Pat dry with a clean tea towel. Set aside.

2 Put the butter, caster sugar and soft light brown sugar in a bowl. Beat until you have a pale and fluffy mixture.

3 Stir in the peanut butter and vanilla. Then, break the egg into a cup, beat it with a fork and stir it into the mixture, too.

A blanched almond

White chocolate

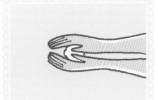

4 Sift the flour onto the mixture in the bowl. Stir it in well, then use your hands to pat and squeeze the mixture into a ball.

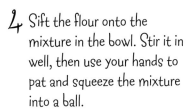

5 Take a teaspoonful of the mixture. Use your hands to roll it into a ball. Put it on a tray. Make more balls, until the mixture is used up. Bake for 10-12 minutes, until golden.

6 While the biscuits are baking, take a small square of kitchen foil. Scrunch it into a ball around 2cm (1in) wide. Pinch one end to make a handle.

7 Take the biscuits out of the oven. Hold the foil ball by its handle. Push it gently into the middle of each biscuit, to make a shallow dimple. The biscuits will crack a little as you do this.

Other flavours

Instead of peanuts, you could top your bites with shelled pistachios, macadamia nuts, blanched almonds or hazelnuts. If the nuts are unsalted, you don't need to rinse them.

Instead of chocolate, you could fill the dimples in your biscuits with the butterscotch filling from page 377. Or, for really nutty bites, fill them with chocolate hazelnut spread.

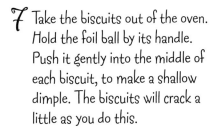

8 Leave the biscuits to cool. Then, melt the chocolate (see page 380). Spoon a little into the dimple in each biscuit. Top with the peanuts you set aside earlier.

The dimple on this biscuit was filled with butterscotch filling – see page 377.

Lace biscuits

Ingredients:

75g (3oz) butter

75g (3oz) porridge oats

100g (4oz) caster sugar

1 medium egg

2 teaspoons plain flour

1 teaspoon baking powder

For the lime mascarpone:

1 lime

250g (9oz) mascarpone

25g (1oz) icing sugar

You will also need 2 baking trays.

Makes around 8

These biscuits spread out as they cook to make a lacy pattern. They have an oaty, buttery taste. You can eat them as they are, or sandwich them with a filling made from mascarpone cheese and lime zest.

1 Heat the oven to 170°C, 325°F or gas mark 3. Grease and line the baking trays, following the instructions on page 10.

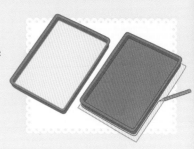

You could make the filling with orange or lemon instead of lime.

2 Put the butter into a saucepan. Place it over a low heat until the butter has melted. Take the pan off the heat. Then, stir in the oats with a wooden spoon.

3 Put the sugar in the pan and stir it in. Leave the mixture to stand for 2 or 3 minutes. This gives the butter enough time to soak into the oats.

4 Break the egg into a small bowl and beat it with a fork. Stir the beaten egg into the oaty mixture. Sift in the flour and baking powder and stir them in.

  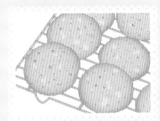

5 Put 4 heaped teaspoons of the mixture onto each tray, making sure they are well spaced out. Bake for 9-10 minutes until they are a deep golden-brown.

6 Leave the biscuits to cool on the baking trays for 5 minutes. Then, carefully lift them off the paper using a blunt knife. Put them onto a wire rack to cool.

7 Leave the baking parchment on the baking trays. Follow steps 5 and 6 to bake more biscuits. Leave all the biscuits on the wire rack to cool completely.

  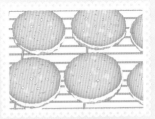

8 While the biscuits are cooling, make the filling, following the recipe on page 376. Spread some of the lime cream onto the flat side of one biscuit.

9 Put another biscuit on top of the filling to sandwich the biscuits together. Sandwich together all the biscuits. Eat them before the filling makes the biscuits soggy.

Yoyo cookies

Ingredients:
175g (6oz) softened butter
40g (1½oz) icing sugar
1 teaspoon vanilla essence
175g (6oz) plain flour
40g (1½oz) cornflour
1 tablespoon cocoa powder

For the chocolate frosting:
40g (1½oz) butter
75g (3oz) plain or milk chocolate

You will also need 2 baking trays
and some sugar sprinkles.

Makes around 12

These round chocolate and vanilla sandwich biscuits look like little yoyos. They are rolled in sugar sprinkles, but you can leave them plain, if you like.

These biscuits were all filled with chocolate frosting, but you could use buttercream (page 376) or butterscotch filling (page 377) instead.

1 Heat the oven to 190°C, 375°F or gas mark 5. Grease or line the baking trays (see page 10).

2 Put the butter in a big bowl. Sift on the icing sugar. Beat until it's smooth. Stir in the vanilla. Sift on the flour and cornflour. Mix well.

3 Put half the mixture in another bowl, sift on the cocoa and mix it in.

4 Take a teaspoon of one mixture. Use your hands to roll it into a ball. Put it on a baking tray. Make more balls. Space them well apart.

5 Use the back of a fork to flatten each of the balls, like this. Bake for 12-14 minutes.

6 Meanwhile, make the chocolate frosting (see page 377).

7 Leave the biscuits on the trays for a few minutes, then move them to a wire rack to cool completely.

8 When the biscuits are cool and the frosting is spreadable, spread frosting on half the biscuits. Press on the rest of the biscuits.

9 Spread some sugar sprinkles on a plate. Roll each biscuit sandwich in the sprinkles.

Chocolate orange hearts

Ingredients:

100g (4oz) self-raising flour

25g (1oz) cocoa powder

75g (3oz) butter, chilled

50g (2oz) caster sugar

1 medium egg

For the orange filling:

50g (2oz) caster sugar

50g (2oz) ground almonds

2 oranges

You will also need a baking tray and a heart-shaped cutter, at least 5cm (2in) across.

Makes 15

When you bite into these crispy chocolate hearts, you'll find a home-made orange-flavoured almond paste filling inside.

1 Grease the baking tray (see page 10). Mix the flour and cocoa in a large bowl. Cut the butter into chunks and add it to the mixture.

2 Rub the butter into the flour (see page 375) until it looks like breadcrumbs. Stir in the sugar. Separate the egg and stir in the yolk. Put the egg white in a cup to use later.

3 Squeeze everything together to make a ball of dough. Wrap it in food wrap. Put it in the fridge for 20 minutes.

4 For the filling, put half the egg white in a bowl with the sugar and ground almonds.

5 Grate the zest from the oranges. Put it in the bowl and mix everything together well.

Dust your hands with icing sugar.

6 Take a teaspoon of the mixture. Roll it into a ball, then flatten it slightly. Make 15 balls. Heat the oven to 200°C, 400°F or gas mark 6.

Dust the rolling pin and surface with icing sugar.

7 Take the dough out of the fridge. Roll it out until it is as thick as your little finger. Press hard as you roll.

8 Cut out 30 hearts. Put half on the tray. Put a ball of filling on each one. Brush the edges of the hearts with egg white. Put a second heart on top and press the edges together.

9 Bake for 8-10 minutes. Leave on the tray for a few minutes, then put the hearts on a wire rack to cool.

These chocolate orange hearts look pretty if you sift a little icing sugar over them.

Contains nuts

Linz biscuits

These delicious hazelnut biscuits are from the city of Linz in Austria. They have a shaped hole cut in the top so the raspberry jam filling shows through.

Ingredients:

100g (4oz) hazelnuts

200g (7oz) plain flour

150g (5oz) caster sugar

150g (5oz) butter, chilled

1 medium egg

½ teaspoon vanilla essence

raspberry jam, or any flavour of jam

You will also need 2 baking trays, a 6cm (2½in) round cutter and some tiny shaped cutters.

Makes around 7

1 Put the nuts into a plastic food bag and seal the end. Use a rolling pin to crush them into small pieces.

2 Put the nuts, flour and sugar into a large bowl. Cut the butter into chunks and rub it into the flour (see page 375) until it looks like breadcrumbs.

Use the white in one of the recipes on pages 148-165.

3 Separate the egg. Put the yolk into the bowl and add the vanilla essence. Mix everything together until it forms a dough.

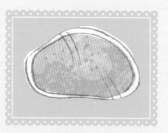

4 Wrap the dough in foodwrap. Put it in the fridge to chill for 30 minutes. Meanwhile, line the trays (see page 10).

Dust the surface and rolling pin with flour.

5 Heat the oven to 200°C, 400°F or gas mark 6. Then, roll out the dough until it is as thick as your little finger.

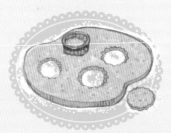

6 Use the round cutter to cut out lots of circles. Squeeze the scraps into a ball. Roll it out and cut more circles.

Linz biscuits are traditionally made with raspberry jam, but you could use other flavours if you like.

7 Use the small cutter to cut holes in half of the circles. Put all the circles onto the trays and bake for 8 minutes.

8 Take the biscuits out of the oven. Leave them on the tray for 2 minutes, then put them on a wire rack to cool.

9 Spread jam on the whole biscuits, as far as the edge. Place a cut-out biscuit on each one and press it down gently.

97

Tray cakes & bakes

Contains coconut

Coconut cake

Ingredients:

200g (7oz) butter or margarine

3 medium eggs

6 tablespoons desiccated coconut

225g (8oz) caster sugar

300g (11oz) self-raising flour

120ml (4floz) milk

For the frosting:

300g (11oz) full-fat cream cheese

100g (4oz) icing sugar

½ teaspoon coconut essence (optional)

For decorating:

2 tablespoons desiccated coconut

pink food dye

3 tablespoons seedless raspberry jam

1 teaspoon lemon juice

You will also need a 27 x 18cm (11 x 7in) rectangular cake tin.

Makes 12-15 squares

This soft coconut traybake is spread with cream cheese frosting and then topped with raspberry sauce and pink desiccated coconut.

1 Take the cream cheese out of the fridge. Heat the oven to 180°C, 350°F or gas mark 4. Grease and line the tin (see page 10).

2 Heat the butter or margarine gently in a small pan until it melts. Leave to cool.

3 Break an egg into a cup, then tip it into a small bowl. Do the same with the other eggs. Beat them with a fork.

4 Put the coconut and sugar in a big bowl. Sift in the flour. Mix. Add the milk, eggs and butter. Mix well.

5 Pour and scrape the mixture into the tin. Bake for 20-30 minutes, or until risen and firm. Test it with your finger (see page 373).

6 Leave the cake for 10 minutes. Then, run a knife around the edge of the tin and turn the cake onto a wire rack. Leave it to cool completely.

When the cake is cool, peel off the parchment.

7 To make the frosting, put the cream cheese in a big bowl. Beat until smooth. Sift on the icing sugar. Add the coconut essence. Mix gently.

Don't beat too much, or it will go watery.

8 For the pink coconut, put the coconut in a small bowl. Add a few drops of food dye and mix it in really well with a teaspoon.

9 For the sauce, push the jam though a sieve into a bowl. Scrape the jam off the back of the sieve, too. Mix in the lemon juice. Add a few drops of pink food dye too, if you like.

Other flavours

You could use other flavours of jam such as apricot or blueberry. Dye the coconut to match the jam.

10 Put the cake on a board. Spread the frosting over the top. Scoop up some sauce on a teaspoon. Drizzle it over the cake in a zigzag shape. Then, scatter over the coconut.

You could pipe on the sauce using a piping gun or bag fitted with a tiny round nozzle.

This cake was decorated with coconut and raspberry flavoured jelly beans.

Iced fancies

Ingredients:

3 medium eggs

2 lemons

175g (6oz) softened butter

175g (6oz) caster sugar

175g (6oz) self-raising flour

1½ tablespoons milk

For the icing:

350g (12oz) icing sugar

25g (1oz) butter

1 teaspoon rose water
(optional)

yellow and pink food dye

You will also need a 20cm (8in)
square cake tin.

Makes 16

For these fancy cakes, you bake a big cake, cut it into squares and ice them. You can make all your cakes lemon flavoured, or add a hint of rose to some of them.

1 Heat the oven to 180°C, 350°F or gas mark 4. Grease and line the cake tin (see page 10). Break the eggs into a bowl. Beat them with a fork.

2 Grate the zest from the outside of the lemons, using the small holes of a grater. Cut the lemons in half, squeeze out the juice and set it aside.

3 Put the zest, butter and sugar in a big bowl. Beat until pale and fluffy. Mix in a little beaten egg. Add the rest of the egg a little at a time, mixing well each time.

4 Sift on the flour. Add the milk. Mix very gently, using a big metal spoon. Spoon the mixture into the tin. Smooth the top with the back of a spoon.

Move the spoon in the... ...shape of a number 8.

5 Bake for 25 minutes, or until risen and firm. Leave for a few minutes. Run a knife around the tin. Turn the cake onto a wire rack. Leave to cool completely.

Peel off the parchment.

6 Put the cake on a board. Cut off the crispy edges. Make 3 cuts across the cake, then 3 more in the other direction, to make 16 squares. Put them on a wire rack with a tray underneath.

7 Sift 175g (6oz) of the icing sugar into a bowl. Put half the butter in a pan. Add 2 tablespoons of lemon juice. Put the pan over a gentle heat.

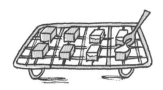

The icing should be pourable. If it's too stiff, stir in a few drops of water.

8 When the butter melts, pour the mixture onto the icing sugar. Add a few drops of yellow food dye. Mix well.

9 Spoon some icing onto half the cakes, covering the tops and letting it drip down the sides.

10 Sift the remaining icing sugar into a bowl. Put the rest of the butter in a pan. Add 5 teaspoons of lemon juice and 1 teaspoon of rose water. Heat as before, then pour onto the icing sugar.

11 Add a few drops of pink food dye. Mix well, as before. Ice the rest of the cakes. Decorate with writing icing or rose decorations (page 382), if you like.

Lemon only

If you don't like rose flavour, you can make all your cakes lemon flavour instead. Follow steps 1-9 as normal. Then, follow steps 8-9 again, to ice the rest of the cakes.

Swiss roll

Swiss roll is a type of sponge cake baked in a tray, spread with a filling and then rolled up. This recipe has a raspberry filling, and both the cake and filling are dairy-free. There are other filling suggestions opposite.

Ingredients:

3 large eggs
125g (4½oz) caster sugar
125g (4½oz) plain flour
1 tablespoon tepid water
2 tablespoons caster sugar

For the filling:
150g (5oz) fresh raspberries
2 tablespoons raspberry jam

You will also need a 35 x 25cm (14 x 10in) Swiss roll tin.

Makes around 10 slices

1 Heat the oven to 200°C, 400°F or gas mark 6. Grease and line the tin (see page 10).

2 Break the eggs into a big bowl. Add the sugar. Beat with a whisk until the mixture is pale and thick and has doubled in volume.

Don't worry if the outside cracks a little. That's how it's supposed to look.

Cut the roll into slices.

3 Sift over half the flour, then fold it in gently, using a big metal spoon. Sift over the rest of the flour, add the water and fold everything together again.

4 Pour the mixture into the tray. Push it into the corners and smooth the top with the back of a spoon. Bake for 10-12 minutes, or until pale golden and springy.

5 Cut a piece of baking parchment slightly bigger than the tray. Lay it out and scatter the caster sugar over it. Run a knife around the tin.

6 Wearing oven gloves, turn the cake onto the parchment. Peel the old parchment off. Carefully roll up the cake from a short end, with the new parchment inside. Leave to cool.

7 For the filling, put the raspberries in a bowl. Use a fork or potato masher to mash them. Mix in the jam.

8 When the cake is cool, carefully unroll it. Spread over the filling, then roll it up again, without the parchment.

Other flavours

You could replace the raspberries with the same weight of chopped fresh peaches or apricots. Use apricot jam instead of raspberry jam.

Instead of a fruit filling, you could use vanilla buttercream and spread on 2 tablespoons of your favourite flavour of jam.

For a chocolate mousse filling, follow the recipe for white chocolate mousse on page 292. Instead of white chocolate, you could use milk or plain chocolate in the mousse.

For a whipped cream and cherry filling, follow the filling recipe on pages 110-111.

Lemon & mango loaf

Ingredients:

150g (5oz) dried mango

2 lemons

100g (4oz) caster sugar

75g (3oz) softened butter

75g (3oz) ground almonds

300ml (½ pint) plain natural yogurt

2 teaspoons vanilla essence

250g (9oz) plain flour

2 teaspoons bicarbonate of soda

For the lemon icing:

175g (6oz) icing sugar

You will also need a 900g (2lb) loaf tin, measuring around 20½ x 12½ x 8cm (8 x 5 x 3⅛in).

Makes 12 slices

This fruity loaf cake contains lemon juice and zest and dried mango, and is covered in sticky lemon icing. There are other combinations of fruit to try too – see the opposite page. This recipe is egg-free.

Use the small holes.

1 Heat the oven to 180°C, 350°F, or gas mark 4. Snip the mango into small pieces. Grease and line the tin (see page 10).

2 Grate the zest from the outside of the lemons. Put it in a big bowl. Cut one lemon in half and squeeze the juice from one half. Put the juice aside.

3 Put the butter and sugar in the big bowl. Beat until they are pale and fluffy.

4 Stir in the ground almonds, 4 rounded tablespoons of the yogurt and the vanilla. Sift over the flour and bicarbonate of soda. Add the remaining yogurt and the mango.

5 Fold the mixture together gently, using a large metal spoon. Stop when all the flour is mixed in.

6 Scrape the mixture into the tin. Bake for 45-50 minutes, or until lightly browned and firm.

You could use extra chopped mango to decorate the top of the loaf.

7 Leave the cake in the tin for 10 minutes, then turn it onto a wire rack. Turn it the right way up, then leave it to cool.

8 For the icing, sift the icing sugar into a big bowl. Mix in 1 tablespoon of the lemon juice. Use a blunt knife to spread the icing onto the cake.

Other flavours

For a lemon and sultana loaf, simply replace the mango with sultanas. You could also try a lemon and blueberry loaf, using dried blueberries.

For a lime and fig loaf, replace the lemons with 4 limes and the mango with dried figs. You could use dates instead of figs.

For an orange and cherry loaf, replace the lemons with oranges and the mango with dried sour cherries – or use dried apricots instead, for an orange and apricot loaf.

Lemon ricotta cake

Ingredients:

2 lemons

3 medium eggs

50g (2oz) softened butter

300g (10oz) caster sugar

250g (9oz) ricotta cheese

175g (6oz) self-raising flour

50g (2oz) white chocolate chips

25g (1oz) plain chocolate chips

You will also need a 20cm (8in) square, deep cake tin.

Makes 9 squares

This tangy lemon cake contains ricotta, a type of soft Italian cheese. It makes the cake especially light and moist. The cake also has a marbled topping, made by sprinkling plain and white chocolate drops over the cake while it is still warm, so they melt. Then, you swirl them together.

1 Grease the tin and line it with baking parchment (page 10). Heat the oven to 180°C, 350°F, gas mark 4. Grate the zest from the lemons using the small holes of a grater.

2 Separate the eggs, following the instructions on page 11. Put the yolks in a cup and put the whites in a big, very clean bowl.

3 Whisk the egg whites with a whisk until they become really thick and foamy. When you lift the whisk up, the egg whites should stand up in stiff points, like this.

4 Put the butter, sugar, egg yolks and lemon zest into another large bowl. Beat them together with a fork. Add the ricotta, a spoonful at a time, beating after each addition.

Move the spoon in the... ...shape of a number 8.

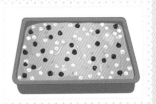

5 Sift the flour over the mixture. Gently fold it in with a metal spoon. Add the egg whites and fold them in too. Then, spoon the mixture into the cake tin.

6 Smooth the top of the mixture with the back of a spoon. Bake the cake in the oven for 45-50 minutes, until it feels firm when you touch it.

7 While the cake is still hot, sprinkle both types of chocolate chips over the top. Follow the instructions on page 381 to make a marbled chocolate topping.

Chocolate roulade

Ingredients:

4 large eggs

125g (5oz) caster sugar

60g (2½oz) ground almonds

1½ tablespoons cocoa powder

1¼ teaspoons baking powder
  (gluten-free types are available)

For the filling:

300ml (½ pint) double cream

1 tin of cherries

You will also need a 35 x 25cm
(14 x 10in) Swiss roll tin.

Makes around 10 slices

This recipe is similar to the Swiss roll on pages 104-105, but this time the cake is made using ground almonds and flavoured with cocoa powder. You can fill it with the cherry cream filling given here, or with vanilla cream (page 377).

1 Heat the oven to 180°C, 350°F or gas mark 4. Grease and line the tin (page 10). Separate the eggs (page 11) so the whites are in one bowl and the yolks are in another.

2 Add the sugar to the yolks. Whisk them together with a fork, until the mixture is pale and thick. Stir in the ground almonds, cocoa powder and baking powder.

Move the spoon in the...
...shape of a number 8.

3 Whisk the egg whites with a whisk, until they are really thick and foamy. When you lift the whisk up, the egg whites should stand up in stiff points, like this.

4 Spoon the egg whites into the mixture. Gently fold them in with a metal spoon. When all the ingredients are well mixed, pour the mixture into the tin.

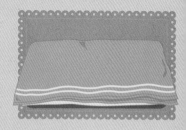

5 Bake for 20-25 minutes, until risen and springy. Leave it in the tin for 10 minutes to cool. Then, cover it with a piece of baking parchment and a clean tea towel.

6 Put the tin in the fridge for at least 2 hours to chill. Meanwhile, whip the cream, following the instructions on page 377.

7 Take the cake out of the fridge. Run a knife around the sides to loosen the edges. Lay the sheet of baking parchment on a work surface. Sieve icing sugar onto it.

8 Turn the cake onto the baking parchment. Peel off the old parchment. Spread the cream over the cake. Use a sieve to drain the syrup from the cherries.

Use the parchment to help you roll up the cake.

9 Remove the cherry stones and scatter the cherries over the cream. Carefully, roll up the cake from one of the short ends. Then, lift the cake onto a plate.

You could sift a little icing sugar over your finished log, to decorate it.

Apple & cinnamon cake

Ingredients:

2 medium eating apples

9 tablespoons sunflower oil

150g (5oz) caster sugar

3 medium eggs

100g (4oz) raisins or sultanas

75g (3oz) wholemeal flour

75g (3oz) self-raising flour

1½ teaspoons baking powder

1½ teaspoons bicarbonate of soda

1½ teaspoons ground cinnamon

1 teaspoon ground ginger

For the topping:

2 tablespoons demerara sugar

½ teaspoon ground cinnamon

You will also need a 27 x 8cm (7 x 11in) rectangular cake tin.

Makes 12 slices

This moist cake is full of raisins, spices and apple pieces, and has a delicious, crunchy cinnamon sugar topping. The apple cooks while the cake is in the oven, so by the time the cake is ready, the pieces of apple have softened.

1 Heat the oven to 180°C, 350°F or gas mark 4. Line the tin with baking parchment (see page 10).

2 Cut each apple in half. Put the halves flat side down and cut them in half again. Cut out the cores, with the knife facing away from you.

3 Throw the cores away. You don't need to peel the apple quarters. Just cut them into bite-sized chunks.

4 Put the sunflower oil and sugar in a large bowl and beat them for a minute with a wooden spoon.

5 Crack one egg into a cup and beat it with a fork. Add it to the oil and sugar mixture and beat it in well. Do the same with the second egg, then the third egg.

6 Put the chopped apple and raisins in the bowl and stir to mix them in well.

7 Sift both types of flour, the baking powder, bicarbonate of soda, cinnamon and ginger over the mixture. If there are any bits left in the sieve, tip them in too.

8 Gently fold everything together with a metal spoon, moving it in the shape of a number 8. Scrape the mixture into the tin and smooth the top.

9 For the topping, mix the sugar and cinnamon and sprinkle it over the cake. Bake for 45 minutes until risen and firm. Leave in the tin for 10 minutes to cool.

0 Hold the tin upside down over a wire rack. The cake should pop out. Peel off the parchment. When the cake is cool, turn it back up the right way and cut it into squares.

Other ideas

You could leave off the cinnamon sugar topping and ice the cake with cream cheese frosting instead, if you like. Follow the recipe for cream cheese frosting given on page 376.

For a pear cake, replace the apples with 2 ripe pears, cut up in the same way as the apples. You could also replace the raisins with plain chocolate chips.

Carrot cake

This is a light, moist cake, with a hint of spice. It is covered with a refreshing cream cheese topping.

Ingredients:

2 medium carrots

3 medium eggs

175ml (6floz) sunflower oil

200g (7oz) caster sugar

100g (4oz) chopped pecans or walnuts (optional)

200g (7oz) plain flour

1½ teaspoons baking powder

1½ teaspoons bicarbonate of soda

1½ teaspoons ground cinnamon

1 teaspoon ground ginger

½ teaspoon salt

For the topping:

50g (2oz) icing sugar

200g (7oz) full-fat cream cheese

1 tablespoon lemon juice

½ teaspoon vanilla essence

For decorating:

pecan or walnut halves (optional)

You will also need a 27 x 18cm (7 x 11in) rectangular, shallow cake tin.

Makes 12 slices

1 Take the cream cheese out of the fridge. Heat the oven to 180°C, 350°F or gas mark 4. Grease and line the tin (see page 10).

2 Wash the carrots and cut off their tops. Hold each carrot firmly and grate it carefully on the biggest holes of a grater.

3 Crack the eggs into a small bowl and beat them with a fork. Put the sunflower oil and sugar into a larger bowl and beat them for a minute with a wooden spoon.

4 Add the beaten eggs to the larger bowl, a little at a time. Beat the mixture well after each addition. Then, stir in the grated carrots and the chopped nuts.

6 Spoon the mixture into the tin. Smooth the top with the back of a spoon. Bake the cake for 45 minutes until it is risen and firm.

5 Sift the flour, baking powder, bicarbonate of soda, cinnamon, ginger and salt over the mixture. Gently fold everything together with a metal spoon.

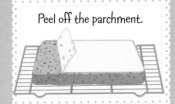

Peel off the parchment.

7 Leave the cake in the tin for 10 minutes, then run a knife around the sides. Carefully turn the cake out onto a wire rack (page 373). Leave the cake to cool completely.

8 Sift the icing sugar into a bowl. Add the cream cheese, lemon juice and vanilla. Beat the mixture well. When the cake has cooled, spoon the topping onto it.

9 Spread the topping over the cake with a blunt knife, making lots of swirly patterns. Then, decorate the cake with pecan or walnut halves, or lemon zest.

These strips of lemon zest were made using a tool called a zester.

Gingerbread cake

Ingredients:

275g (10oz) golden syrup

100g (4oz) dark muscovado sugar

100g (4oz) butter

225g (8oz) self-raising flour

1 tablespoon ground ginger

1 teaspoon ground cinnamon

2 medium eggs

2 tablespoons milk

For decorating:

100g (4oz) icing sugar

You will also need a 900g (2lb) loaf tin, measuring around 20 x 12 x 8cm (8 x 5 x 3½in).

Makes around 12 slices

This soft, loaf-shaped cake is flavoured with ginger, syrup, and brown sugar. If you keep it for a few days, it will become deliciously moist and sticky.

1 Heat the oven to 170°C, 325°F or gas mark 3. Grease and line the tin (see page 10).

2 Put the syrup, sugar and butter in a saucepan. Put it over a low heat. Stir now and then, until the butter melts. Take it off the heat.

3 Sift the flour, ginger and cinnamon into big bowl. Make a hollow in the middle.

4 Break an egg into a cup. Tip the egg into a jug. Do the same with the other egg. Add the milk and beat with a fork until mixed.

5 Pour the syrup mixture into the flour. Start mixing. When half the flour is mixed in, add the egg mixture. Keep stirring until everything is well mixed.

The top of the cake may crack but this doesn't matter.

6 Pour the mixture into the tin. Bake for 50 minutes. Test with a skewer to check it is cooked.

When the cake is cool, peel off the parchment.

7 Leave to cool for 15 minutes, then turn the cake out of the tin onto a wire rack. Leave it upside down to cool.

8 To make the icing, sift the icing sugar into a bowl. Add 1 tablespoon of cold water and mix to a smooth paste.

9 Spoon the icing over the cake, so it dribbles down the sides (see page 378). Wait until it dries before you add any decorations.

Other flavours

For a richer, darker flavour, use just 200g (7oz) golden syrup and add 75g (3oz) black treacle at the same time.

For a zesty icing, replace the water with lemon or lime juice.

You'll find instructions on page 384 for making houses like these, to decorate your cake.

This roof was decorated with patterns piped in glittery writing icing.

For a snowy roof, spread on white writing icing, then scatter on white sprinkles or sparkling sugar.

Add details like these using the side or end of a cocktail stick.

You could scatter sparkling sugar on top of your cake and serving plate.

Chocolate party cake

Ingredients:

100g (4oz) self-raising flour

40g (1½oz) cocoa powder

1½ teaspoons baking powder

150g (5oz) softened butter
 or soft margarine

150g (5oz) soft light brown sugar

1 teaspoon vanilla essence

3 tablespoons milk

3 large eggs

For the chocolate buttercream:

100g (4oz) softened unsalted butter
 or margarine

175g (6oz) icing sugar

40g (1½oz) cocoa powder

1 tablespoon milk

½ teaspoon vanilla essence

You will also need a 27 x 18cm
(11 x 7in) rectangular cake tin.

Makes 12-15 squares

This chocolate cake can be cut up into lots of squares so it's great for handing around at parties. The cake shown here is decorated with chocolate beans and drizzled white chocolate, but you can use any decorations you like.

1 Heat the oven to 180°C, 350°F or gas mark 4. Grease and line the tin (see page 10).

2 Sift the flour, cocoa and baking powder into a big bowl. Put the butter and sugar in another bowl.

3 Beat the butter or margarine and sugar until pale and fluffy. Mix in the vanilla and milk.

4 Crack an egg into a cup. Tip it into the butter and sugar mixture. Add 1 tablespoon of the floury mixture. Beat well. Do this with each egg.

Move the spoon in the....
...shape of a number 8.

5 Add the rest of the floury mixture and stir it in gently, using a big metal spoon.

6 Scrape the mixture into the tin and level the top with the back of a spoon. Bake for 30-35 minutes, until risen and springy.

If you tie a ribbon around the cake, remember to take it off before you cut the cake.

It will be easier to cut your cake if you take out any candles first, too.

7 When the cake is cooked, leave it in the tin for a few minutes, then turn it out onto a wire rack (see page 373).

Peel off the parchment

8 To make the chocolate buttercream, see page 376.

9 When the cake is cold, spread the buttercream over the top.

10 Decorate with drizzled chocolate (see page 381), chocolate beans and candles too, if you like. To eat, cut into 12 or 15 squares.

Chocolate traybake

This chocolate cake doesn't contain wheat, gluten or nuts, and you can make it dairy-free too, so it's a good choice if you're cooking for someone who can't eat those foods. Read the allergy advice on page 388 first.

1 Heat the oven to 190°C, 375°F or gas mark 5. Grease and line the tin (see page 10).

2 Beat the butter or margarine and sugar together in a large bowl, until they are pale and fluffy.

3 Break the eggs into a small bowl and beat them with a fork. Add them to the beaten mixture a little at a time, beating it again after each addition.

You could decorate your finished traybake with shapes cut from chocolate paste (page 381).

Peel off the parchment.

4 Sift the cocoa and baking powder into the bowl. Add the cornmeal, vanilla and a tablespoon of water. Mix well.

5 Spoon the mixture into the tin, pushing it into the corners with the back of a spoon. Bake for 25-30 minutes until the cake is firm and springy. Leave for 5 minutes, to cool.

6 Shake the tin upside down over a wire rack. The cake should pop out. While it is still hot, make the marbled chocolate topping (see page 381 for instructions).

If you're cooking this cake for someone with food allergies, use allergy-free chocolate for the topping.

7 When the topping has set, put the cake on a board, then cut it into around 12 squares.

121

Christmas log

Ingredients:

4 large eggs

125g (4½oz) caster sugar

60g (2½oz) ground almonds

2½ tablespoons cocoa powder

1¼ teaspoons baking powder

For the chocolate buttercream:

100g (4oz) softened butter
   or margarine

225g (8oz) icing sugar

1 tablespoon warm water

1 tablespoon cocoa powder

For the raspberry cream filling:

200ml (7fl oz) whipping cream

150g (5oz) fresh raspberries

1½ tablespoons caster sugar

You will also need a 35 x 25cm
(14 x 10in) Swiss roll tin.

Makes 10 slices

This is a festive version of the chocolate roulade recipe on pages 110-111. The outside of the log is decorated with chocolate buttercream and sifted with icing sugar, to make it look more like a real log dusted in snow, but it tastes good at any time of year.

1 Heat the oven to 180°C, 350°F or gas mark 4. Grease and line the tin (page 10). Separate the eggs (page 11) so the whites are in one bowl and the yolks are in another.

2 Beat the sugar with the yolks until they are pale and thick. Stir in the ground almonds, cocoa and baking powder.

3 Using a whisk, whisk the egg whites, until they are really thick and foamy. When you lift up the whisk, they should stand up in stiff points, like this.

Move the spoon in the...
...shape of a number 8.

4 Gently fold the whites into the yolk mixture. Pour into the tin. Bake for 20-25 minutes until firm.

5 Then, leave the cake in the tin for ten minutes. Cover it with a clean tea towel. Put it in the fridge for an hour.

6 For the buttercream, beat the butter and icing sugar in a bowl until they are smooth. Mix the water and cocoa. Stir them into the buttercream.

7 For the filling, whip the cream (see page 377). Mash the raspberries with a fork. Stir them into the cream, with the sugar.

8 Take the cake out of the fridge. Run a knife around the edges. Sift some icing sugar onto a surface and turn the cake onto it.

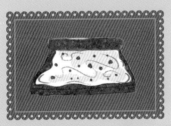

9 Peel the parchment off the top of the cake. Spread the filling over the cake. Carefully roll it up from one of the short ends. Lift it onto a plate.

0 Spread the chocolate buttercream all over the cake.

You could sift over icing sugar and decorate your Christmas log with fresh mint leaves and raspberries.

Other ideas

For a dairy-free version, use dairy-free margarine for the buttercream and for a filling, mash 150g (5oz) fresh raspberries into 2 tablespoons raspberry jam. To make the cake wheat-free and gluten-free, use gluten-free and wheat-free baking powder. See the allergy advice on page 388 first.

Honey spice cake

Ingredients:

1 lemon

1 orange

150g (5oz) soft light brown sugar

150g (5oz) softened butter or margarine

3 medium eggs

2 teaspoons baking powder

150g (5oz) semolina or fine cornmeal (polenta)

2 teaspoons ground cinnamon

½ teaspoon ground allspice

150g (5oz) ground almonds

4 tablespoons runny honey

You will also need a 27 x 18cm (11 x 7in) rectangular cake tray.

Makes 12-15 squares

This sticky cake tastes of honey, cinnamon and lemon. You can make it wheat- and gluten-free by using cornmeal and wheat- and gluten-free baking powder. To make it dairy-free, use dairy-free margarine.

1 Heat the oven to 180°C, 350°F or gas mark 4. Grease and line the tray (see page 10).

2 Squeeze the juice from the orange and lemon. Put it in a jug.

3 Put the sugar and butter or margarine in a big bowl. Beat until you have a pale and fluffy mixture.

4 Break an egg into a bowl and beat it. Stir it into the mixture in the big bowl. Do the same with the other eggs. Don't worry if it looks lumpy.

5 Put the baking powder, semolina or cornmeal, cinnamon, allspice and ground almonds in a bowl and mix. Tip them into the large bowl.

6 Add 4 tablespoons of juice from the jug and stir. Scrape the mixture into the tray and level the top with the back of a spoon. Bake for 30-35 minutes.

You could decorate your cake with flower or bee shapes cut from sugarpaste or marzipan – see page 382.

To stick decorations to the cake, brush a dab of honey on the back of each one, then press it onto the cake.

Don't worry if it doesn't all mix in.

7 Meanwhile, put the honey in the jug and mix it in. When the cake is risen and firm, take it out of the oven.

8 Give the mixture in the jug a stir, then pour it over the cake. Leave the cake in the tray to cool, then cut it into 12-15 squares.

Other ideas

You can use the same recipe to make cupcakes, instead of a tray cake. At step 1, heat the oven to 200°C, 400°F or gas mark 6. Line a 12-hole deep muffin tray with 12 paper muffin cases. At step 6, spoon the mixture into the cases and bake for 15-20 minutes.

Moist fruit cake

Ingredients:

125g (4½oz) softened butter

125g (4½oz) dark muscovado sugar

2 large eggs

1 orange

1 lemon

200g (7oz) mixture of dried figs, prunes, apricots and dates

50g (2oz) mixture of dried cranberries and glacé cherries

250g (9oz) mixture of currants, raisins and sultanas

25g (1oz) chopped mixed peel

125g (4½oz) plain flour

½ teaspoon baking powder

2 teaspoons mixed spice

To decorate:

2 tablespoons smooth apricot jam

400g (14oz) marzipan (optional)

400g (14oz) icing sugar

You will also need a 20cm (8in) square cake tin.

Makes 25 squares

This moist fruit cake is covered with marzipan and icing, but it also tastes delicious without any topping. For a nut-free version, leave out the marzipan.

1 Heat the oven to 180°C, 350°F or gas mark 4. Line the tin with parchment (page 10). Cut another square of parchment the same size to use later.

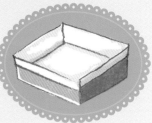

2 Cut two strips of parchment 35cm (14in) long and 12cm (5in) wide. Use the strips to line the sides of the tin.

The mixture will look lumpy.

3 Beat the butter and sugar in a large bowl. Beat the eggs in a cup, then add them to the bowl a little at a time, beating well between each addition.

4 Grate the zest from the orange and lemon. Squeeze the juice from the orange. Add the zest and juice to the mixture.

6 Add the cranberries, cherries, currants, raisins, sultanas, mixed peel, flour, baking powder and mixed spice. Mix everything together well.

5 Remove the date stones if there are any. Use scissors to snip the figs, prunes, apricots and dates into small pieces. Put the fruit in the bowl.

You could decorate each square with half a glacé cherry.

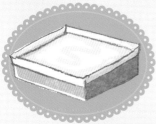

7 Spoon the mixture into the tin. Use the spoon to push it into the corners and smooth the top. Lay the square of parchment on top.

8 Bake for 50-60 minutes. Peel off the parchment. Test the cake with a skewer (see page 373) to see if it's cooked. If not, cook for 10 minutes more, then test again.

9 Leave the cake in the tin until it's cool. Turn it onto a wire rack. Peel off the parchment. Spread jam over the cake.

10 Roll out the marzipan until it is bigger than the cake. Fold it over the rolling pin and lift it onto the cake.

11 Use scissors to trim the edges off the marzipan. For the icing, sift the icing sugar into a bowl. Mix in 4 tablespoons of warm water. Spread over the cake.

12 Leave the icing to dry. Use a sharp knife to cut 4 lines across the cake in one direction and 4 lines in the other direction, to make 25 squares.

Bars & Brownies

Cherry crumble bars

These bars have a crumbly top and a sponge base with streaks of jam inside. You can use any type of jam, but brightly-coloured ones look more attractive.

Ingredients:

For the topping:

75g (3oz) plain flour

25g (1oz) porridge oats

25g (1oz) sunflower seeds (optional)

75g (3oz) soft light brown sugar

50g (2oz) butter

For the sponge:

200g (7oz) self-raising flour

1 teaspoon cinnamon

½ teaspoon baking powder

pinch of salt

125g (4½oz) caster sugar

40g (1½oz) butter

2 large eggs

200ml (7fl oz) soured cream

375g (15oz) red cherry jam

You will also need a 27 x 18cm (11 x 7in) rectangular cake tin, at least 4cm (1¾in) deep.

Makes 12

1 Heat the oven to 180°C, 350°F or gas mark 4. Grease and line the tin (page 10). For the topping, sift the flour into a big bowl. Stir in the oats, seeds and sugar.

2 Put the butter in a saucepan and heat it until it has just melted. Remove the pan from the heat. Carefully, pour the butter over the ingredients in the bowl.

3 Use a fork to stir everything together. Then, put the bowl in the fridge to chill, while you make the mixture for the sponge.

4 Sift the flour, cinnamon, baking powder and salt into another big bowl. Stir in the sugar. Heat the butter in a saucepan. When it has just melted, pour it into a jug.

5 Crack the eggs into a small bowl and beat them with a fork. When the butter in the jug has cooled, add the eggs and the soured cream. Stir them together.

6 Pour the mixture from the jug into the dry ingredients. Beat everything together with a wooden spoon until it is smooth. Spoon the mixture into the tin.

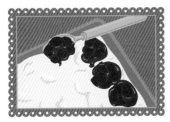

7 Use a spoon to push the mixture into the corners of the tin. Put the jam into a bowl and beat it with a fork. Then, drop teaspoonfuls of jam on top of the sponge.

Make sure the jam is pushed down into the sponge.

8 When the top of the sponge is almost covered with jam, swirl the jam through the mixture with a knife. This will make a marbled pattern when the bars are cooked.

9 Take the topping out of the fridge. Break it up and sprinkle it evenly over the sponge. Bake for 40 minutes. Leave in the tin to cool before cutting into 12 bars.

Apple flapjacks

Ingredients:

2 eating apples

175g (6oz) butter

175g (6oz) demerara sugar

2 tablespoons golden syrup

½ teaspoon ground cinnamon

50g (2oz) sultanas

225g (8oz) porridge oats

2 tablespoons sunflower seeds
(optional)

You will also need an 18 x 27cm
(7 x 11in) tin.

Makes 12

These fruity flapjacks contain fresh apple, sultanas and cinnamon. To make flapjacks, you melt some of the ingredients together in a pan, before putting them in the oven.

1 Heat the oven to 160°C, 325°F or gas mark 3. Grease the tin, then line it with baking parchment (see page 10).

2 Cut the apple into quarters. Peel them, then cut out the cores. Cut the quarters into small chunks.

Use a wooden spoon... ...to stir the mixture.

3 Put the chunks of apple in a saucepan with 25g (1oz) of the butter. Cook them over a low heat for 10 minutes, stirring every now and then, until the apple is soft.

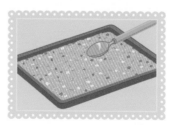

4 Add the rest of the butter with the sugar, syrup, cinnamon and sultanas. Heat gently until the butter has melted. Then, take the pan off the heat.

5 Stir in the oats and seeds. Stir everything together. Spoon the mixture into the tin and spread it out. Smooth the top with the back of a spoon.

6 Bake for 25 minutes. Take the tin out of the oven, leave it for 10 minutes to cool. Then, cut the mixture into 12 flapjacks.

Flapjacks should be dark golden-brown and soft when you take them out of the oven. If you cook them too long, they may be dry and not so chewy.

Chocolate fudge brownies

Ingredients:

100g (4oz) plain chocolate

2 large eggs

125g (5oz) softened butter

275g (10oz) caster sugar

½ teaspoon vanilla essence

50g (2oz) self-raising flour

25g (1oz) plain flour

2 tablespoons cocoa powder

100g (4oz) walnuts or pecans (optional)

You will also need a 20cm (8in) square cake tin and a heatproof bowl that fits snugly into a saucepan.

Makes 9

Brownies originated in America. They are baked chocolatey treats that have a crisp, sugary top and a gooey centre. Traditionally, brownies contain lots of pecans or walnuts, but you can leave them out if you don't like nuts, or if you can't eat them.

Wear oven gloves.

1 Heat the oven to 180°C, 350°F or gas mark 4. Grease and line the tin (see page 10). Break up the chocolate and put it in the heatproof bowl.

2 Fill the saucepan a quarter full of water. Heat until the water bubbles. Take the pan off the heat. Carefully lower in the heatproof bowl.

3 Stir with a wooden spoon until the chocolate has melted. Then, wearing oven gloves, carefully lift the bowl out of the pan.

4 Break the eggs into a small bowl and beat them. Put the butter, sugar and vanilla in a big bowl. Beat until they are fluffy. Add the eggs a little at a time, beating well each time.

5 Sift both types of flour and the cocoa powder into the bowl. Add the melted chocolate and mix well.

6 Put the nuts on a chopping board. Cut them into small pieces. Stir them into the mixture. Spoon the mixture into the tin. Smooth the top with the back of a spoon.

7 Bake the brownies for 35 minutes. They are ready when they have risen slightly and a crust has formed on top, but they should still be soft in the middle.

8 Leave the brownies in the tin for 20 minutes. Then, cut across the tin 3 times in one direction, and 3 times in the other direction, to make 9 squares.

Find out how to stencil icing sugar shapes on top of your brownies on page 383.

Cherry chocolate brownies

Ingredients:

100g (4oz) plain chocolate

2 large eggs

125g (4½oz) softened butter or margarine

275g (10oz) caster sugar

½ teaspoon vanilla essence

50g (2oz) self-raising flour

25g (1oz) plain flour

2 tablespoons cocoa powder

100g (4oz) dried cherries

100g (4oz) walnut or pecan pieces (optional)

You will also need a 20cm (8in) square cake tin and a heatproof bowl that fits snugly into a saucepan.

Makes 12 to 16

These brownies have a crispy top and a squidgy middle studded with nuts and dried cherries. Leave out the nuts if you prefer. You could eat these brownies while they're still warm, with a scoop of vanilla ice cream and chocolate sauce, made by following the recipe given on the opposite page.

1 Heat the oven to 180°C, 350°F or gas mark 4. Grease and line the tray (see page 10).

2 Melt the chocolate, following the instructions on page 380.

3 Break the eggs into a small bowl. Beat them with a fork.

4 Put the butter or margarine, sugar and vanilla in a big bowl. Beat until they are fluffy. Add the eggs a little at a time, beating well each time.

5 Sift both types of flour and the cocoa powder into the bowl. Add the melted chocolate. Mix well.

6 Mix in the cherries and nuts. Scrape the mixture into the tin. Smooth the top with the back of a spoon.

The chocolate sauce goes hard on the cold ice cream.

You could cut up some fresh cherries to eat with your brownies. Cut them in half, running the knife around the central stone.

If you prefer more traditional brownies, just leave out the cherries.

7 Bake for 35 minutes, until slightly risen. It should have a crust on top but a soft middle.

8 Leave in the tin for 20 minutes to cool.

Chocolate sauce

You will need 100g (4oz) chocolate, 2 tablespoons of golden syrup or honey and 1 tablespoon of water.

Break up the chocolate. Put all the ingredients in a pan over a low heat. Stir until you have a glossy mixture. Leave to cool for a few minutes before eating.

Chocolate chip brownies

Ingredients:

100g (4oz) plain chocolate

2 large eggs

125g (5oz) softened butter

275g (10oz) caster sugar

½ teaspoon vanilla essence

50g (2oz) self-raising flour

25g (1oz) plain flour

2 tablespoons cocoa powder

100g (4oz) chocolate chips or
chocolate

100g (4oz) walnut or pecan pieces
(optional)

You will also need a 20cm (8in)
square cake tin and a heatproof bowl
that fits snugly into a saucepan.

Makes 9

This is a luxurious recipe for rich chocolate brownies containing a generous helping of chocolate chips. You can use whatever flavour of chocolate chips you like – plain, milk or white. Or you could buy a bar of your favourite chocolate and cut it up to make your own chips. Leave the nuts out, if you prefer.

1 Heat the oven to 180°C, 350°F or gas mark 4. Put the tin onto a piece of baking parchment. Draw around it and cut out the shape.

2 Use a paper towel to wipe a little cooking oil over the insides of the tin and put the paper square into the tin.

3 Break up the plain chocolate and put it in the heatproof bowl. Fill the saucepan a quarter full with water. Heat the water until it bubbles. Take the pan off the heat.

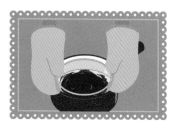

4 Wearing oven gloves, lower the bowl into the pan. Stir the chocolate until it melts, then, wearing oven gloves, take the bowl out of the pan.

5 Break the eggs into a small bowl. Beat well. Put the butter, sugar and vanilla in a big bowl. Beat until fluffy. Add the eggs, a little at a time, beating well each time.

6 Sift both types of flour and the cocoa into the bowl. Then, add the melted chocolate and mix it all together. If you're using a chocolate bar to make chips, break it up into small pieces.

7 Add the pieces or chips, and the nuts, to the mixture. Stir well. Then, spoon the mixture into the tin and smooth the top with the back of a spoon.

8 Bake the brownies for 35 minutes. They're ready when they have risen slightly and a crust has formed on top. They will still be soft inside.

These brownies are *delicious* eaten while they're still *slightly warm*, as the chocolate chips will be *gooey*.

9 Leave the brownies in the tin for 20 minutes to cool, then cut them into 9 squares.

Chocolate peanut brownies

Ingredients:

100g (4oz) salted, roasted peanuts

100g (4oz) plain chocolate

2 large eggs

125g (4½oz) softened butter or margarine

275g (10oz) soft light brown sugar

½ teaspoon vanilla essence

50g (2oz) self-raising flour

25g (1oz) plain flour

2 tablespoons cocoa powder

You will also need a 20cm (8in) square cake tin and a heatproof bowl that fits snugly into a saucepan.

Makes 8-12

Chocolate and peanuts taste delicious together in these fudgy chocolate brownies. Try them warm with peanut butter sauce and ice cream. For more traditional brownies, use pecans instead of the peanuts, or leave out the nuts altogether.

1 Heat the oven to 180°C, 350°F or gas mark 4. Grease and line the tin (see page 10).

2 Melt the chocolate, following the instructions on page 380. Wearing oven gloves, take the bowl out of the pan.

3 Put the peanuts in a sieve and rinse them well under a cold tap, to remove the salt. Then, pat them dry with a clean tea towel.

4 Break the eggs into a small bowl. Beat them with a fork.

5 Put the butter or margarine, sugar and vanilla in a big bowl. Beat until they are fluffy. Add the beaten eggs a little at a time, beating well each time.

6 Sift both types of flour and the cocoa powder into the bowl. Add the melted chocolate and the peanuts. Mix well.

7 Scrape the mixture into the tin. Smooth the top with the back of a spoon. Bake for 35 minutes, until slightly risen. They will have a crust on top but a soft middle.

Peanut butter sauce

To make a simple peanut butter sauce to eat with your brownies, you will need 150g (5oz) smooth peanut butter. Put it in a small saucepan over a low heat for 5 minutes, stirring every now and then, until the peanut butter becomes soft and runny.

8 Leave in the tin for 20 minutes to cool. Then cut into 8-12 pieces.

White chocolate brownie bites

Ingredients:

200g (7oz) white chocolate or white chocolate chips

75g (3oz) butter

3 medium eggs

175g (6oz) caster sugar

1 teaspoon vanilla essence

175g (6oz) plain flour

75g (3oz) dried cranberries

You will also need a 20cm (8in) square cake tin and a heatproof bowl that fits snugly into a saucepan.

Makes around 25

Made with white chocolate and tangy cranberries, these little bites are a pale and interesting alternative to traditional brownies. White chocolate brownies like these are sometimes called 'blondies'.

1. Heat the oven to 180°C, 350°F or gas mark 4. Grease and line the tin (page 10). Fill the saucepan a quarter full of water and heat it gently. When the water bubbles, take the pan off the heat.

Wear oven gloves.

2. If you're using chocolate in a bar, break it into small pieces. Put half the pieces or chips in the heatproof bowl. Cut the butter into chunks. Add them too. Put the bowl in the pan.

3. Stir until the butter and chocolate have melted. Then, wearing oven gloves, lift the bowl out of the pan.

4. Beat the eggs in a large bowl. Stir in the sugar and vanilla essence. Add the chocolate mixture a little at a time, beating well between each addition.

Move the spoon in the...

...shape of a number 8.

5 Add the flour, the cranberries and the rest of the chocolate pieces or chips. Fold everything together gently.

6 Spoon the mixture into the tin. Bake for 25 minutes for soft, gooey brownies, or 30 minutes to make them firmer.

7 Leave in the tin for 20 minutes. Then, cut into 25 little squares. Sift icing sugar over the top, if you like.

Other flavours

Instead of dried cranberries, you could use other dried fruits such as blueberries, currants, chopped ready-to-eat dried apricots or tropical dried fruits such as mango, pineapple or papaya.

Instead of the dried fruit, you could add plain or milk chocolate chips or pieces.

Ice cream & brownie cake

Ingredients:

50g (2oz) plain chocolate

1 medium egg

65g (2½oz) softened butter or margarine

125g (4½oz) soft dark brown sugar

25g (1oz) self-raising flour

15g (½oz) plain flour

1 tablespoon cocoa powder

1½ litres (2½ pints) ice cream, or 2 litres (4 pints) soft-scoop ice cream

You will also need a 20cm (8in) square cake tin, a heatproof bowl that fits snugly into a saucepan and a 900g (2lb) loaf tin, measuring around 20½ x 12½ x 8cm (8 x 5 x 3½in).

Makes 10 slices

To make this cake, you bake a chocolate brownie and then sandwich it between layers of ice cream. You can use whatever flavour (or flavours) of ice cream you like.

1 Heat the oven to 180°C, 350°F or gas mark 4. Grease and line the square cake tin (see page 10). Melt the chocolate, following the instructions on page 380.

2 Break the egg into a cup. Beat it with a fork. Put the butter and sugar into a big bowl. Beat until fluffy.

3 Add a spoonful of egg and beat it in. Add the rest of the egg a spoonful at a time, beating well each time.

4 Sift both types of flour and the cocoa into the bowl. Add the melted chocolate. Mix well. Spoon into the tin. Spread it out with the back of a spoon.

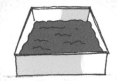 

You can eat the edges later – they're delicious!

5 Bake for 20 minutes, until slightly risen with a crust on top. Leave in the tin to cool. When it is cold, take the ice cream out of the freezer and leave it for 10 minutes.

6 Run a knife around the brownie and shake it onto a board. Turn it the right way up. Use a sharp knife to cut off the raised edges. Then, cut the brownie in half.

7 Line the loaf tin with a big piece of plastic food wrap. Leave the ends of the wrap hanging over the sides of the tin.

Chocolate sauce

You will need 40g (1½oz) plain or milk chocolate and 75ml (3floz) double or whipping cream. To make the sauce, follow step 8 on page 231.

8 Fill the tin one third full of ice cream. Push it into the corners and pack it down well. Then, smooth the top with the back of a spoon.

You could top your ice cream cake with chocolate sauce (see box above) and chocolate beans.

If the brownie breaks – piece it back together in the tin.

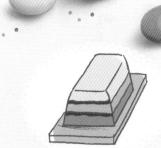

9 Put one half of the brownie on top. You may need to trim off the end to make it fit. Spoon in more ice cream so the tin is two-thirds full. Smooth the top.

10 Put the other piece of brownie on top. Trim it if you need to. Add more ice cream to fill the tin. Smooth the top. Fold the ends of food wrap over the top. Freeze for at least 4 hours.

11 Peel the food wrap off the top. Put the tin upside down on a board. Rub a hot, damp cloth over the outside of the tin. The cake will pop out. Remove the tin and the food wrap.

Meringues & macaroons

Filled meringues

Ingredients:

2 medium eggs

100g (4oz) caster sugar

For the raspberry cream (optional):

125g (5oz) fresh raspberries

150ml (¼ pint) double cream

You will also need 2 baking trays.

Makes around 20

Meringues are made of whisked egg whites and sugar, baked until the outsides are crisp, while the insides stay deliciously chewy. Eat them just as they are, or sandwich pairs together with raspberry cream.

1 Heat the oven to 110°C, 225°F or gas mark ¼. Then, line the baking trays (see page 10).

2 Separate the eggs (see page 11). Put the whites in the large bowl. You don't need the yolks for this recipe – you could use them in the recipe on pages 26-27.

3 Beat the egg whites very quickly with a whisk, until they become very thick and foamy. If the foam stays in a point, like this, when you lift up the whisk, you have whisked it enough.

4 Add a heaped teaspoonful of sugar and whisk until it is all mixed in. Keep on adding spoonfuls of sugar and whisking them in, until all the sugar is mixed in.

5 Scoop up a heaped teaspoon of the mixture. Use another spoon to push it onto a tray. Put more blobs on the trays, until the mixture is used up. Space the blobs out well.

6 Bake for 40 minutes. Turn off the oven. Leave the meringues inside for 15 minutes. Then, lift them out and leave them to cool.

7 Meanwhile, make the raspberry cream. Rinse the raspberries in a sieve and shake them dry. Put them in a bowl and mash them until they are squashed and juicy.

148

8 Pour the cream into a large bowl and beat it very quickly with a whisk. Carry on until it becomes thick. Try lifting up the whisk – if the cream stays in a floppy point, like this, you have whisked it enough.

9 Add the mashed raspberries to the cream and mix them in gently with a metal spoon. When the meringues are cold, spread the flat side of one with some raspberry cream. Then, press the flat side of another meringue to the filling.

Other ideas

If you use refined, white caster sugar, your meringues should come out almost white. If you use unrefined, golden caster sugar they will be a very pale golden colour.

Other fillings

Replace the raspberries with 3 ripe, wrinkly passionfruits. Cut the passionfruits in half and scoop out the seeds and juice with a spoon. At step 9, add the passionfruit seeds and juice to the cream instead of the raspberries.

Multicoloured meringues

Ingredients:

2 medium eggs

1 pinch cream of tartar (optional)

100g (4oz) caster sugar

sugar sprinkles

different food dyes

You will also need 2 baking trays.

Makes around 18

These colourful little meringues are decorated with bright swirls of food dye and sugar sprinkles before they are baked.

1 Heat the oven to 110°C, 225°F or gas mark ⅛. Line the trays with baking parchment – see page 10.

2 Crack one egg on the side of a bowl. Open the shell and let the egg slide onto a plate. Cover the yolk with an egg cup.

3 Hold the plate and egg cup over a big, clean bowl. Tip the plate, so the egg white slides into the bowl. Separate the other egg in the same way.

You don't need the yolks... ...use them in the recipe on page 26.

4 Sprinkle the cream of tartar over the egg whites. Whisk them very quickly with a whisk.

5 Keep whisking until they are really thick and foamy. The egg whites should stay in a stiff point when you lift up the whisk.

6 Add a heaped teaspoon of the sugar. Whisk it in well. Keep whisking in spoonfuls of sugar, until you have used it up.

Don't mix the dye in.

7 Scoop up a heaped teaspoon of the mixture. Use another spoon to push it onto a tray. Fill the tray with more blobs. Scatter on the sugar sprinkles.

8 Spoon the remaining mixture into 3 clean bowls. Dot drops of different food dyes over the mixture in each bowl. Put a blob of mixture on the second tray.

These meringues were coloured using gel food dyes. If you use liquid food dyes, your swirls will be paler.

9 Swirl the back of the spoon around the outside of the blob, to make the food dye swirly. Fill the tray with more blobs in the same way.

10 Bake for 40 minutes. Turn off the oven and leave them inside for 15 minutes. Then, take them out and leave them on the trays to cool.

Other ideas

You could serve these meringues with a bowl of whipped cream to dip them into. Whisk 150ml (¼ pint) double cream quickly, until it stands in a floppy point when you lift up the whisk.

151

Meringue nests

Ingredients:

2 medium eggs

100g (4oz) caster sugar

For the filling:

150ml (¼ pint) double cream

½ teaspoon vanilla essence

225g (8oz) fresh berries, such as
strawberries, raspberries
and blueberries, or a mixture of
different berries

You will also need 2 baking trays.

Makes 8

These meringue nests can be made a day or two before you want to eat them. Just keep them in an airtight container, then fill them with cream and fruit.

1 Heat the oven to 110°C, 225°F, gas mark ¼. Line the baking trays, following the instructions on page 10.

2 Separate the eggs, following the instructions on page 11. Put the whites in a big, very clean bowl. You don't need the yolks – use them in the recipe on pages 26-27.

3 Whisk the egg whites until they become really thick and foamy. When you lift the whisk up, the egg whites should stand up in stiff points, like this.

4 Add a heaped teaspoon of sugar. Whisk it in well. Keep adding spoonfuls of sugar and whisking them in, until you have added all the sugar.

5 Scoop up a dessertspoonful of the mixture. Then, using a teaspoon, push the spoonful off onto one of the baking trays.

6 Using the back of the teaspoon, make a shallow hollow in the middle. Then, make seven more nests, leaving spaces between them.

152

7 Bake for 40 minutes, then turn off the oven, leaving them inside. After 15 minutes, take them out.

8 For the filling, pour the cream into a big bowl. Add the vanilla. Whisk it very quickly (see page 377), until it stands up in floppy points when you lift the whisk.

9 Wash the berries and dry them on a paper towel. Then, when the nests are cold, fill the hollow in each one with cream and decorate them with berries.

Other flavours

You could replace the berries with tropical fruits such as pineapple pieces, kiwi fruit slices and pulp scooped from a ripe, wrinkly passionfruit.

Chocolate swirl meringues

Ingredients:

50g (2oz) plain chocolate

2 medium eggs

100g (4oz) caster sugar

You will also need 2 baking trays and a heatproof bowl that fits snugly into a saucepan.

Makes around 12

These meringues have melted chocolate stirred through them before they are baked. This gives the finished meringues a marbled appearance and a delicious, chocolatey flavour.

1 Heat the oven to 110°C, 225°F, gas mark ½. Line the baking trays with baking parchment, following the instructions on page 10.

2 Break up the chocolate and put it in the heatproof bowl. Fill the saucepan ¼ full of water. Heat the water until it bubbles, then take the pan off the heat.

3 Wearing oven gloves, lower the bowl into the pan. Stir the chocolate until it melts. Wearing oven gloves, take the bowl out of the pan. Leave it to cool.

You don't need the yolks – use them in the recipe on pages 26-27.

4 To separate the first egg, break the egg on the edge of a big bowl. Slide the egg slowly onto a small plate. Then, put an egg cup over the yolk.

5 Hold the egg cup and tip the plate over the bowl, so that the egg white dribbles into it. Do the same with the other egg, so that both the whites are in the bowl.

6 Whisk the egg whites with a whisk until they are really thick and foamy. When you lift the whisk up, the egg whites should stand up in stiff points, like this.

You could dip the bases of your finished meringues in 50g (2oz) melted plain chocolate.

7 Add a heaped teaspoon of sugar. Whisk it in well. Keep adding spoonfuls of sugar and whisking them in, until you have added all the sugar.

8 Drizzle teaspoons of the melted chocolate over the meringue mixture. Stir once or twice to swirl the chocolate through the mixture.

9 Scoop up a dessertspoonful of the mixture. Using a teaspoon, push it off onto one of the trays. Make more meringues.

10 Bake for 40 minutes. Turn off the oven and leave them inside. After 15 minutes, take them out. Leave them to cool on the trays.

Mini meringues

Ingredients:

2 medium eggs
100g (4oz) caster sugar
pink or red food dye
150ml (¼ pint) double cream

You will also need 2 baking trays.

Makes around 30

This recipe shows you how to make tiny, crisp and chewy pink and white meringues. They are delicious eaten plain, but you can also follow the instructions here to sandwich them together in pairs using whipped cream.

1 Heat the oven to 110°C, 225°F, gas mark ¼. Line the trays with baking parchment, following the instructions on page 10.

2 Crack one egg on the edge of a bowl, then pour it slowly onto a plate. Hold an egg cup over the yolk. Tip the plate over a big, very clean bowl so the egg white dribbles into it.

3 Do the same with the other egg, so that the two egg whites are in the bowl. You don't need the yolks in this recipe. You could use them in the recipe on pages 26-27.

4 Whisk the egg whites with a whisk until they are really thick and foamy. They should stand up in stiff points when you lift the whisk up, like this.

5 Add a heaped teaspoon of sugar to the egg whites and whisk it in well. Repeat this until you have added all the sugar.

6 Scoop up a teaspoon of the meringue mixture. Then, use another teaspoon to push it off onto the baking tray.

Move the spoon in the... ...shape of a number 8.

7 Make 15 meringues, leaving gaps between them. Then, add a few drops of food dye to the rest of the mixture.

8 Gently fold the food dye into the mixture using a spatula or a big metal spoon. Then, when the mixture is pink, make 15 more meringues.

9 Put the meringues in the oven and bake them for 40 minutes. Then, turn off the oven, leaving the meringues inside.

10 After 15 minutes, carefully lift the baking trays out of the oven. Leave the meringues on the trays to cool.

11 Pour the cream into a bowl, then whisk it very quickly. Carry on until the cream stands up in floppy points when you lift up the whisk.

12 Using a blunt knife, spread some cream on the flat side of a meringue. Then, press another meringue on the top.

If you sandwich your meringues with cream, eat them on the same day.

Raspberry macaroons

Ingredients:

100g (4oz) icing sugar

2 medium eggs

1 pinch cream of tartar

¼ teaspoon pink food dye

25g (1oz) caster sugar

100g (4oz) ground almonds

For the filling:

100g (4oz) fresh raspberries

150g (5oz) full-fat cream cheese

2 tablespoons icing sugar

You will also need 2 baking trays.

Makes around 12

These macaroons are made of whisked egg whites mixed with ground almonds and baked so the outside goes crisp while the inside stays chewy. They have a creamy raspberry filling, but for a dairy-free alternative you could fill them with raspberry jam.

1 Line the baking trays (see page 10). Sift the icing sugar into a big bowl.

You don't need the yolks – use them in the recipe on pages 26-27.

2 Separate the eggs (see page 11). Put the egg whites in a large, clean bowl.

3 Whisk the egg whites until they stand up in peaks (see page 11). Whisk in the cream of tartar, food dye and 2 tablespoons of the icing sugar.

Move the spoon in the... ...shape of a number 8.

Use another spoon to push the blob off.

4 Add the rest of the icing sugar a tablespoon at a time, whisking well each time.

5 Add the caster sugar and ground almonds. Use a metal spoon to fold them in very gently.

6 Scoop up almost a teaspoon of the mixture. Put it on a tray. Make more blobs, spacing them out well.

7 Tap each tray sharply on the work surface, twice. Leave for 30 minutes.

8 Heat the oven to 110°C, 225°F or gas mark ¼. Bake for 30 minutes. Turn off the oven. Leave the macaroons in for 15 minutes. Then, leave them on the trays to cool.

9 To make the filling, mash the raspberries with a fork. Stir in the cream cheese and icing sugar.

10 Spread some filling on the flat side of a macaroon. Press on another macaroon. Fill the rest in the same way.

A mint chocolate macaroon

This macaroon is lemon flavoured.

A raspberry macaroon

Other flavours

For lemon macaroons, replace the pink food dye with yellow food dye. For the filling, replace the raspberries with the grated zest of 1 lemon and 2 tablespoons of lemon juice squeezed from the lemon. Mix a few drops of yellow food dye into the filling, too.

For mint chocolate macaroons, replace the pink food dye with green. For the filling, make some chocolate ganache (see pages 161-162) and stir in a few drops of peppermint essence.

Chocolate macaroons

Ingredients:

100g (4oz) icing sugar

2 medium eggs

1 pinch cream of tartar

25g (1oz) cocoa powder

25g (1oz) caster sugar

75g (3oz) ground almonds

For the ganache:

75g (3oz) plain chocolate

4 tablespoons double cream

You will also need 2 baking trays.

Makes around 8

These chocolate macaroons have crisp yet chewy chocolate shells and are spread with creamy chocolate filling known as ganache.

1 Line two large baking trays with baking parchment (see page 10). Sift the icing sugar into a bowl.

2 Separate the eggs, following the instructions on page 11. Put both egg whites in a big, very clean bowl. You don't need the yolks – use them in the recipe on pages 26-27.

3 Whisk the egg whites until they become thick and foamy. When you lift up the whisk, the foam should stay in a floppy point.

Move the spoon in the...

...shape of a number 8.

4 Whisk in the cream of tartar and 2 tablespoons of the icing sugar. Add the rest of the icing sugar, a tablespoon at a time, whisking well each time.

5 Sift the cocoa over the mixture. Add the caster sugar and ground almonds. Use a metal spoon to fold everything together very gently.

6 Scoop up a teaspoon of the mixture and put it on a tray. Put more blobs on the trays, spacing them out well.

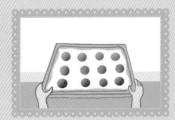

7 Tap each tray sharply on the work surface, twice. Leave for 30 minutes. Make the ganache, following the instructions on page 381.

8 Heat the oven to 110°C, 225°F or gas mark ¼. Bake for 30 minutes. Turn off the oven. Leave them in for 15 minutes. Take them out and leave on the trays to cool.

Other ideas

Instead of plain chocolate ganache for the filling, you could use milk or white chocolate ganache. Follow the instructions on page 381 to make them.

9 Spread some ganache onto the flat side of a macaroon. Press on another macaroon. Fill all the macaroons the same way.

This macaroon was decorated using a stencil and coloured icing sugar (see page 383).

Macaroon creams

These crisp, golden macaroons will simply melt in your mouth. They are filled with pretty, pastel shades of sweet buttercream.

Ingredients:

2 medium eggs

175g (6oz) caster sugar

125g (4½oz) ground almonds

25g (1oz) ground rice

For the buttercream:

50g (2oz) softened butter or margarine

100g (4oz) icing sugar

pink, green and yellow food dyes

You will also need 2 baking trays.

Makes around 18

1 Heat the oven to 150°C, 300°F, gas mark 2. Line the baking trays (see page 10).

2 Break one egg on the edge of a bowl. Slide the egg slowly onto a small plate. Then, put an egg cup over the yolk.

Use the yolks instead in the recipe on pages 26-27.

3 Holding the egg cup, tip the plate over the bowl, so that the egg white dribbles into it. Do the same with the other egg, so that both the whites are in the bowl.

4 Whisk the egg whites until they are really thick and foamy. When you lift up the whisk, they should stand up in stiff points, like this.

Move the spoon in the... ...shape of a number 8.

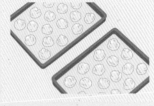

5 Add the caster sugar, ground almonds and ground rice to the egg whites. Then, use a metal spoon to fold the ingredients together gently.

6 Scoop up a slightly rounded teaspoon of the mixture. Using another teaspoon, push the mixture off the spoon and onto one of the baking trays.

7 Make more macaroons in the same way, making sure they are well spaced out on the trays. Bake for 20 minutes, until they are pale golden.

8 Leave the macaroons on the trays for 5 minutes. Then, lift them onto a wire rack and leave them to cool.

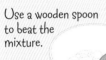

Use a wooden spoon to beat the mixture.

9 For the buttercream, put the butter in a bowl. Beat it until it is smooth. Sift on the icing sugar, then beat until fluffy.

10 Divide the mixture between three bowls. Drop a few drops of food dye into each bowl, to tint each portion a different shade. Mix it all in.

Use a blunt knife to spread the buttercream.

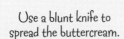

11 Spread some buttercream on the flat side of a macaroon. Press another macaroon on top. Sandwich all the macaroons.

Other flavours

For flavoured fillings, mix a few drops of flavouring essence into each bowl of buttercream at step 10. Try vanilla essence with the yellow buttercream, peppermint essence with the green buttercream and almond essence or rose water with the pink buttercream.

Butterscotch macaroons

These little macaroons have shells made from egg whites and ground almonds, filled with a creamy butterscotch filling. You'll find other flavours on the opposite page.

Ingredients:

50g (2oz) icing sugar

1 medium egg

1 pinch cream of tartar

15g (½oz) soft dark brown sugar

50g (2oz) ground almonds

For the butterscotch filling:

15g (½oz) butter

40g (1½oz) soft dark brown sugar

100g (4oz) full-fat cream cheese

You will also need a baking tray.

Makes around 6 pairs

1 Line the tray with baking parchment (see page 10). Sift the icing sugar into a bowl. Take the cream cheese out of the fridge.

2 Separate the egg (see page 11). Put the white in a large, clean bowl.

3 Whisk the egg white (see page 11) until it stays in a floppy point when you lift up the whisk.

4 Whisk in the cream of tartar and 1 tablespoon of the icing sugar. Add the rest of the icing sugar a tablespoon at a time, whisking well each time.

5 Sift the soft dark brown sugar and ground almonds into the bowl. Squash any soft lumps through with a spoon. Throw away any hard bits left in the sieve.

Move the spoon in the...

...shape of a number 8.

6 Use a metal spoon to fold everything together very gently.

Use another spoon to push off each blob.

7 Put a teaspoonful of the mixture on the tray. Make more blobs, spacing them out well. Tap the tray sharply on the work surface, twice.

A butterscotch macaroon

A lime macaroon

A strawberry macaroon

8 Leave the shells for 30 minutes. Meanwhile, make the butterscotch filling, following the instructions on page 377. Put it in a bowl in the fridge to chill.

9 Heat the oven to 110°C, 225°F or gas mark ¼. Bake the macaroons for 30 minutes. Turn off the oven. Leave them in for 15 minutes, then take them out. Leave on the tray to cool.

10 Spread some filling on the flat side of a macaroon shell. Press on the flat side of another shell. Fill the rest in the same way.

Lime macaroons

For the macaroons, replace the soft dark brown sugar with 15g (½oz) caster sugar and add a few drops of green food dye at the same time. For the filling, you will need 1 lime, 3 tablespoons full-fat cream cheese and 4 teaspoons icing sugar. Follow the instructions for lemon macaroons on page 159, but use the lime instead of the lemon.

Strawberry macaroons

For the shells, replace the soft dark brown sugar with 15g (½oz) caster sugar and add a few drops of pink or red food dye at the same time. For the filling you will need 1 tablespoon of smooth strawberry jam, 3 tablespoons of full-fat cream cheese and a few drops of red or pink food dye. Mix them together in a bowl.

Muffins & whoopie pies

Iced muffins

Ingredients:

300g (10oz) plain flour

2 teaspoons baking powder

150g (5oz) caster sugar

1 lemon

50g (2oz) butter

225ml (8 floz) milk

1 medium egg

100g (4oz) seedless raspberry jam

For decorating:

175g (6oz) icing sugar

small sweets and sugar sprinkles

You will also need a 12-hole deep muffin tin.

Makes 10

These delicious muffins are filled with jam, covered in icing and then decorated with sprinkles and sweets.

1 Heat the oven to 200°C, 400°F or gas mark 6.

Use a pastry brush.

2 Brush some oil in 10 of the holes in the muffin tin. Then, cut a small circle of baking parchment to put in the bottom of each hole.

3 Sift the flour and baking powder into a large bowl. Add the caster sugar, then mix everything together with a metal spoon.

4 Grate the zest from the outside of the lemon, using the small holes on a grater. Then, cut the lemon in half and squeeze out the juice.

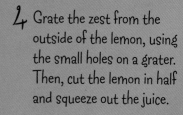

5 Put 2 tablespoons of juice on one side, for the icing. Then, cut the butter into pieces and put it in a pan with the lemon zest.

6 Add 4 tablespoons of the milk and heat the pan gently until the butter melts. Then, take it off the heat and add the rest of the milk.

7 Break the egg into a cup and beat it with a fork, then stir it into the butter mixture. Pour the mixture into the bowl.

Use a
sharp knife.

8 Stir everything together
with a fork. Then, nearly
fill the 10 holes with the
mixture and bake the
muffins for 15 minutes.

9 Leave the muffins in the tin
for 3 minutes, then loosen
them with a blunt knife. Put
them on a wire rack to cool.

10 Turn each muffin on
its side and cut it in half.
Then, spread jam on the
bottom half and put the top
half back on.

11 Sift the icing sugar
into a bowl. Mix in the lemon
juice you set aside. Spoon icing
onto the muffins. Scatter on
sweets and sprinkles.

If you are having a birthday
party, you could decorate
some of the muffins
with little candles.

169

Chocolate muffins

Ingredients:

200g (7oz) plain, milk or white chocolate

275g (10oz) self-raising flour

1½ teaspoons of baking powder

25g (1oz) cocoa powder

100g (4oz) caster sugar

100ml (4floz) sunflower oil

250ml (9floz) milk or soya milk

1 medium egg

1 teaspoon vanilla essence

You will also need a 12-hole deep muffin tin and 12 muffin cases.

Makes 12

The main recipe here is for muffins made with chocolate muffin dough studded with chocolate chips. On the opposite page are instructions for making other flavours of muffin, too. You could top your finished muffins with a drizzle of melted chocolate.

1 Heat the oven to 200°C, 400°F or gas mark 6. Put a case in each hole of the muffin tin. Break or chop the chocolate into small pieces.

2 Sift the flour, baking powder and cocoa into a large bowl. Add the sugar and chocolate pieces. Stir everything together.

3 Measure the oil and milk in a jug. Break the egg into a cup and beat it with a fork. Put it in the jug, along with the vanilla essence.

4 Pour the milky mixture into the bowl. Mix everything together quickly with a fork. Stop when there are no pockets of flour left.

5 Divide the mixture between the paper cases. Bake for 20 minutes, or until the muffins are risen and firm.

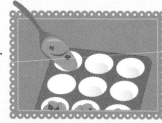

6 Leave the muffins in the tin for 10 minutes. Then, put them on a wire rack to cool.

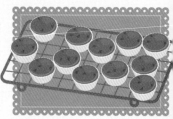

Lemon & white chocolate muffins

First, grate the zest from the outside of a lemon on the small holes of a grater. Cut the lemon in half. Squeeze the juice from one half. In step 2, use white chocolate, leave out the cocoa and add 25g (1oz) extra self-raising flour and the lemon zest. In step 3, when you measure out the milk, put back 2 tablespoons of it and add 2 tablespoons of the lemon juice instead.

Vanilla & fruit muffins

In step 2, replace the cocoa powder and chocolate with 25g (1oz) extra self-raising flour, 50g (2oz) extra caster sugar and 150g (5oz) fresh or frozen blueberries or raspberries. If you use frozen berries, there's no need to defrost them.

171

Spiced apple muffins

Ingredients:

3 eating apples

100g (4oz) butter

3 cloves

250g (9oz) self-raising flour

1½ teaspoons baking powder

1½ teaspoons ground cinnamon

25g (1oz) cornflour

200g (7oz) caster sugar

2 medium eggs

175ml (6floz) milk

For the topping:

1 small lemon

1 small orange

50g (2oz) demerara sugar

You will also need a 12-hole deep muffin tin and 12 muffin cases.

Makes 12

These apple muffins are gently spiced with cinnamon, cloves, orange and lemon, and drizzled with syrup to make them deliciously moist.

1 Heat the oven to 190°C, 375°F or gas mark 5. Put a paper case in each hole in the tin.

Make sure the knife is facing away from you.

2 Use a peeler to peel the skin off an apple. Cut it into quarters. Put them on a board. Make two cuts in each one, in a V-shape, to cut out the core. Then, cut the quarters into chunks.

3 Do the same with the other apples. Put them in a pan with the butter and cloves. Cook over a low heat for 5 minutes. Turn off the heat.

Stir every now and then.

4 In a large bowl, mix the flour, baking powder, cinnamon, cornflour and sugar. Beat the eggs and milk in a jug.

5 Use a spoon to remove the cloves from the pan. Pour the apple mixture and egg mixture into the flour.

6 Stir until everything is just mixed. It should still look quite lumpy.

These muffin cases were made by pressing squares of baking parchment into the holes of a muffin tray.

7 Spoon the mixture into the paper cases. Bake for 18-20 minutes until firm and golden.

8 Squeeze the juice from half the lemon and half the orange. Mix it with the sugar. Spoon it over the hot muffins. Leave to cool.

Other flavours

At step 4, you could add a handful of raisins or dried cranberries, or a few chopped walnuts or hazelnuts.

Marbled muffins

Ingredients:

100g (4oz) plain, milk or white
  chocolate in a bar

2 lemons

300g (11oz) self-raising flour

1½ teaspoons baking powder

125g (4½oz) caster sugar

100ml (4floz) sunflower oil

a little milk or soya milk

1 medium egg

25g (1oz) cocoa powder

You will also need a 12-hole deep
muffin tin and 12 muffin cases.

Makes 12

These muffins are made using lemon and chocolate
muffin mixtures to create a swirly pattern. There's
a chunk of chocolate hidden inside each muffin, too.

1 Heat the oven to 200°C, 400°F or gas mark 6.
   Put a paper case in each hole of the muffin tin.
   Break or cut the chocolate into 12 chunks.

2 Grate the zest from the
   lemons using the small
   holes of a grater. Squeeze
   the juice from the lemons.

3 Sift the flour and baking
   powder into a big bowl.
   Add the sugar and
   lemon zest and mix.

The mixture
should look
lumpy.

4 Put the juice in a jug. Add enough
   milk to bring it up to the 250ml
   (9floz) mark. Break the egg into a
   cup. Beat it with a fork, put it in
   the jug, add the oil and mix.

5 Pour the contents of the jug
   into the bowl. Mix quickly with
   a fork. Stop when there are no
   lumps of flour left.

6 Pour half the mixture into
   another bowl. Sift the cocoa
   powder over it. Mix it in
   quickly with a fork.

If you eat these muffins while they're warm, the chocolate will be soft and gooey.

7 Spoon a teaspoon of chocolate mixture into each case. Then, spoon in a teaspoon of lemon mixture. Keep on adding alternate teaspoons, until the cases are a third full.

These are plain chocolate chunks, but you could use milk or white if you prefer.

8 Put a chocolate chunk in each one. Cover with alternate teaspoons of the lemon and chocolate mixtures, until they are used up.

9 Bake for 20 minutes, or until risen and firm. Leave them in the tin for 10 minutes, then put them on a wire rack to cool.

Other flavours

For chocolate and orange or chocolate and lime marbled muffins, replace the lemons with 2 oranges or 3 limes.

Lemon & berry muffins

Ingredients:

1 lemon

250g (9oz) self-raising flour

1 teaspoon bicarbonate of soda

150g (5oz) caster sugar

90ml (3½floz) sunflower oil

150g (5oz) carton low-fat lemon
    flavoured yogurt

2 medium eggs

150g (5oz) fresh berries

75g (3oz) icing sugar

You will also need a 12-hole deep
muffin tin and 12 muffin cases.

Makes 12

These delicious muffins are made using lemon yogurt and fresh berries. You could use blackberries, blueberries or raspberries, or a mixture. You could even use frozen berries – no need to defrost them first.

1 Put a muffin case into each hole of the tin. Heat the oven to 190°C, 375°F or gas mark 5. Use the small holes of a grater to grate the zest from the outside of the lemon.

2 Sift the flour and bicarbonate of soda into a large mixing bowl and stir in the caster sugar.

3 Measure the oil into a jug. Add the lemon yogurt and the zest. Cut the lemon in half and squeeze the juice from one half. Add the lemon juice to the oil mixture.

4 Break the eggs into a small bowl and beat them well. Add them to the oil mixture too. Use a metal spoon to mix the ingredients until they are well blended.

5 Pour the oil mixture into the big bowl. Stir all the ingredients for a few seconds. Add the berries, then gently mix everything together.

6 Spoon the mixture into the paper cases. Fill each one almost to the top. Bake the muffins for 15-18 minutes, until they are golden and firm to touch.

7 Leave the muffins in the tin for 5 minutes. Lift them onto a wire rack. Sift some icing sugar over them. To make lemon glacé icing to drizzle over them, see page 377.

For a special occasion or a gift, you could tie card and ribbon around your muffins.

Banana fudge muffins

Ingredients:

250g (9oz) self-raising flour

1 teaspoon baking powder

100g (4oz) fudge

100g (4oz) soft light brown sugar

75g (3oz) butter

125ml (4½floz) milk

1 teaspoon vanilla essence

2 ripe, medium-sized bananas

2 medium eggs

2 tablespoons runny honey

You will also need a 12-hole deep muffin tin and 12 muffin cases.

Makes 12

Chunks of fudge melt into these muffins and give them a lovely, moist texture. They are delicious topped with honey and eaten while they are still warm.

1 Heat the oven to 190°C, 375°F or gas mark 5. Put a muffin case in each hole of the tin. Sift the flour and baking powder into a big bowl.

2 Put the fudge on a chopping board and cut it into chunks. Add the sugar and fudge to the flour and stir them in.

3 Put the butter in a saucepan. Heat it gently over a low heat until the butter has melted. Remove the pan from the heat and add the milk and vanilla essence.

4 Peel the bananas and put them into a small bowl. Mash them with a fork until they are fairly smooth. Break the eggs into another bowl and beat them with a fork.

5 Add the bananas and the beaten eggs to the pan. Stir the ingredients in the pan. Then, pour the mixture into the big bowl.

6 Stir until everything is just mixed. The mixture should still look quite lumpy. Then, spoon it into the paper cases.

7 Bake for 20 minutes, until the muffins are risen and firm. Leave them in the tin for 5 minutes. Brush the tops with honey, then lift them onto a wire rack.

Your muffins will have a better banana flavour if you use very ripe or even over-ripe bananas.

Vanilla whoopie pies

Ingredients:

75g (3oz) butter

1 large egg

150g (5oz) caster sugar

150ml (¼ pint) soured cream

2 teaspoons vanilla essence

3 tablespoons milk

275g (10oz) plain flour

¾ teaspoon bicarbonate of soda

For the buttercream filling:

50g (2oz) softened butter

100g (4oz) icing sugar

1 teaspoon of vanilla essence

You will also need 2 baking trays.

Makes 12

Whoopie pies are from America. They are round, flat sponge cakes sandwiched together with buttercream or other fillings. Their name is supposed to have come about because people enjoyed eating them so much, they shouted 'whoopie!'

1 Heat the oven to 180°C, 350°F or gas mark 4. Line the baking trays with parchment (see page 10).

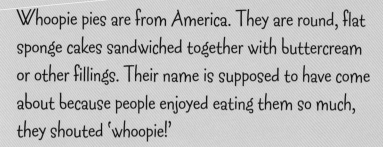

2 Put the butter in a small pan. Heat gently until the butter melts. Take it off the heat.

3 Break the egg into a big bowl. Add the sugar. Whisk for 2-3 minutes, until thick and pale.

4 Add the melted butter, soured cream, vanilla and milk. Mix them in gently using a big metal spoon, moving it in the shape of an 8.

Find out how to make chocolate whoopie pies on pages 182-183.

5 Sift the flour and bicarbonate of soda over the mixture. Mix them in gently.

Use another spoon to push each blob off.

6 Put heaped teaspoons of the mixture on the trays, making sure the blobs are well spaced out. Bake for 10-12 minutes, or until golden and just firm.

7 Leave on the trays for 5 minutes. Then, put them on a wire rack to cool.

8 Make the buttercream (see page 376). Spread some on the flat side of a sponge. Gently press another one on top. Make more pies in the same way.

This buttercream was tinted with food dye and piped in a flat spiral (see page 379).

Sifted cocoa powder

Roll a pie over a plate of chocolate drops or sugar sprinkles, to make it look like this.

Plain buttercream

Drizzled melted chocolate (see page 381)

This pie was rolled in chopped nuts.

Chocolate whoopie pies

Ingredients:

75g (3oz) butter
1 large egg
150g (5oz) caster sugar
150ml (¼ pint) soured cream
2 teaspoons vanilla essence
3 tablespoons milk
225g (8oz) plain flour
50g (2oz) cocoa powder
¾ teaspoon bicarbonate of soda
some ice cream, for filling

You will also need 2 baking trays.

Makes around 15

This recipe is for chocolate whoopie pies filled with ice cream. If you prefer, you could fill your pies with vanilla buttercream by following the recipe on the previous page – or you could try the other fillings mentioned on the opposite page.

1 Heat the oven to 180°C, 350°F or gas mark 4. Put the baking trays on some baking parchment. Draw around them. Cut out the shapes and put them on the trays.

2 Put the butter in a small pan. Heat gently until the butter just melts. Take the pan off the heat.

3 Break the egg into a large bowl. Add the sugar. Whisk for 2-3 minutes, until the mixture is thick and pale.

4 Add the melted butter, sour cream, vanilla and milk. Mix them in gently using a big metal spoon, moving it in the shape of an 8.

Use another spoon to push each blob off.

5 Sift the flour, cocoa and bicarbonate of soda over the mixture. Mix them in gently, still moving the spoon in the shape of a number 8.

6 Put teaspoonfuls of the mixture on the trays, making sure the blobs are well spaced out. Bake for 10-12 minutes, or until just firm.

7 Leave on the trays for 5 minutes. Then, put them on 2 wire racks to cool. Don't fill the pies until they are completely cold

8 To fill a pie, spread some ice cream on the flat side of a sponge. Press another sponge on top. Wrap the pie in plastic food wrap and put it in the freezer. Do the same with the others.

9 Leave the pies in the freezer for 1 hour, or longer if you prefer. When you want to eat one, put it in the fridge for 10 minutes, to soften a little.

Use different flavours of ice cream for a multicoloured effect.

Other fillings

For chocolate buttercream, you will need 50g (2oz) softened butter or margarine, 75g (3oz) icing sugar, 25g (1oz) cocoa powder, 1 teaspoon vanilla essence and 1 teaspoon milk or water. To make it, follow the instructions on page 376.

For white chocolate ganache, you will need 200g (7oz) white chocolate and 100ml (3½floz) double cream. To make it, follow the instructions for ganache on page 381.

Little cakes

Tiny cupcakes

Ingredients:

40g (1½oz) caster sugar

40g (1½oz) softened butter or margarine

40g (1½oz) self-raising flour

1 medium egg

1½ teaspoons cocoa powder

1 tablespoon white chocolate chips

1 tablespoon milk chocolate chips

For the vanilla buttercream:

50g (2oz) softened butter or margarine

100g (4oz) icing sugar

1 teaspoon vanilla essence

For the chocolate buttercream:

50g (2oz) softened butter or margarine

75g (3oz) icing sugar

25g (1oz) cocoa powder

1 teaspoon milk or water

You will also need around 24 tiny paper cake cases, 2 baking trays and a piping gun or bag with a star- or flower-shaped nozzle.

Makes around 24

This recipe is for tiny vanilla and chocolate cupcakes topped with buttercream. You could decorate them with sugar sprinkles, melted chocolate and chocolate buttons.

1. Heat the oven to 180°C, 350°F or gas mark 4. Arrange the paper cases on the baking trays.

2. Put the sugar and butter or margarine in a big bowl. Sift in the flour. Break the egg into a cup, then pour it in. Mix well.

3. Spoon half the mixture into another bowl. Sift the cocoa powder over it. Add the white chocolate chips. Mix. Put the milk chocolate chips in the first bowl. Mix.

4. Spoon the chocolate mixture into half the paper cases and the plain mixture into the others. Each case should be around two-thirds full.

5. Bake for 10-12 minutes, or until risen and firm. Leave the cakes for a few minutes, then put them on a wire rack to cool.

This cake was topped with a blob of buttercream, some melted chocolate and sugar strands.

If you use margarine or dairy-free spread in your buttercream, it's best to spread it onto your cakes instead of piping it.

6 While the cakes are cooling, make the vanilla buttercream, then the chocolate buttercream, following the instructions on page 376.

7 When the cakes are cool, pipe chocolate buttercream onto some and vanilla buttercream onto others, following the instructions for piping swirls on page 379.

8 If you want to scatter on sugar sprinkles or add chocolate buttons, do it straight away, while the buttercream is still sticky.

Little red velvet cakes

Ingredients:

50g (2oz) caster sugar

25g (1oz) softened butter

1 rounded teaspoon runny honey or golden syrup

7 tablespoons plain natural yogurt

2 teaspoons red food dye

1 teaspoon vanilla essence

100g (4oz) plain flour

1 teaspoon bicarbonate of soda

1½ teaspoons cocoa powder

For the cream cheese frosting:

40g (1½oz) softened butter

75g (3oz) full-fat cream cheese

250g (9oz) icing sugar

½ teaspoon vanilla essence

1 tablespoon lemon juice

You will also need 2 baking trays and around 60 tiny paper cake cases.

Makes around 30

Red velvet cakes originated in America. These little red velvet cakes have a velvety texture and contain a little liquid food dye to make them a rich, deep red.

1 Take the cream cheese out of the fridge. Heat the oven to 180°C, 350°F or gas mark 4. Arrange around 30 paper cases on the baking trays. Tuck a second case inside each one.

Move the spoon in the... ...shape of a number 8.

2 Put the sugar, butter and honey or syrup in a bowl. Beat to mix them together well. Add the yogurt, food dye and vanilla and mix them in.

3 Sift on the flour, bicarbonate of soda and cocoa powder. Stir them in gently, using a big metal spoon.

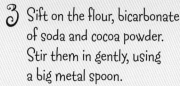

4 Spoon the mixture into the paper cases. Each paper case should be around half full. Bake for 14-15 minutes, or until risen and firm.

5 Leave the cakes for a few minutes, then put them on a wire rack to cool completely.

6 To make the frosting, put the butter and cream cheese in a bowl. Sift on the icing sugar. Add the vanilla and lemon juice. Mix gently.

Don't beat too hard, or it will go watery.

Bow decorations

To make a bow decoration, you will need a cocktail stick and some ribbon. Carefully cut the cocktail stick in half with scissors. Lay half the stick across the ribbon. Tie a half knot around the stick, then tie a bow. Slide the bow up to the cut end of the stick. Push the pointed end into a cake.

To make a bow decoration, follow the instructions in the box on the left.

These bows were made from red velvet ribbon.

Take out the bow decoration before you eat the cake.

7 Take the cases off the cakes. Use a knife to scrape the crumbs off the paper, until you have around 2 tablespoons of crumbs.

8 Put a sieve over a bowl. Push the crumbs through the sieve – use the back of a spoon to help them through.

9 Spread some frosting on each cake, making swirls and peaks with the knife. Then, sprinkle on some sieved crumbs.

Chocolate fudge cupcakes

Ingredients:

175g (6oz) dairy-free margarine

175g (6oz) caster sugar

3 medium eggs

40g (1½oz) cocoa powder

125g (4½oz) fine cornmeal
   (or polenta)

1½ teaspoons wheat- and
   gluten-free baking powder

1 teaspoon vanilla essence

For the chocolate fudge topping:

150g (5oz) plain chocolate

75g (3oz) dairy-free margarine

75g (3oz) icing sugar

You will also need a 12-hole deep muffin tin, 12 paper muffin cases and a heatproof bowl that fits snugly into a saucepan.

Makes 12

These moist, crumbly cupcakes are spread with a delicious chocolate fudge topping. You could decorate them with fresh berries, if you like. This recipe doesn't contain any wheat, gluten, dairy products or nuts, so it's a good choice if you're allergic to any of these things, but read the allergy advice on page 388 first.

1 Heat the oven to 190°C, 375°F or gas mark 5. Put a paper case into each hole of the muffin tin. Put the margarine and sugar in a bowl. Beat until fluffy.

2 Break the eggs into a small bowl and beat them with a fork. Add the eggs to the mixture a little at a time, beating it well each time.

3 Add the cocoa, cornmeal, baking powder, vanilla and 1 tablespoon of water. Mix well. Spoon the mixture into the muffin cases.

4 Bake for 20 minutes, until risen and firm. Leave them in the tin for 5 minutes, then put them on a wire rack to cool.

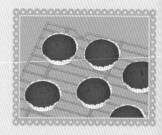

As the icing sets, it goes glossy.

These cakes were decorated with a mixture of raspberries, blueberries and redcurrants.

5 For the topping, break the chocolate into the heatproof bowl. Add the margarine. Fill the pan a quarter full of water. Heat until the water bubbles. Take the pan off the heat.

6 Wearing oven gloves, put the bowl in the pan. When everything has melted, take the bowl out, wearing oven gloves. Sift in the icing sugar.

7 Mix in the icing sugar. When the cakes are cool, spoon on the topping, then add any decorations. Leave the topping to set for around 30 minutes.

Maple syrup cupcakes

Contains optional nuts

Ingredients:

50g (2oz) pecan nuts (optional)
100g (4oz) softened butter
50g (2oz) soft light brown sugar
100g (4oz) self-raising flour
2 medium eggs
6 tablespoons maple syrup

For the buttercream:
100g (4oz) softened butter
225g (8oz) icing sugar
1 tablespoon warm water
½ teaspoon vanilla essence

You will also need a 12-hole shallow bun tin and 12 paper cupcake cases.

Makes 12

These cupcakes are flavoured with maple syrup and topped with a swirl of buttercream. They are delicious made with or without pecan nuts.

1 Put the nuts in a plastic food bag and seal the end with an elastic band. Crush the nuts into small pieces with a rolling pin.

2 Heat the oven to 190°C, 375°F or gas mark 5. Beat the butter and sugar in a large bowl until they are light and fluffy. Sift in the flour.

3 Beat the eggs in a cup. Pour them into the bowl, then add the nuts and maple syrup, too. Stir until everything is well mixed.

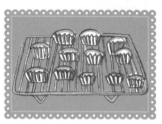

4 Put a paper case in each hole in the tin. Use a teaspoon to divide the mixture between the paper cases. Bake for 12-15 minutes until risen and firm.

5 Leave the cupcakes in the tin for a few minutes. Then, lift each one onto a wire rack. Leave them to cool completely.

6 For the buttercream, put the butter, icing sugar, warm water and vanilla in a bowl. Beat until smooth. Spread some over each cake.

Make different colours of buttercream by mixing a few drops of food dye into some of the buttercream.

You could decorate your cupcakes with whole or chopped nuts, or with small sweets or sprinkles.

193

Upside-down berry cakes

Ingredients:

2 oranges

100g (4oz) softened butter or margarine

100g (4oz) caster sugar

2 medium eggs

1 teaspoon wheat- and gluten-free baking powder

100g (4oz) fine cornmeal (polenta)

6 large (or 12-18 small) fresh or frozen raspberries, blackberries or blueberries (if they're frozen there's no need to defrost them)

For the berry icing:

100g (4oz) icing sugar

50g (2oz) smooth berry jam – use whatever flavour you like

For decorating:

a few fresh berries (optional)

You will also need a 6-hole deep muffin tin.

Makes 6

These moist upside-down cakes have berries in the middle and berry icing on top. The recipe is wheat- and gluten-free, and can be made dairy-free, too.

1 Heat the oven to 190°C, 375°F or gas mark 5. Grease the inside of each hole of the muffin tin (see page 10) using a little softened butter or margarine.

2 Grate the zest from the outside of the oranges. Then, cut the oranges in half and squeeze out the juice.

3 Put the zest in a bowl. Add the butter or margarine and the sugar. Beat until the mixture is pale and fluffy.

4 Break an egg into a cup. Beat it with a fork. Stir it into the mixture. Then, do the same with the other egg.

5 Add the baking powder and cornmeal and 2 teaspoons of the orange juice. Mix everything together gently.

6 Spoon the mixture into the holes of the muffin tin. Poke 1 large berry (or 2-3 small ones) into the middle of each one.

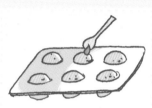

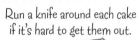

7 Bake for 20 minutes, or until firm and risen. Carefully, pour 2 teaspoons of the orange juice over each cake. Leave to cool.

8 To make the icing, sift the icing sugar into a bowl. Add the jam. Mix it in until you have a smooth paste.

9 When the cakes are cold, put a board over the muffin tin. Turn the tin and board over together, so the tin is on top. Lift off the tin. Leave the cakes upside down.

Each of these cakes was topped with icing made from a different type of jam – strawberry, raspberry and blueberry.

10 Spoon some icing onto each cake. Top with the fresh berries.

Raspberry jam icing

Berry cupcakes

For berry cupcakes that aren't upside-down, bake the cakes in paper cases. At step 9, turn them the right way up, then spoon the icing on top. Or, pipe on swirls of buttercream – see page 376 for buttercream recipes and page 379 for piping tips.

Butterfly cakes

Ingredients:

1 medium egg
50g (2oz) self-raising flour
¼ teaspoon baking powder
50g (2oz) caster sugar
50g (2oz) soft margarine

For the topping:
40g (1½oz) softened butter or
    margarine
¼ teaspoon vanilla essence
75g (3oz) icing sugar
4 teaspoons smooth raspberry jam

You will also need a 12-hole shallow
bun tin and 8 paper cupcake cases.

Makes 8

These cakes are topped with butterflies made by cutting the tops off the cakes and then sticking them back on so they look like butterfly wings.

1 Heat the oven to 190°C, 375°F or gas mark 5. Break the egg into a mug. Then, sift the flour and baking powder into a large bowl. Add the egg, caster sugar and margarine.

2 Stir all the ingredients together with a wooden spoon. Carry on until you have a smooth mixture.

3 Put the paper cases into 8 of the holes of the tin. Then, use a teaspoon to half-fill each case with the mixture.

Use a wooden spoon.

4 Bake the cakes for 16-18 minutes. Then, carefully lift them out of the oven and put them on a wire rack to cool.

5 To make the topping, put the butter or margarine in a bowl and add the vanilla. Stir until the mixture is really smooth.

6 Sift in one third of the icing sugar and stir it in. Then, sift on the remaining icing sugar and stir it in, too.

You could sift a little extra icing sugar over the top of your cakes, if you like.

Leave an edge around the circle.

7 Using a sharp knife, carefully cut a circle from the top of each cake. Then, cut each circle in half.

8 Spread some buttercream on top of each cake. Then, spoon half a teaspoon of jam in a line across the icing.

9 Take two of the slices made from the cake tops. Gently push them into the buttercream, so they look like butterfly wings.

Little coconut cakes

Ingredients:

2 limes

65g (2½oz) butter or margarine

2 tablespoons desiccated coconut

75g (3oz) caster sugar

100g (4oz) self-raising flour

1 medium egg

2 tablespoons milk

For the lime frosting:

25g (1oz) softened butter

50g (2oz) full-fat cream cheese

175g (6oz) icing sugar

40g (1½oz) desiccated coconut

You will also need 2 baking trays and around 60 tiny paper cake cases.

Makes around 30

These little, moist cakes are made with a sweet and tangy combination of coconut and lime. They are topped in creamy frosting and then dipped in coconut.

1 Heat the oven to 180°C, 350°F or gas mark 4. Arrange around 30 paper cases on the trays. Tuck a second case inside each one. Take the cream cheese out of the fridge.

2 Grate the zest from the outside of the limes using the small holes of a grater. Cut the limes in half and squeeze out the juice. Put half the zest in a big bowl.

3 Put the butter or margarine in a small pan. Heat gently until it melts. Then, take it off the heat.

4 Put the coconut and sugar in the bowl with the zest. Sift in the flour. Stir everything together.

5 Break the egg into a cup and beat it with a fork. Pour it into the big bowl. Add the milk, the melted butter and 1 teaspoon of the lime juice. Mix well.

6 Spoon the mixture into the paper cases. Each one should be two-thirds full. Bake for 10-12 minutes, or until risen and firm.

These curls of lime zest were made using a tool known as a zester.

7 When the cakes are cooked, set aside 2 teaspoons of the lime juice for the frosting. Spoon the remaining lime juice over the hot cakes. Leave to cool.

8 To make the lime frosting, put the butter and cream cheese in a big bowl. Mix them together. Sift in half the icing sugar. Mix it in.

9 Sift in the rest of the icing sugar. Add the 2 teaspoons of the lime juice you set aside. Mix everything together.

10 Put the coconut in a small bowl. Spread some frosting on top of a cake. Hold the cake by the case and dip it in the coconut.

11 Frost the rest of the cakes in the same way. Sprinkle the remaining lime zest over the cakes.

Flower cupcakes

Ingredients:

175g (6oz) softened butter or
  margarine

175g (6oz) caster sugar

3 medium eggs

1½ teaspoons wheat- and
  gluten-free baking powder

165g (5½oz) fine cornmeal (polenta)

4 tablespoons milk or soya milk

1 teaspoon orange flower water
  or vanilla essence

For the glacé icing:

175g (6oz) icing sugar

You will also need a 12-hole deep
muffin tin and 12 muffin cases.

Makes 12

These moist cupcakes are wheat- and gluten-free. For a delicate, flowery taste, you can flavour them with orange flower water, which is made using blossoms from orange trees. Decorate them with bought sugar flowers, or make your own – see the page opposite.

1 Heat the oven to 190°C, 375°F or gas mark 5. Put a muffin case in each hole of the tin.

2 Put the butter or margarine and the caster sugar in the bowl. Stir them together, then beat quickly until the mixture is pale and fluffy.

3 Break an egg into a small bowl and beat it with a fork. Add it to the large bowl and mix it in well. Do the same with the other eggs, too. Beat the mixture well each time.

4 Put the baking powder and cornmeal in the bowl. Add the milk and orange flower water or vanilla. Mix gently with a metal spoon, moving it in the shape of a number 8.

5 Divide the mixture between the paper cases. Bake for 20 minutes, or until risen and golden-brown. Leave in the tin for a few minutes, then move to a wire rack to cool.

6 Sift the icing sugar into a bowl. If there are any lumps left in the sieve, squash them through with the back of a spoon. Add 1½ tablespoons of warm water and mix to a smooth paste.

Flower decorations

You will need some kitchen foil (optional), a little icing sugar, some coloured marzipan or ready-to-roll icing (see page 382) and a small flower cutter. Marzipan contains nuts.

1 Sprinkle icing sugar over a clean surface and a rolling pin. Put some icing or marzipan on the surface and roll over it, until it is half as thick as your little finger.

2 Cut out lots of flower shapes. For flat flowers, use them right away, or put them on a plate to dry.

3 To make a curved flower, take a large sheet of foil and scrunch it into a ball. Drape a flower over the ball and leave it to dry.

You could press tiny balls of coloured icing into the middle of your flowers.

7 When the cakes are cold, spread a little icing onto each one. Top with a flower decoration while the icing is still wet.

Apricot sprinkle cakes

Ingredients:

1 orange

150g (5oz) ready-to-eat dried apricots

150g (5oz) caster sugar

150g (5oz) softened butter

3 medium eggs

2 teaspoons baking powder (gluten-free types are available)

150g (5oz) semolina or fine cornmeal (polenta)

150g (5oz) ground almonds

For the apricot cream:

300ml (½ pint) double or whipping cream

2 tablespoons smooth apricot jam

red and yellow food dye

sugar sprinkles

You will also need a 12-hole deep muffin tin and a piping gun or bag fitted with a medium star-shaped nozzle.

Makes 12

These moist little cakes contain dried apricots and are covered with apricot cream and sprinkles. To make them wheat- and gluten-free, see pages 388 and 391.

1 Heat the oven to 180°C, 350°F or gas mark 4. Grease the inside of each hole of the muffin tin (see page 10).

2 Grate the zest from the outside of the orange using the small holes of a grater. Then, squeeze the juice from the orange.

3 Using kitchen scissors, cut the apricots into small pieces. Put them in a bowl. Add the orange zest and juice.

4 Put the sugar and butter in a big bowl. Beat with a wooden spoon until pale and fluffy.

5 Break an egg into a cup, then tip it into the buttery mixture. Mix it in. Do the same with the other eggs.

6 Put the baking powder, semolina or cornmeal and ground almonds in a bowl. Mix. Tip into the big bowl. Add the apricots, juice and zest. Mix well.

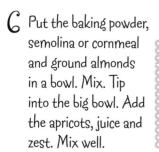

Don't worry if it looks lumpy.

7 Spoon the mixture into the holes of the muffin tin. Bake for 20-25 minutes, until risen and firm. Leave for 10 minutes, then turn the cakes onto a wire rack. Leave to cool completely.

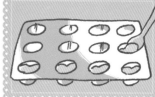

8 For the apricot cream, pour the cream into a big bowl. Add the jam and a few drops of food dye. Whisk until it thickens. It should stay in a floppy peak when you lift the whisk.

You could decorate your cakes with paper cake toppers. Find out how to make them on page 383.

Other ideas

For a traybake version of this recipe, bake the mixture in a 27 x 18cm (11 x 7in) rectangular tin for 30-35 minutes. Cool on a wire rack. Spread the apricot cream on top, scatter on some sprinkles and cut into 12-15 squares.

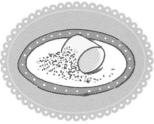

9 Pour some sprinkles onto a plate. Spread a very thin layer of cream around the sides of a cake. Roll the sides in the sprinkles. Put the cake on a plate. Do the same with the other cakes.

10 Spoon the remaining cream into your piping bag or gun. Pipe a flat spiral onto each cake – see page 379 for tips. Or, just spread on the cream.

Lemon & lime cupcakes

These little cakes are drizzled with lemon and lime syrup, then covered with a luscious layer of icing.

Ingredients:

90g (4oz) self-raising flour

90g (4oz) caster sugar

90g (4oz) softened butter or margarine

1 tablespoon milk

2 medium eggs

For the lemon and lime syrup:

1 lemon

1 lime

25g (1oz) caster sugar

For the lemon and lime icing:

175g (6oz) icing sugar

15g (½oz) butter

You will also need a 12-hole shallow bun tin and 12 paper cupcake cases.

Makes 12

1 Heat the oven to 190°C, 375°F or gas mark 5. Put a paper case in each hole of the tin. Sift the flour into a big bowl.

2 Put the sugar, butter or margarine and milk in the bowl. Break the eggs into a cup. Put them in the bowl too. Stir until fluffy.

3 Spoon the mixture into the paper cases. Bake for 12 minutes, or until golden. Leave for a few minutes, then lift the cakes onto a wire rack to cool.

4 To make the syrup, grate the zest from the outside of the lemon and lime using the small holes on a grater, or use a zester, if you have one.

5 Put two-thirds of the lemon and lime zest onto a small plate. Cover it with plastic food wrap and put it to one side. Put the rest of the zest in a small pan.

6 Squeeze the juice from the lemon and lime. Put the sugar and 3 tablespoons of the juice in the pan. Heat it gently until the sugar has dissolved.

7 Take the pan off the heat and leave to cool. Then, pour the syrup through a small sieve into a jug. Throw away the zest left in the sieve.

8 Pour a little syrup over each cake. Leave the cakes on the wire rack until they are completely cold.

9 For the icing, sift the icing sugar into a bowl. Put the butter and 3 tablespoons of juice in a small pan. Heat the pan gently until the butter has melted.

10 Stir the melted mixture into the icing sugar. Spread the icing over the cakes. Decorate each cake with the remaining lemon and lime zest.

You will get long strands of zest like this if you scrape them from the fruit using a zester.

Chocolate cupcakes

Ingredients:

100g (4oz) self-raising flour

40g (1½oz) cocoa powder

1½ teaspoons baking powder

150g (5oz) softened butter or
    margarine

150g (5oz) soft light brown sugar

1 teaspoon vanilla essence

3 tablespoons milk or water

3 large eggs

For the buttercream:

100g (4oz) softened butter or
    margarine

225g (8oz) icing sugar

1 tablespoon milk or water

½ teaspoon vanilla essence

different shades of food dye
    (optional)

You will also need a 12-hole
deep muffin tin and 12 paper
muffin cases.

Makes 12

These chocolate cupcakes are topped with a swirl of buttercream. Decorate them with sugar sprinkles, or look at pages 382-385 for more decorating ideas.

1 Heat the oven to 180°C, 350°F or gas mark 4. Put a paper case in each hole of the tin.

2 Sift the flour, cocoa and baking powder into a big bowl. Put the butter or margarine and sugar in another bowl.

3 Beat the butter or margarine and sugar until they are pale and fluffy. Mix in the vanilla and milk or water.

4 Crack an egg into a cup. Tip it into the butter and sugar mixture. Add 1 tablespoon of the flour mixture. Beat well. Do this with each egg.

5 Add the rest of the flour mixture and stir it in gently, using a big metal spoon.

Move the spoon in the...

...shape of a number 8.

6 Spoon the mixture into the paper cases. Bake for 12-15 minutes, until the cakes are risen and firm. Leave them in the tin for a few minutes. Then, put them on a wire rack to cool.

7 For the buttercream, put the butter, margarine or spread in a bowl. Beat with a wooden spoon until soft. Sift in one third of the icing sugar. Stir it in.

If you're using sugar sprinkles, scatter them on as soon as you've spread on the buttercream.

8 Sift in the rest of the icing sugar. Add the milk or water and vanilla. Beat quickly until the mixture is fluffy. Leave one third of the buttercream, and spoon the rest into two separate bowls.

9 Dye two of the bowls of buttercream, by mixing a few drops of food dye into each of them. When the cakes are cool, spread on the buttercream.

Chocolate buttercream

For chocolate buttercream, use just 175g (6oz) icing sugar. At step 8, sift in 40g (1½oz) cocoa powder at the same time as the icing sugar. Leave out the food dye.

Tiny butterfly cakes

Ingredients:

40g (1½oz) caster sugar

40g (1½oz) soft margarine

40g (1½oz) self-raising flour

1 medium egg

1½ teaspoons cocoa powder

For the plain chocolate ganache:

40g (1½oz) plain or milk chocolate

2 tablespoons double cream

For the white chocolate ganache:

60g (2½oz) white chocolate

2 tablespoons double cream

You will also need a baking tray, around 50 tiny paper cake cases and some chocolate beans, sugar sprinkles and different shades of chocolate writing icing, for decorating the cakes.

Makes around 25

These mini cakes are spread with a creamy chocolate topping called ganache, and the top of the cake is used to make wings shaped like a butterfly's. You can make bug-shaped cakes too, or just decorate your cakes with sugar sprinkles or chocolate buttons.

1 Heat the oven to 180°C, 350°F or gas mark 4. Arrange around 25 paper cases on the tray. Tuck another case inside each one.

2 Put the sugar and margarine in a big bowl. Sift in the flour. Break the egg into a cup, then pour it in. Mix it all together.

3 Spoon half the mixture into another bowl. Sift the cocoa powder over it. Mix it in.

Use two teaspoons, one to spoon and one to scrape.

Each case should be around half full.

4 Spoon the chocolate mixture into half the paper cases, and the vanilla mixture into the rest of the cases. Bake for 10-12 minutes, or until risen and firm.

Scatter on some sugar sprinkles, to decorate the butterfly's body.

5 Leave for a few minutes, then put on a wire rack to cool. Meanwhile, make the plain chocolate ganache and the white chocolate ganache (see page 381).

6 When the cakes are cold, take them out of their cases. Slice the top off each cake. Then, cut each top into 2 semicircles, like this.

To make a bug, put the wings on like this. You could pipe on dots, too.

7 Spread some ganache on top of each cake. Gently push 2 semicircles into the ganache on each cake, to make wings.

8 You could make a head from a chocolate bean and pipe on dots of chocolate writing icing for eyes.

Just spread on some ganache and top with a chocolate button.

Little chocolate gateaux

Ingredients:

50g (2oz) self-raising flour

20g (¾oz) cocoa powder

½ teaspoon baking powder

75g (3oz) softened butter or margarine

75g (3oz) caster sugar

2 medium eggs

½ teaspoon vanilla essence

1½ tablespoons milk or water

For the filling and topping:

150ml (¼ pint) double cream

4 tablespoons cherry jam

a block of plain chocolate

6 fresh cherries (optional)

You will also need a 6-hole deep muffin tin.

Makes 6

This recipe is for miniature chocolate cakes layered with cherry jam, whipped cream and grated chocolate. There are also suggestions for other flavours, opposite.

1 Heat the oven to 180°C, 350°F or gas mark 4. Grease each hole of the muffin tin with butter or margarine (see page 10).

2 Sift the flour, cocoa and baking powder into a big bowl. Put the butter or margarine and sugar in another bowl.

3 Beat the butter or margarine and sugar until the mixture becomes pale and fluffy.

4 Crack an egg into a cup. Tip it into the butter and sugar mixture. Add 1 tablespoon of the flour mixture. Beat well. Do the same with the other egg, too.

Move the spoon in the shape of a number 8.

Run a knife around each cake if it's hard to get them out.

5 Add the rest of the flour mixture, and the vanilla and milk or water. Stir everything together gently, using a big metal spoon.

6 Spoon the mixture into the tin. Bake for 12-15 minutes, until risen and firm. Leave to cool for a few minutes.

7 Hold the tin upside down over a wire rack. Shake until the cakes pop out. Turn them the right way up. Leave to cool.

To make this version, don't cut your cake. Spread chocolate hazelnut spread around the sides. Roll it in chopped nuts. Spoon more spread on top. Decorate with a hazelnut.

A little chocolate hazelnut gateau

Don't beat too much, or the cream will go hard.

8 Whip the cream, following the instructions on page 377.

9 When the cakes are cold, cut them in half, like this. Spread some cream and then some jam on the bottom halves. Put the top halves back on.

To make this little chocolate raspberry gateau, follow the instructions in the box below.

A little chocolate cherry gateau

0 Spread more cream on the tops. Grate some chocolate over the tops, using the big holes on a grater. Put a cherry on each.

Little chocolate raspberry gateaux

To top and fill 6 cakes, you will need 100g (4oz) softened butter or margarine, 200g (7oz) icing sugar and 100g (4oz) raspberries. Put the butter or spread in a bowl. Sift on the icing sugar, mash in 6 raspberries and mix. Cut each cake into 3 layers. Spread some buttercream on each one. Stack them up. Decorate with the remaining raspberries.

Tiny citrus cakes

Ingredients:

1 orange or 1 lemon or 2 limes

100g (4oz) caster sugar

100g (4oz) softened butter or margarine

100g (4oz) self-raising flour

2 medium eggs

For the icing:

100g (4oz) icing sugar

You will also need around 60 tiny paper cases and 2 baking trays.

Makes around 30

This recipe is for tiny cakes flavoured with the juice and zest of lemons, oranges or limes. The cakes are topped with a layer of smooth icing.

1. Heat the oven to 180°C, 350°F or gas mark 4. Put around 30 paper cases on the trays. Tuck a second case inside each one.

2. Grate the zest from the outside of the fruit, using the small holes of a grater. Then, squeeze the juice from the fruit.

3. Put the zest, sugar and butter, margarine or spread in a bowl. Sift in the flour.

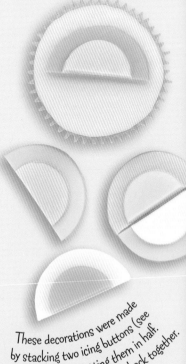

4. Break one egg into a cup, then pour it in. Do the same with the other egg. Add 2 tablespoons of the fruit juice. Mix everything together well.

5. Divide the mixture between the paper cases. Each paper case should be around two-thirds full. Bake for 10-12 minutes, or until risen and firm.

6. Set aside 3 teaspoons of the fruit juice for the icing. Spoon a teaspoon of the remaining juice onto each cake. Leave the cakes to cool.

These decorations were made by stacking two icing buttons (see page 382), then cutting them in half. You could put contrasting halves back together.

To make grapefruit-flavoured cakes, grate half the zest from a pink grapefruit, then cut it in half and squeeze the juice from one half.

Lemon and lime juice make white icing. To colour it, you could mix in a little yellow or green food dye.

7 While the cakes are cooling, make the icing. Sift the icing sugar into a bowl. Add the fruit juice you set aside. Mix to make a spreadable paste.

8 Spread some icing onto each cake. To make it really smooth, dip the blade of a blunt knife in warm water, then run it over the icing. Leave to dry a little before adding other decorations.

Christmas cupcakes

Ingredients:

3 clementines

90g (3½oz) caster sugar

90g (3½oz) softened butter

2 medium eggs

90g (3½oz) self-raising flour

For the icing:

175g (6oz) icing sugar

You will also need a 12-hole shallow bun tin and 12 paper cupcake cases.

Makes 12

These clementine-flavoured cupcakes look festive topped with holly decorations, but you could make them at any time of year and use other decorations.

Use the small holes.

1 Heat the oven to 190°C, 375°F or gas mark 5. Put a paper case in each hole in the tin. Grate the zest from the outside of the clementines.

2 Beat the sugar, butter and zest in a big bowl. Break the eggs into a cup. Put the eggs and flour in the bowl. Mix well.

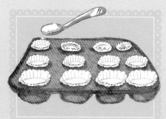

3 Use a teaspoon to divide the mixture between the cases. Bake for 15 minutes until risen and firm.

4 Squeeze the juice from the clementines. Spoon it over the cupcakes while they are still warm.

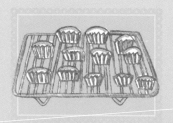

5 Put the cakes on a wire rack. Leave them until they are completely cool, then make the icing.

6 Sift the icing sugar into a bowl and mix in 1½ tablespoons of warm water. Spread it onto the cakes with a blunt knife.

Use a holly leaf cutter to cut shapes from green ready-to-roll icing or marzipan (page 382). Marzipan contains nuts.

For holly berries, roll little balls from red ready-to-roll icing or marzipan.

Little raspberry cakes

Ingredients:

2 medium eggs

75g (3oz) caster sugar

110g (4oz) ground almonds

½ teaspoon wheat- and gluten-free baking powder

For the topping:

150g (5oz) icing sugar

around 150g (5oz) fresh raspberries

You will also need a 12-hole shallow bun tin and 12 paper cupcake cases.

Makes 12

These light, moist little cakes are made from whisked egg whites and ground almonds, topped with raspberry glacé icing and fresh raspberries. These cakes are wheat- and gluten-free but they contain nuts.

1 Heat the oven to 170°C, 325°F or gas mark 3. Put a case in each hollow of the bun tin.

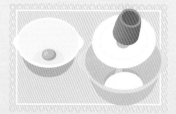 

2 Separate the eggs (see page 11), so all the whites are in one bowl and all the yolks are in another.

3 Put the sugar in the bowl with the egg yolks. Use a fork to stir the sugar into the yolks until it is all mixed in.

4 Beat the egg whites very quickly with a whisk, until they become very thick and foamy. Lift up the whisk. If the foam stays in a point, you have whisked it enough.

5 Scrape the egg whites into the bowl with the egg yolk mixture. Mix them in very gently with a metal spoon, stirring it in the shape of a number 8.

6 Add the almonds and baking powder and stir them in gently, still using the metal spoon. Divide the mixture between the paper cases.

7 Bake for 20-25 minutes, until risen and golden-brown on top. Leave them in the tin for 10 minutes, then move them to a wire rack to cool completely.

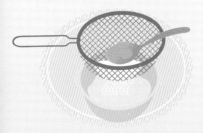

8 To make the topping, put the icing sugar in a sieve over a bowl. Shake the sieve so the icing sugar falls through. Squash any lumps through with the back of a spoon.

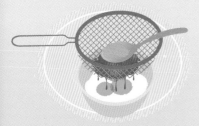

9 Put 4 raspberries in the sieve. Squash them with the back of a spoon, so the juice goes through into the bowl and the pips stay in the sieve. Scrape off any juice clinging to the back of the sieve and put that in the bowl too.

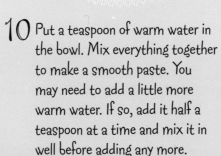

10 Put a teaspoon of warm water in the bowl. Mix everything together to make a smooth paste. You may need to add a little more warm water. If so, add it half a teaspoon at a time and mix it in well before adding any more.

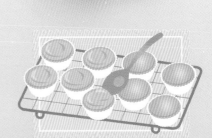

11 Use a teaspoon to spread some icing on top of each cake. Then, arrange the raspberries on top of the icing.

Orange drizzle cupcakes

Ingredients:

3 oranges

175g (6oz) softened butter or margarine

175g (6oz) caster sugar

3 medium eggs

1½ teaspoons wheat- and gluten-free baking powder

165g (5½oz) fine cornmeal (polenta)

For the orange glacé icing:

175g (6oz) icing sugar

You will also need a 12-hole deep muffin tin and 12 paper muffin cases.

Makes 12

These moist, tangy cupcakes are drizzled with orange juice and orange icing. They are made with cornmeal instead of flour, which means they are wheat- and gluten-free. You can also make them dairy-free – see pages 388 and 391 for instructions.

1 Heat the oven to 190°C, 375°F or gas mark 5. Put a paper case in each hollow of the muffin tin.

2 Grate the zest from the outside of the oranges using the small holed on a grater. Put the zest in a big bowl.

3 Squeeze the juice from the oranges. Put 1½ tablespoons of juice in a bowl and the rest in a jug.

4 Put the butter or margarine and caster sugar in the bowl with the zest. Beat until the mixture is pale and fluffy.

5 Break an egg into a small bowl. Beat it with a fork. Tip it into the big bowl and mix it in. Do the same with the other eggs.

6 Put the baking powder and cornmeal in the bowl. Add one tablespoon of orange juice from the jug. Mix gently.

7 Spoon the mixture into the paper cases. Bake for 20 minutes, until golden and firm.

Lemon or lime drizzle cupcakes

Replace the oranges with 3 lemons or 6 limes.

Chocolate orange cupcakes

At step 6, use just 125g (4½oz) cornmeal and sift 40g (1½oz) cocoa powder into the bowl too. Instead of the icing, melt 100g (4oz) chocolate (see page 380) and drizzle it over the top.

8 Carefully pour the juice from the jug over the hot cakes. Leave them in the tin to cool.

These cupcakes had extra grated orange zest sprinkled on top.

For drizzling, you need to use quite runny glacé icing.

9 Sift the icing sugar into a big bowl. Add the juice you put in the bowl earlier. Mix to make a smooth icing.

10 Scoop up some icing. Hold the spoon over a cake. Tip the spoon, then move it over the cake, leaving a trail of icing.

Mocha butterfly cakes

Ingredients:

100g (4oz) softened butter or margarine

100g (4oz) soft light brown sugar

2 medium eggs

1½ teaspoons instant coffee granules

75g (3oz) self-raising flour

25g (1oz) cocoa powder

For the vanilla buttercream:

40g (1½oz) softened butter or margarine

1 teaspoon vanilla essence

75g (3oz) icing sugar

You will also need a 12-hole shallow bun tin and 12 paper cupcake cases.

Makes 12

The combination of chocolate and coffee is known as mocha. These mocha butterfly cakes are filled with vanilla buttercream and dusted with icing sugar.

1 Heat the oven to 180°C, 350°F or gas mark 4. Put the butter and sugar in a big bowl. Beat them with a wooden spoon until the mixture is light and fluffy.

2 Break the eggs into a small bowl and beat them with a fork. Put the coffee granules in a cup with 1 teaspoon of warm water. Stir, then add the mixture to the eggs.

3 Pour the egg mixture into the big bowl a little at a time, beating well each time. Sift in the flour and cocoa. Fold in the flour (see page 11).

4 Put a paper case in each hole of the tin. Spoon the mixture into the paper cases.

5 Bake for 15 minutes, until firm. Leave them in the tin for 5 minutes, then lift them onto a wire rack to cool.

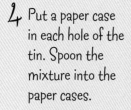

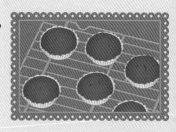

You could sift a little icing sugar over your finished cakes.

6 Using a sharp knife, carefully cut a circle from the top of each cake. Cut each circle in half. Follow the instructions on page 376 to make the vanilla buttercream.

7 Spread some buttercream onto each cake. Take two of the slices made from the cake tops. Push them into the buttercream, so they look like wings.

Chocolate orange cakepops

Ingredients:

1 orange

40g (1½oz) softened butter or
   margarine

40g (1½oz) soft light brown sugar

1 medium egg

25g (1oz) self-raising flour

15g (½oz) cocoa powder

½ teaspoon baking powder

For the frosting:

25g (1oz) butter

50g (2oz) milk chocolate

For the coating:

200g (7oz) milk or white chocolate

sugar sprinkles and chocolate
   strands (optional)

You will also need a 6-hole deep
muffin tin, 3 paper muffin cases
and around 15 wooden skewers
or lollipop sticks.

Makes around 15

Cakepops are little balls of cake on lollipop sticks. These cakepops are flavoured with chocolate and orange, and decorated with chocolate strands and sugar sprinkles.

1 Heat the oven to 180°C, 350°F or gas mark 4. Put the 3 paper cases in the muffin tin.

2 Grate the zest from the orange, using the small holes of a grater. Then, squeeze the juice from half the orange. Save the zest for later.

3 Put the butter, margarine or spread and sugar in a bowl. Beat until you have a pale and fluffy mixture. Stir in 2 teaspoons of the orange juice.

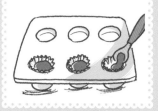

4 Break an egg into a cup, then tip it into the bowl. Sift on the flour, cocoa and baking powder. Mix gently.

5 Spoon the mixture into the 3 paper cases. Bake for 12-15 minutes, until risen and firm. Put on a wire rack to cool.

6 To make the frosting, follow the instructions on page 377. Then, stir in the orange zest.

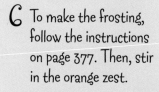

7 Take off the cases. Crumble the cakes into a bowl, until all the cake is in small crumbs. Mix in the frosting.

8 Scoop up a teaspoonful of the mixture. Roll it into a ball. Put it on a plate. Make more cake balls. Put the plate in the fridge for 30 minutes.

9 Pour some sprinkles onto a plate. Put out some cups or glasses to stand the finished cakepops in.

10 For the coating, melt the chocolate (see page 380). Take a cakepop. Push a lollipop stick into the flattened part that was in contact with the plate.

11 Dip the cakepop in the chocolate. Spoon on more chocolate, to cover the cakepop. Hold it over the bowl and shake it gently, so any excess chocolate drips off.

12 Hold the cakepop over the plate and scatter sprinkles all over it. Stand the stick in a glass. Make more cakepops. Chill for 15 minutes, so the chocolate sets.

You could stand cakepops in jam jars, or stick them into half oranges.

Mini cheesecakes

These little cheesecakes are topped with sliced peaches or nectarines, but you could use 150g (5oz) fresh raspberries or blueberries instead, and swap the jam in the topping for raspberry jam. They are also delicious with no topping at all.

Ingredients:

175g (6oz) digestive biscuits

75g (3oz) butter

450g (1lb) full-fat cream cheese

125g (4½oz) caster sugar

2 large eggs

2 teaspoons vanilla essence

For the topping:

½ lemon

4 tablespoons smooth peach or apricot jam

2 ripe peaches or nectarines

You will also need a 12-hole deep muffin tray and 12 muffin cases.

Makes 12

1 Heat the oven to 150°C, 300°F, gas mark 2. Put the muffin cases in the tray. Take the cream cheese out of the fridge.

2 Put the biscuits in a clean plastic food bag. Seal the end with an elastic band.

3 Roll a rolling pin over the bag to crush the biscuits into small pieces.

4 Put the butter in a saucepan. Put the pan over a low heat. When the butter melts, mix in the biscuit crumbs.

5 Divide the mixture evenly between the cases in the tin. Press it down firmly, using the back of a teaspoon.

6 Put the tin in the fridge so the bases will become firm. Meanwhile, make the cheesecake filling.

7 Put the cream cheese and sugar in a big bowl. Mix them together. Put the eggs and vanilla extract in a small bowl. Beat them with a fork.

8 Add the egg mixture to the cheese mixture a little at a time, beating well each time. Spoon the mixture into the cases.

9 Bake for 25 minutes. Turn off the oven and leave the tin in for another 30 minutes. Then, take it out.

10 Move the cheesecakes to a wire rack to cool. Put them in the fridge to chill for at least 2 hours. Then, make the topping.

11 Squeeze the juice from the lemon. Put it in a bowl and mix in the jam. Spread it onto the cheesecakes.

12 Cut the peaches or nectarines in half, running the knife around the stone. Remove the stone. Cut the fruit into thin slices. Put them on the cheesecakes.

Remove the muffin cases before you eat the cheesecakes.

Little pink cakes

Ingredients:

1 medium egg
50g (2oz) self-raising flour
40g (1½oz) soft margarine
40g (1½oz) caster sugar
small paper cases
a baking tray

For the icing:
50g (2oz) icing sugar
pink or red food dye

You will also need a baking tray
and 48 tiny paper cake cases.

Makes 24

These tiny cakes are covered in pink glacé icing –
though you could make your icing any colour you like.
When the cakes are iced, you can then decorate them
with writing icing and little sweets and sprinkles.

1 Heat the oven to 180°C, 350°F or gas mark 4.

Use a wooden spoon.

2 Break the egg into a mug.
Then, sift the flour into a
large bowl and add the egg,
margarine and caster sugar.

3 Stir everything together well,
until the mixture is smooth.
Arrange 24 paper cases on
the tray. Then, tuck a second
case inside each one.

The cakes will turn
golden-brown.

4 Using a teaspoon, spoon the
cake mixture into the paper
cases until each case is just
under half full.

5 Bake the cakes for about 12
minutes, until risen and golden-
brown. Lift them onto a wire
rack and leave them to cool.

6 For the icing, sift the icing
sugar into a bowl. Add 1
tablespoon of water and mix
until the icing is smooth.

Add a little more food colouring to make brighter pink icing.

7 Add a few drops of food dye. Then, mix it in well.

Some of these cakes have two different layers of icing on them.

8 Spoon a little icing onto the top of each cake. Then, spread out the icing with the back of the spoon.

9 Leave the icing for a little while to set. Then, draw decorations on the cakes, using the white writing icing.

If you'd like to make white icing, don't add any food colouring.

Other ideas

Instead of using writing icing, you could spoon some of the icing into a piping gun or bag and pipe it onto your cakes. Follow the instructions on pages 378-379.

You could decorate cakes with sweets or write letters on them, to spell out your name.

Little rose cakes

Ingredients:

1 lemon

175g (6oz) caster sugar

175g (6oz) softened butter
  or margarine

175g (6oz) self-raising flour

3 medium eggs

For the rose syrup:

1 tablespoon caster sugar

1 teaspoon rose water

For the rose buttercream:

150g (5oz) softened butter
  or margarine

350g (12oz) icing sugar

1 tablespoon lemon juice

2½ teaspoons rose water

pink food dye

You will also need a 12-hole deep
muffin tin, 12 paper muffin cases
and a piping bag fitted with a big
snowflake-shaped nozzle.

Makes 12

Piped two-tone buttercream roses make a spectacular topping for these little rose-flavoured cakes. You can leave out the rose water if you don't like the taste.

1 Heat the oven to 180°C, 350°F or gas mark 4. Put a paper case in each hole of the muffin tray. Grate the zest from the lemon on the small holes of a grater. Cut the lemon in half, squeeze out the juice and put it in a jug.

2 Put the lemon zest, sugar and butter or margarine in a big bowl. Beat until fluffy. Sift on the flour.

3 Break one egg into a cup, then add it to the mixture. Do the same with each of the other eggs. Mix until smooth. Spoon into the paper cases.

4 Bake for 20-25 minutes. While the cakes are baking, make the syrup. Stir the sugar and rose water into the lemon juice in the jug.

5 When the cakes are risen and firm, spoon a little syrup onto each one. Put them on a wire rack to cool.

6 To make the buttercream, put the butter or margarine in a bowl. Beat with a wooden spoon until it's smooth. Sift on half the icing sugar. Mix it in.

7 Sift on the rest of the icing sugar. Add the lemon juice and rose water. Beat until fluffy.

These cakes were all iced with different shades of pink buttercream.

8 Mix a few drops of food dye into the buttercream to make a pale pink shade. Put 1 tablespoon of buttercream in a small bowl. Mix in more dye, to make a strong pink shade.

9 Spoon the strong pink buttercream into the piping bag. Put the bag on a surface and flatten it with your hand. Pull the bag open again. Spoon in the pale pink buttercream.

10 Pipe a rose onto each cake, starting in the middle. For tips on piping roses, see page 379.

Party cupcakes

Ingredients:

125g (4½oz) butter or margarine

2 medium eggs

150g (5oz) caster sugar

200g (7oz) self-raising flour

100g (4oz) chocolate chips
   (optional)

75ml (3floz) milk

For the buttercream:

100g (4oz) softened butter
   or margarine

225g (8oz) icing sugar

1 tablespoon milk or water

1 teaspoon vanilla essence

different shades of food dye

For the chocolate sauce:

40g (1½oz) plain or milk chocolate

75ml (3floz) double cream

You will also need a 12-hole deep muffin tin, 12 paper muffin cases, some sugar sprinkles and some cake toppers (see page 383).

Makes 12

These simple cupcakes make a great party activity. Bake them in advance, then let your party guests add buttercream, sauce, sprinkles and cake toppers.

1 Heat the oven to 180°C, 350°F or gas mark 4. Put a paper case in each hole of the muffin tray.

2 Put the butter or margarine in a small pan. Heat gently until it melts. Leave it to cool.

3 Break an egg into a cup, then tip it into a bowl. Break the other egg into the cup. Tip it into the bowl. Beat with a fork.

4 Put the sugar in a big bowl. Sift on the flour. Add the chocolate chips. Mix. Add the milk, eggs and butter or margarine. Mix well.

5 Divide the mixture between the paper cases. Bake for 12-15 minutes, until risen and firm. Leave for 10 minutes, then put on a wire rack. Leave to cool completely.

6 For the buttercream, put the butter or margarine in a bowl. Sift on one third of the icing sugar. Beat until soft. Sift on the rest of the icing sugar.

7 Add the milk or water and the vanilla. Beat until fluffy. Divide the buttercream between several bowls. Mix some food dye into each portion.

8 For the sauce, break up the chocolate. Put the cream in a small pan. Heat gently until it starts to steam. Take it off the heat. Add the chocolate, and stir until it melts.

9 Put out the cakes, bowls of buttercream, sauce, sprinkles and cake toppers. Your guests can spoon some buttercream onto a cupcake, pour on some sauce and then add sprinkles and toppers.

Other ideas

You could buy chocolate sauce – or other sauces such as toffee or strawberry.

If you'd prefer to make chocolate cupcakes, simply follow the recipe on pages 206-207. Or, bake both recipes so you'll have 12 of each flavour.

Little banana cakes

Contains optional nuts

Ingredients:

125g (4½oz) softened butter
  or margarine
150g (5oz) soft dark brown sugar
2 large eggs
1 teaspoon vanilla essence
4 large, ripe bananas
250g (9oz) self-raising flour
½ teaspoon baking powder
1 teaspoon lemon juice

For the cream cheese frosting:
50g (2oz) icing sugar
200g (7oz) full-fat cream
  cheese, at room temperature
1 tablespoon lemon juice

You will also need a 12-hole deep
muffin tray, 12 paper muffin cases
and some walnut pieces or extra
banana to decorate (optional).

Makes 12

These little cakes contain fresh banana, which makes them moist and juicy. The riper the bananas, the more flavour your cakes will have. To make these cakes dairy-free, use dairy-free margarine and top with buttercream (page 376) made with dairy-free margarine.

1 Heat the oven to 180°C, 350°F or gas mark 4. Fill the tray with paper cases.

2 Put the butter and sugar in a big bowl. Beat them together until the mixture is pale and fluffy.

3 Break an egg into a cup, then put it in a small bowl. Do the same with the other egg. Add the vanilla essence. Mix with a fork.

4 Put a spoonful of the egg in the big bowl. Beat it in well. Add the rest of the egg, a spoonful at a time, beating well each time.

5 Peel the bananas and put them in a bowl. Mash them with a fork or potato masher. Mix in the lemon juice. Tip the mixture into the big bowl and mix it in.

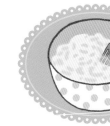

6 Sift the flour and baking powder over the mixture. Mix it in well.

7 Spoon the mixture into the cases. Bake for 20-25 minutes, or until browned and firm.

8 Leave the cakes for 5 minutes, then put them on a wire rack and leave them to cool.

9 Make the cream cheese frosting (see page 376). Spread it over the cakes. Decorate with slices of fresh banana or walnut pieces, if you like.

Banana slices

If you're decorating your cakes with banana slices, mix them in a bowl with a tablespoon of lemon juice first. This will stop them turning brown.

These cakes taste delicious even without a topping.

Vanilla cupcakes

Ingredients:

175g (6oz) self-raising flour
175g (6oz) soft margarine
175g (6oz) caster sugar
1 teaspoon vanilla essence
3 medium eggs

For the buttercream:
100g (4oz) softened butter or
   margarine
225g (8oz) icing sugar
1 tablespoon milk
1½ teaspoons vanilla essence
food dye (optional)

You will also need a 12-hole deep
muffin tray and 12 muffin cases.

Makes 12

These pretty cupcakes are topped with buttercream tinted in pastel shades. You can spread the buttercream onto the cakes, or pipe it on in swirly patterns using a piping bag or gun.

1 Heat the oven to 180°C, 350°F or gas mark 4. Put a paper case in each hole in the tray.

2 Sift the flour into a large mixing bowl. Add the margarine, sugar and vanilla essence.

3 Break the eggs into a cup, then pour them into the bowl. Stir until you have a smooth mixture.

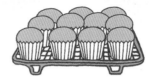

4 Spoon the mixture into the paper cases, dividing it evenly between them. Bake for 20-25 minutes, or until firm and golden on top.

5 Leave the cooked cakes in the tray for a few minutes. Then, put them on a wire rack to cool. Meanwhile, make the buttercream (see page 376).

6 When the cakes are completely cool, spread or pipe on some buttercream (see page 379 for piping instructions).

A mini cupcake with a small piped swirl

You could decorate your cupcakes with small sweets or sugar sprinkles.

This buttercream was spread on with a knife.

This cupcake has a piped swirly topping.

Mini cupcakes

Use the recipe for tiny butterfly cakes on pages 208-209. Follow steps 1-2, spoon the mixture into the cases and bake for 10-12 minutes. Then, follow steps 6-7 here, to cool and decorate them.

Very chocolatey cupcakes

Ingredients:

1½ tablespoons milk

¼ teaspoon lemon juice

65g (2½oz) rice flour

2 tablespoons cocoa powder

½ teaspoon baking powder
(gluten-free types are available)

a pinch of bicarbonate of soda

125g (4½oz) caster sugar

65g (2½oz) plain or milk chocolate

65g (2½oz) butter

1 medium egg

For the white chocolate cream:

150g (5oz) white chocolate

25g (1oz) unsalted butter

75ml (3floz) double cream

You will also need a baking tray, around 60 tiny paper cake cases and a piping bag or gun fitted with a star-shaped nozzle.

Makes around 30

These little chocolate cakes are moist, rich and wheat- and gluten-free (see page 388). They're topped with white chocolate cream and chocolate decorations.

1 Heat the oven to 170°C, 325°F or gas mark 3. Put around 30 tiny paper cases on the baking tray. Tuck a second case inside each one. Pour the milk into a jug and stir in the lemon juice.

2 Sift the rice flour, cocoa, baking powder and bicarbonate of soda into a large bowl. Add the sugar and stir.

3 Break up the chocolate. Put it in a pan. Add the butter and 1½ tablespoons of cold water. Heat gently until the chocolate and butter melt.

4 Break the egg into a cup and beat it with a fork. Stir it into the mixture in the jug. Then, pour the mixture into the big bowl.

5 Add the chocolate mixture too. Stir until smooth. Spoon into the paper cases. Bake for 15 minutes, then test with a skewer – see page 373.

6 Leave the cakes for 5 minutes, then move them to a wire rack to cool. Meanwhile, make the white chocolate cream.

7 Break up the chocolate and put it in a bowl. Put the butter and cream in a small pan. Heat gently until the butter melts. Pour the hot cream onto the chocolate.

8 Leave for 2 minutes, then stir until the chocolate melts. Refrigerate for 30 minutes, or until it's like soft butter. Then, beat it with a whisk until pale and fluffy, like whipped cream.

9 Spoon it into your piping gun or bag. Pipe a swirl onto each cupcake, following the instructions on page 379. Add chocolate shapes or sprinkles.

To make chocolate stars or hearts like these, follow the instructions on page 384.

This cupcake was topped with plain chocolate cream – see the box below.

Other flavours

To make plain or milk chocolate cream, you will need 150g (5oz) plain or milk chocolate and 75ml (3floz) double cream. Follow steps 7-9, but leave out the butter.

Mini crispy buns

Ingredients:

100g (4oz) soft margarine

50g (2oz) softened butter

50g (2oz) light soft brown sugar

1 medium egg

1 teaspoon vanilla essence

125g (5oz) self-raising flour

50g (2oz) corn flakes

200g (7oz) white chocolate

sugar sprinkles, for decorating

You will also need 2 baking trays and a heatproof bowl that fits snugly into a saucepan.

Makes around 20

This recipe is for tiny buns that contain corn flakes to make them crispy. They are topped with a delicious layer of white chocolate.

1 Heat your oven to 190°C, 375°F or gas mark 5. Grease the baking trays with cooking oil (page 10). Cut a large piece of baking parchment and put it on a chopping board, too.

2 Put the margarine and butter into a bowl and stir them until they are smooth. Add the sugar and beat the mixture until it is fluffy.

3 Break the egg into a cup and add the vanilla. Stir the mixture with a fork, then pour half of it into the bowl.

Leave lots of space between the buns.

4 Stir in the egg mixture. Then, add the rest and stir that in, too. Sift the flour into the bowl and stir everything well.

5 Crush the corn flakes a little with your fingers and put them onto a plate. Scoop up a teaspoon of the mixture and put it on top.

6 Roll the mixture in the corn flakes to cover it. Then, put it on a greased baking tray and make more buns in the same way.

7 Bake the buns for 12-14 minutes. Leave them on the trays for two minutes, then lift them onto a wire rack to cool.

8 Fill a large pan a quarter full of water and heat it until the water bubbles. Take the pan off the heat.

9 Break up the chocolate and put it in the heatproof bowl. Then, wearing oven gloves, carefully put the bowl into the pan of water.

Wear oven gloves.

10 After 2 minutes, stir the chocolate until it has melted. Carefully lift the bowl out of the pan.

11 Put the buns onto the chopping board. Spread a teaspoon of the melted chocolate over each bun.

12 Sprinkle sugar sprinkles on the buns. Then, put them in the fridge for 20 minutes, for the chocolate to set, or eat them straight away.

Mint choc chip cakes

Ingredients:

40g (1½oz) caster sugar

40g (1½oz) soft margarine

40g (1½oz) self-raising flour

1 tablespoon cocoa powder

1 medium egg

1 tablespoon plain chocolate chips

1 tablespoon white chocolate chips

For the peppermint icing:

175g (6oz) icing sugar

1 teaspoon peppermint essence

green food dye

You will also need a baking tray and around 50 tiny paper cake cases.

Makes around 25

These tiny chocolate chip cakes are topped with a delicious minty icing. You can decorate them with more chocolate chips, if you like.

1 Heat the oven to 180°C, 350°F or gas mark 4. Put around 25 paper cases on the tray. Tuck a second case inside each. Put the sugar and margarine in a big bowl.

2 Sift the flour and cocoa powder into the bowl. Break the egg into a cup, then tip it into the bowl. Stir the mixture until it is smooth.

3 Spoon half the mixture into another bowl. Put the plain chocolate chips in one bowl and the white chocolate chips in the other. Stir them in.

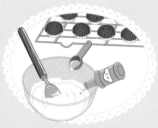

4 Using two teaspoons, spoon all the mixture into the paper cases. Bake for 12 minutes, until they are firm. Lift the cakes onto a wire rack to cool.

5 For the icing, sift the icing sugar into a bowl. Add 1½ tablespoons of warm water, the peppermint essence and a few drops of green food dye.

6 Stir the icing until it is smooth. Use a teaspoon to spread a little icing onto each cake. Decorate the cakes with more chocolate chips, if you like.

You could decorate your cakes with different types of chocolate. See page 380 to find out how to make chocolate curls.

Fairy cakes

Ingredients:

90g (3½oz) self-raising flour
90g (3½oz) caster sugar
90g (3½oz) soft margarine
2 medium eggs
½ teaspoon vanilla essence

For the icing:
175g (6oz) icing sugar
yellow food dye

You will also need a 12-hole shallow bun tin and 12 paper cupcake cases.

Makes 12

These pretty cakes are really easy to make because all the ingredients are simply beaten together. You can ice them with different colours of icing and decorate them with sweets, sugar flowers, fresh fruit or piped icing.

1 Heat the oven to 190°C, 375°F, or gas mark 5. Put a paper case into each hole in the tin. Sift the flour into a large bowl. Add the sugar, margarine and vanilla.

2 Break the eggs into a cup, then add them to the bowl. Stir with a wooden spoon until the mixture is smooth.

3 Use a teaspoon to divide the mixture between the paper cake cases. Bake for 15 minutes, until they are firm and golden.

4 Leave the cakes in the tin for a few minutes. Then, lift them out of the tin onto a wire rack to cool.

5 To make white icing, sift the icing sugar into a bowl. Stir in 1½ tablespoons of warm water to make a smooth paste. Spoon icing onto four of the cakes.

6 To make pale yellow icing, mix a few drops of yellow food dye into the icing. Use a teaspoon to ice four more cakes with pale yellow icing.

7 To make darker yellow icing, mix in a few more drops of yellow dye. Spread it onto the last four cakes. Then decorate all the cakes.

Small strawberry sponge cakes

Ingredients:

75g (3oz) caster sugar

75g (3oz) softened butter or
  margarine

½ teaspoon vanilla essence

2 medium eggs

75g (3oz) self-raising flour

For the filling:

25g (1oz) softened butter or
  margarine

50g (2oz) icing sugar

½ teaspoon vanilla essence

4 tablespoons smooth
  strawberry jam

For decorating:

2 tablespoons icing sugar

You will also need a 6-hole deep
muffin tin.

Makes 6

These cakes are miniature versions of a popular cake often known as a Victoria sponge. They are filled with luscious vanilla buttercream and strawberry jam.

1 Heat the oven to 180°C, 350°F or gas mark 4. Grease the inside of each hole of the muffin tin (see page 10) using a little softened butter or margarine.

2 Put the sugar and the butter or margarine in a big bowl. Beat until you have a fluffy mixture. Add the vanilla.

3 Break one egg into a cup. Pour it into the bowl and mix. Do the same with the other egg. Sift over the flour and mix it in gently.

Run a knife around each cake if it's hard to get them out.

4 Spoon the mixture into the holes of the muffin tin. Bake for 20-25 minutes, or until firm and risen. Leave the cakes to cool for 10 minutes.

5 Hold the muffin tin upside down over a wire rack and shake, so the cakes pop out. Turn them the right way up again. Leave to cool completely.

6 While the cakes are cooling, use the butter, icing sugar and vanilla to make the vanilla buttercream, following the instructions on page 376.

7 When the cakes are cool, cut each one in half, like this.

8 Spread a little buttercream over each bottom half, then spread on some jam. Put the top halves back on.

9 To decorate the cakes, spoon the icing sugar into a small sieve. Hold it over each cake and tap the sieve gently.

All these cakes were filled with strawberry jam, but you could use other flavours.

These cakes look pretty topped with a slice of strawberry.

Big cakes

Classic sponge cake

Ingredients:

225g (8oz) softened butter

225g (8oz) caster sugar

4 medium eggs

225g (8oz) self-raising flour

For the filling:

150ml (¼ pint) whipping cream
or double cream

4 tablespoons jam or lemon curd

You will also need two 20cm (8in)
round, shallow cake tins.

Makes 12 slices

The main recipe here is for a traditional light sponge cake, made by beating together butter and caster sugar until they are light and fluffy. The cake is cooked in 2 layers which are sandwiched together with jam and whipped cream.

1 Heat the oven to 180°C, 350°F or gas mark 4. Line the tins with baking parchment (see page 10).

2 Put the butter and sugar in a large bowl and mix them together. Then, beat them very quickly until you have a fluffy mixture.

3 Break one egg into a cup and beat it with a fork. Pour it into the large bowl and beat the mixture to mix it in well. Do the same with the other eggs, beating well each time.

Move the spoon in the...

...shape of a number 8.

4 Sift the flour into the bowl. Mix the flour into the egg mixture very gently, using a metal spoon.

5 Divide the mixture between the cake tins. Smooth the top of the mixture with the back of the spoon.

6 Put the cakes in the oven. Bake for 20 minutes. Test with a finger (see page 373), to see if they are cooked.

7 When the cakes are cooked, leave them in their tins for 5 minutes. Then, turn the cakes out onto a wire rack to cool.

8 For the filling, pour the cream into a big bowl. Whisk it quickly until it becomes very thick and stays in a floppy point when you lift the whisk.

9 Put one cake on a plate with the flat side up. Spread on the jam or curd, then spread the cream on top.

10 Put the other cake on top, flat side down. Press the cakes together gently.

11 You could sift a little icing sugar over the top of your cakes, or stencil on a doily pattern in icing sugar – see page 305.

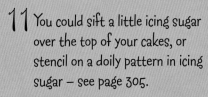

If you're going to stencil a pattern onto your cake, like this, put the second layer on flat side up.

Quick sponge cake

Ingredients:

225g (8oz) self-raising flour

225g (8oz) caster sugar

225g (8oz) soft margarine

4 medium eggs

For the vanilla buttercream:

100g (4oz) softened butter or
  soft margarine

225g (8oz) icing sugar

1 tablespoon of milk

½ teaspoon of vanilla essence

You will also need two 20cm (8in)
round, shallow cake tins.

Makes 12 slices

This is a quick sponge cake recipe, made by mixing all the ingredients in one bowl. The main recipe is for a plain cake sandwiched with vanilla buttercream. You'll find other fillings and flavours opposite.

1 Heat the oven to 180°C, 350°F or gas mark 4. Grease and line the tins (see page 10).

2 Sift the flour into a big bowl. Add the sugar and margarine. Break an egg into a cup, then tip it into the bowl. Do the same with the other eggs.

3 Stir until you have smooth mixture. Spoon half into each cake tin and smooth the tops with the back of the spoon.

4 Bake for 25 minutes, or until the cakes are risen and firm to the touch. Leave in the tins for 5 minutes.

5 Run a knife around the tins, then turn the cakes onto a wire rack (see page 373).

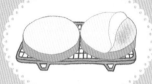

6 Peel off the parchment. Turn the cakes the right way up. Then, make the buttercream (instructions on page 376).

7 When the cakes are cool, put one on a plate, flat side up. Spread on the buttercream. Put the other cake on top, flat side down. Press gently.

Sprinkle on a little caster sugar, if you like.

Other flavours

Chocolate sponge
Replace 40g (1½oz) of the flour with cocoa powder.

Coffee sponge
Mix 1 rounded tablespoon of instant coffee with 1 tablespoon of hot water. Cool and add after step 2.

Citrus sponge
Grate the zest of 2 lemons, limes or oranges and add it after step 2.

Sugar and spice sponge
Add 2 teaspoons of ground cinnamon and 1 teaspoon of ground ginger at step 2. This goes well with a vanilla buttercream filling.

Other fillings

Jam and buttercream
Spread 4 tablespoons of jam on top of the buttercream at step 7.

Fruity filling
For a dairy-free raspberry filling, see the Swiss roll recipe on pages 104-105.

Creamy fillings
Use a flavoured buttercream from page 376, or 150ml (¼ pint) whipped cream (see page 377). You could spread on 4 tablespoons of jam before the cream.

Lime filling
You could fill your cake with tangy lime mascarpone (see page 376).

Lemon sponge filled with lemon buttercream

Plain sponge with jam and buttercream

Chocolate sponge filled with raspberry cream

Lemon layer cake

Ingredients:

1 lemon
225g (8oz) self-raising flour
1 teaspoon baking powder
4 medium eggs
225g (8oz) soft margarine
225g (8oz) caster sugar

For the lemon curd:
2 medium eggs
75g (3oz) caster sugar
1 lemon
50g (2oz) unsalted butter

For the lemon icing:
1 lemon
125g (5oz) icing sugar

You will also need three 20cm (8in) round, shallow cake tins and a heatproof bowl that fits snugly into a saucepan.

Makes 10 slices

Layers of lemon cake are sandwiched together with home-made lemon curd, then topped with tangy lemon icing.

Use the small holes of a grater.

1 Heat the oven to 180°C, 350°F or gas mark 4. Grease and line the tins (page 10). Grate the zest from the outside of the lemon, then squeeze the juice from the lemon.

2 Sift the flour and baking powder into a big bowl. Break the eggs into a cup, then put them in the bowl. Add the margarine and sugar. Beat well.

3 Stir in the lemon juice and zest. Divide the mixture between the tins. Bake for 20 minutes, until firm. Then, turn the cakes out onto a wire rack to cool.

4 For the lemon curd, break the eggs into the heatproof bowl. Beat with a fork. Add the sugar. Grate the zest from the lemon and squeeze out the juice. Put the zest and juice in the bowl.

5 Cut the butter into chunks. Add them, too. Fill the saucepan ¼ full of water. Heat until it is just bubbling. Wearing oven gloves, lower the bowl into the pan.

6 Keep stirring all the time. After around 20 minutes, the mixture should have thickened enough to coat the back of the spoon in a thin, even layer. Take the pan off the heat. Leave to cool.

Don't worry if some curd oozes out.

7 Spread one of the cakes with half of the lemon curd. Put another cake on top. Spread the rest of curd over that cake. Then, put the final cake on top.

8 For the icing, grate the zest from the lemon, or scrape some off with a zester. Put the zest to one side. Cut the lemon in half and squeeze the juice from one half.

9 Sift the icing sugar into a big bowl. Add the juice. Mix well. Spread it over the cake, so it drips down the sides (see page 378). Sprinkle the zest on top of the cake.

Coffee cake

Ingredients:

2 dessertspoons instant coffee granules

175g (6oz) softened butter or margarine

175g (6oz) caster sugar

3 large eggs

175g (6oz) self-raising flour

1½ teaspoons baking powder

200g (7oz) walnut or pecan pieces (optional)

For the buttercream:

175g (6oz) softened butter or margarine

200g (7oz) icing sugar

You will also need a 20cm (8in) round, deep cake tin, preferably with a loose base.

Makes 12 slices

Coffee buttercream

Put the butter or margarine in a big bowl. Beat until fluffy. Sift over one third of the icing sugar and stir it in. Then, sift on the rest of the icing sugar. Add the rest of the coffee from step 5. Beat quickly, until pale and fluffy.

This coffee cake can be cut it in half and filled and topped with coffee buttercream. If you don't want to cut it in half, just leave the cake whole, make half the amount of buttercream and spread it on top. Leave out the nuts if you prefer.

1 Heat the oven to 180°C, 350°F or gas mark 4. Grease and line the tin (see page 10).

2 Put the coffee granules in a cup and add 2 dessertspoons of boiling water. Mix.

3 Put the butter or margarine and sugar in a big bowl. Beat until the mixture is pale and fluffy. Break the eggs into a bowl and beat them with a fork.

4 Add a spoonful of egg to the buttery mixture and stir it in. Add the rest of the egg a spoonful at a time, mixing well each time.

5 Sift the flour and baking powder over the bowl. Stir them in. Add half the coffee and the nuts. Mix well.

6 Scrape the mixture into the tin. Smooth the top with the back of a spoon. Bake for 30-35 minutes, until firm. Leave in the tin for 10 minutes to cool slightly.

7 Remove the cake from the tin, following the instructions on page 373.

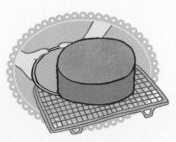

8 Transfer the cake to a wire rack. Leave it to cool completely.

9 Cut the cake into two layers, steadying it gently with one hand and cutting very carefully with a serrated knife.

10 Make the coffee buttercream, following the instructions on the right.

11 Spread half the buttercream on the bottom layer. Put the top back on and spread the rest of the buttercream over it.

Scatter extra nuts over the top of your cake, if you like.

255

Strawberry jam cake

Ingredients:

1 lemon

175g (6oz) smooth
 strawberry jam

2 tablespoons red food dye

225g (8oz) softened butter or
 margarine

175g (6oz) caster sugar

275g (10oz) self-raising flour

4 medium eggs

1 teaspoon baking powder

For the buttercream:

150g (5oz) softened butter or
 margarine

75g (3oz) smooth strawberry jam

1 tablespoon lemon juice

250g (9oz) icing sugar

For decorating:

2 tablespoons smooth
 strawberry jam

a few drops of red food dye

You will also need a 20cm (8in)
round, deep cake tin and a
cocktail stick.

Makes 14-16 slices

This moist cake has strawberry jam in every bit
of it. The cake has jam baked into it. The icing is
strawberry jam buttercream and the decorations
are shiny jam hearts.

1 Heat the oven to 180°C, 350°F or gas mark 4. Grease and line
the tin (see page 10).

2 Grate the zest from the lemon
on the fine holes of a grater. Mix
the zest, jam and food dye in a
small bowl. Squeeze the juice
from the lemon and set it aside.

3 Put the butter or margarine
and sugar in a big bowl. Beat
until fluffy. Add the jam
mixture and 1 tablespoon of
the flour. Beat well.

4 Break the eggs into a cup.
Beat with a fork. Tip into the
big bowl. Sift in the rest of the
flour and the baking powder.
Stir until smooth. Spoon into
the tin. Smooth the top.

5 Bake for 45 minutes, then
cover with kitchen foil. Bake
for 10-15 minutes more. Push
a skewer into the middle. If it
comes out clean, the cake is
cooked. If not, cook for 10 more
minutes, then test again.

When the cake is cool, peel off the parchment.

6 Leave the cake for 15 minutes. Remove it from the tin (see page 373). Put it on a wire rack to cool.

7 For the buttercream, put the butter or margarine in a big bowl. Add the jam and lemon juice and beat until fluffy. Sift in the icing sugar. Mix well.

8 When the cake is cool, put it on a serving plate. Spread the buttercream over the sides and top of the cake. Smooth the surface with a blunt knife.

9 To decorate the cake, push the jam though a sieve into a bowl. Scrape the jam off the back of the sieve, too. Mix in the food dye and 1 teaspoon of lemon juice.

10 Use a cocktail stick to mark three circles, one inside the other, on the cake. Drop ¼ teaspoon of the jam mixture onto one of the circles.

11 Drop more blobs all along the circles, 2½cm (1in) apart. Drag the point of the cocktail stick along each circle, through the blobs of jam. They will become hearts.

You could use other jam flavours, such as apricot or cherry. Choose a food dye to match.

Luscious lemon cake

Ingredients:

2 lemons

3 medium eggs

50g (2oz) softened butter
  or margarine

300g (11oz) caster sugar

250g (9oz) ricotta cheese

175g (6oz) self-raising flour

For the lemon buttercream:

1 lemon

200g (7oz) softened butter
  or margarine

350g (12oz) icing sugar

You will also need two 15cm (6in)
round, shallow cake tins.

Makes 12 slices

This tangy cake is covered with luscious lemon buttercream. You could decorate it with cake flags – find out how to make them on page 383.

1 Heat the oven to 180°C, 350°F or gas mark 4. Grease and line the cake tins (page 10). Grate the zest from the lemons on the small holes of a grater. Squeeze the juice from one of the lemons.

2 Separate the eggs (page 11). Put the whites in a big bowl. Put the yolks in another big bowl.

Move the spoon in the...

...shape of a number 8.

3 Add the zest, butter or margarine and sugar to the yolks. Mix well. Add the ricotta a spoonful at a time, mixing it in well with a fork each time.

4 Sift the flour over the ricotta mixture. Use a spatula or a big metal spoon to fold it in gently.

5 Whisk the egg whites until they are thick and foamy. They should stay in a point when you lift the whisk. Add them to the ricotta mixture. Fold them in gently.

6 Divide the mixture between the tins. Level the tops with the back of a spoon. Bake for 40-45 minutes, until risen and firm. Test with a finger (see page 373).

7 Put the tins on a wire rack. Poke holes all over the tops of the cakes with the skewer. Pour over the lemon juice. Leave them to cool.

Use the small holes on a grater.

8 For the buttercream, grate the zest from the lemon, then squeeze out the juice. Put the zest in a big bowl. Add the butter or margarine.

9 Sift on half the icing sugar. Mix well. Sift on the rest of the icing sugar. Add 1½ tablespoons of lemon juice. Beat until fluffy.

0 Put one cake on a plate. Spread on a quarter of the buttercream. Put the other cake on top, upside down. Spread the rest of the buttercream over the top and sides of the cake.

If you don't have two 15cm (6in) cake tins, use one deep 20cm (8in) round tin instead. Bake for 45-55 minutes.

These curls of lemon zest were made using a tool known as a zester.

After this cake was iced, a blunt knife was used to make stripes in the buttercream.

Chocolate orange cake

Ingredients:

1 medium orange

175g (6oz) soft margarine

175g (6oz) caster sugar

3 medium eggs

2 tablespoons cocoa powder

1 teaspoon baking powder

200g (7oz) self-raising
   wholemeal flour

5 tablespoons plain natural yogurt

For the topping:

100g (4oz) milk chocolate

175g (6oz) plain chocolate

150ml (¼ pint) soured cream

You will also need a 20cm (8in)
round, deep cake tin and a
heatproof bowl that fits snugly
into a saucepan.

Makes 8-10 slices

Chocolate and orange taste delicious together.
Wholemeal flour makes this cake crunchy around
the edges, while yogurt makes it light in the middle.

1 Heat the oven to 170°C, 325°F
or gas mark 3. Grease and line
the tin (see page 10).

2 Grate the zest from the
outside of the orange, using
the small holes of the grater.
Cut the orange in half and
squeeze out the juice.

3 Put the margarine in a big
bowl. Beat it until it is soft and
smooth. Stir in the sugar and
orange rind. Beat the mixture
until it is light and fluffy.

4 Crack the eggs into a small
bowl and beat them well with a
fork. Pour the eggs into the large
mixing bowl, a little at a time.
Beat well after each addition.

5 Put the cocoa into a small
bowl. Stir 2 tablespoons of
warm water to make a
smooth paste. Scrape it into
the large bowl and stir it in.

Move the spoon in the shape of a number 8.

6 Sift the baking powder and about half of the flour over the mixture. Then, add half of the yogurt. Gently fold the ingredients together.

7 Sift the remaining flour into the bowl. If there are bits left in the sieve, tip them into the bowl too. Add the rest of the yogurt and fold it in. Add the orange juice and fold it in too.

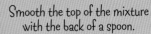

Smooth the top of the mixture with the back of a spoon.

8 Spoon the mixture into the tin. Bake for one hour. Test it with a finger, to find out if it is cooked (see page 373).

Peel the baking parchment off the cake.

9 Leave the cake in the tin for 10 minutes. Then, run a knife around the sides of the tin. Turn out the cake onto a wire rack to cool.

10 For the topping, melt the chocolate, following the instructions on page 380. Then, wearing oven gloves, take the bowl out of the pan and pour in the soured cream.

11 Use a whisk to mix in the cream. Leave it to cool for a few minutes, then spread it over the cake so it drips down the sides (see page 378).

You could decorate your cake with chocolate curls. See page 380 for how to make them.

Pink layer cake

Ingredients:

around 200g (7oz) plain flour

2¼ teaspoons baking powder

150g (5oz) caster sugar

6 tablespoons sunflower oil

6 teaspoons vanilla essence

a little milk

pink liquid food dye

6 medium eggs

a little cream of tartar

For the vanilla cream:

300ml (½ pint) double or
    whipping cream

2 tablespoons icing sugar

1 teaspoon vanilla essence

You will also need a 20cm (8in)
round, shallow cake tin.

Makes 14-18 slices

This spectacular layer cake in shades of pink is filled
and topped with vanilla cream. Each of the layers is
made separately, and baked one after the other.

1 Heat the oven to 170°C, 325°F, gas mark 3. Cut a circle
of baking parchment to fit the bottom of the tin (see page
10), then cut two more the same. Grease and line the tin.

2 Sift 65g (2½oz) of flour and
¾ teaspoon of baking powder
into a big bowl. Add 75g
(3oz) of sugar and stir it in.

3 Put 2 tablespoons of sunflower
oil, 2 teaspoons of vanilla,
5½ teaspoons of milk and ½
teaspoon of food dye in a jug.

4 Separate 2 eggs. Put the
whites in a large bowl. Put
the yolks in the jug and
beat with a fork.

5 Sprinkle a pinch of cream of tartar over the egg whites. Whisk until they become thick and foamy. The foam should stay in a point when you lift the whisk.

6 Pour the oil and milk mixture into the flour mixture. Mix well. Spoon in one third of the egg whites.

Move the spoon in the... ...shape of a number 8.

7 Use a spatula or metal spoon to fold them in gently. Add the rest of the egg whites. Fold until just mixed. Scrape into the tin.

8 Bake for 20 minutes. Test with a skewer (page 373) to make sure it's cooked. Leave for 5 minutes. Turn the cake onto a wire rack. Wash and dry the tin.

9 Grease and line the tin again. Follow step 2. Put 2 tablespoons of sunflower oil, 2 teaspoons of vanilla, 4 teaspoons of milk and 2 teaspoons of food dye in the jug. Follow steps 4-8.

Use the same bowls and jug – you don't need to wash them.

10 Grease and line the tin again. Follow step 2. Put 2 tablespoons of sunflower oil, 2 teaspoons of vanilla, 3 teaspoons of milk and 3 teaspoons of food dye in the jug. Follow steps 4-8.

Don't beat too much, or it will go hard.

11 For the vanilla cream, pour the cream into a bowl. Sift on the icing sugar and add the vanilla. Whisk until the cream stands in a floppy point when you lift the whisk.

12 When the cakes are cold, put one on a board. Use a sharp knife to trim off the browned edges all the way around. Do the same with the other cakes.

Decorate the top with sugar sprinkles if you like.

13 Put the first cake on a serving plate. Spread on one third of the cream. Put the second cake on top. Spread on half the remaining cream. Put the third cake on top and spread on the rest of the cream.

263

Vanilla cheesecake

This smooth vanilla cheesecake is made with cream cheese and baked in the oven until it sets firm. It's delicious on its own, but you could add a tangy fruit topping (see the page opposite). You'll also find a recipe for an easy lemon cheesecake on the opposite page. It's simpler to make because it sets in the fridge and doesn't need to be baked in the oven.

1 Heat the oven to 150°C, 300°F or gas mark 2. Wipe a little cooking oil over the inside of the tin with a paper towel.

2 Put the biscuits in a clean plastic bag. Seal the end with an elastic band. Use a rolling pin to crush the biscuits into pieces the size of large breadcrumbs.

3 Put the butter in a saucepan and put it over a low heat. When the butter has melted, turn off the heat.

4 Add the biscuit crumbs to the butter and mix. Spoon the mixture into the tin. Press it down with the back of a spoon. Put the tin in the fridge to chill.

5 Meanwhile, put the cream cheese and sugar in a bowl and mix. Break the eggs into a small bowl, add the vanilla and mix them together with a fork.

6 Add a little of the egg to the cheese mixture and mix it in well. Do this again and again until the egg is all used up.

Berry topping

You will need around 150g (5oz) mixed berries, 4 tablespoons of seedless raspberry jam and 1 tablespoon of lemon juice. Wash and dry the berries. Pile the fruit onto the cheesecake. To glaze the fruit, mix the jam and lemon juice and brush the mixture over the fruit. The glaze is optional.

Easy lemon cheesecake

Instead of the eggs and vanilla, you will need 150ml (¼ pint) double cream and 2 large lemons. At step 5, put just 350g (12oz) cream cheese in a bowl with the cream and sugar. Mix. Grate the zest from the lemons on the small holes of a grater. Squeeze the juice from the lemons. Put the zest and juice in the bowl and mix. Spoon the mixture over the biscuit base, level the top and chill for at least 2 hours.

7 Pour the cheese mixture into the tin. Level the top with the back of a spoon. Bake for 30 minutes. Turn off the oven and leave the cheesecake in for 30 minutes more.

8 Take the cheesecake out of the oven and leave it to cool on a wire rack. Then, put it in the fridge for at least 2 hours.

9 Remove the sides of the tin (see page 373). Then, slide the cheesecake onto a plate.

Sticky chocolate cake

Ingredients:

For the sticky chocolate icing:

150g (5oz) plain chocolate

150ml (¼ pint) double cream

For the chocolate sponge cake:

200g (7oz) self-raising flour

½ teaspoon baking powder

4 tablespoons cocoa powder

4 medium eggs

225g (8oz) soft margarine

225g (8oz) light soft brown sugar

1 tablespoon milk

You will also need a heatproof bowl that fits snugly into a saucepan and two 20cm (8in) round, shallow cake tins.

Makes 8-10 slices

This light chocolate sponge cake is made by mixing all the ingredients in the same bowl. It's baked in two layers, which are sandwiched together and covered with a delicious layer of sticky chocolate icing.

1 For the icing, break the chocolate into pieces. Put the pieces into the heatproof bowl and add the cream. Then, fill the saucepan a quarter full with water.

2 Heat the water until it bubbles. Take the pan off the heat. Wearing oven gloves, put the bowl into the pan. Stir until the mixture is smooth. Wearing oven gloves, take the bowl out of the pan.

3 Let the icing cool for a few minutes. Then, put it in the fridge for around 1 hour, stirring it every now and then. It will thicken gradually. Meanwhile, make the cake.

4 Heat the oven to 180°C, 350°F or gas mark 4. Pour a little cooking oil into each tin and wipe it over the insides. Then, put the tins on some baking parchment.

5 Draw around the tins, cut out the circles and put them into the tins. Then, sift the flour, baking powder and cocoa into a large bowl.

6 Break the eggs into a cup. Put them in the large bowl, then add the margarine, sugar and milk. Stir everything well. Spoon the mixture into the tins and smooth the tops.

7 Bake for around 25 minutes. Take the cakes out of the oven, then test them with a finger, to see if they are cooked (see page 373).

8 Leave the cakes in the tins for 5 minutes. Run a knife around them and turn them out onto a wire rack. Peel off the parchment. Leave to cool.

9 Spread some of the icing over the top of one of the cakes, then put the other cake on top. Then, spread the rest of the icing over the outside of the cake.

Keep the cake in the fridge until you are ready to eat it.

Other flavours

If you like the taste of milk chocolate, you could use it in the sticky chocolate icing, instead of plain chocolate. Your cake will taste a little lighter.

Pineapple cake

Ingredients:

250g (9oz) plain flour

2 teaspoons of baking powder

125g (4½oz) soft dark brown sugar

2 teaspoons of ground cinnamon

150ml (¼ pint) sunflower oil or other cooking oil

3 large eggs

1 teaspoon vanilla essence

a 400g (14oz) can of crushed pineapple

For the cream cheese frosting:

400g (14oz) full-fat cream cheese, at room temperature

150g (5oz) icing sugar

You will also need two 20cm (8in) round, shallow cake tins.

Makes 12 slices

This moist, light cake is made using canned crushed pineapple. It's filled and topped with cream cheese frosting flavoured with pineapple juice and pieces.

1. Heat the oven to 180°C, 350°F or gas mark 4. Grease and line the tins (see page 10).

2. Mix the flour, baking powder, sugar and cinnamon in a big bowl. Put the oil in another bowl and add the eggs and vanilla, then beat them with a fork.

3. Put 2 tablespoons of pineapple from the can in a small bowl. Add the rest of the contents of the can to the oil mixture. Stir it in.

4. Mix the oil mixture into the flour mixture. Divide between the cake tins. Bake for 25 minutes, until risen and golden brown.

5. Leave the cakes in their tins for 10 minutes. Then, turn them out onto a wire rack. Leave to cool.

When the cakes are cool...

...peel off the parchment.

6. Make the cream cheese frosting (see page 376). Mix in the pineapple you set aside earlier.

Stir very gently.

7 When the cakes are cold, put one on a plate, flat side down. Spread over half the frosting. Put the other cake on top, flat side down. Spread on the remaining frosting.

Other flavours

For a nutty version, add 50g (2oz) pecan or walnut pieces to the oil mixture in step 3. You could decorate the top of the finished cake with pecan or walnut halves or pieces.

You could decorate your cake with dried pineapple pieces.

Make swirls in the frosting as you spread it on.

Don't worry if your cakes look a little uneven – the frosting will cover up any bumps.

Pumpkin cake

Ingredients:

a piece of pumpkin or squash weighing around 350g (12oz)

1 orange

175ml (12 tablespoons) sunflower oil

200g (7oz) soft light brown sugar

4 medium eggs

225g (8oz) self-raising flour

1 teaspoon baking powder

1 teaspoon bicarbonate of soda

3 teaspoons ground cinnamon

2 teaspoons ground ginger

¼ teaspoon ground nutmeg or mace (optional)

a pinch of ground cloves (optional)

100g (4oz) plain or milk chocolate chips

For the topping:

1 orange

50g (2oz) softened butter or margarine

100g (4oz) icing sugar

red and yellow food dye

100g (4oz) plain or milk chocolate

¼ teaspoon ground cinnamon

¼ teaspoon ground ginger

You will also need a 20cm (8in) round, deep cake tin.

Makes 12-16 slices

This cake is made with spices, chocolate chips and grated pumpkin. You can't really taste the pumpkin but it makes the cake extra light and moist.

1 Heat the oven to 180°C, 350°F or gas mark 4. Grease and line the tin (see page 10).

2 Use a vegetable peeler to peel the rind from the pumpkin. Scoop out the seeds with a spoon. Grate the pumpkin on the big holes of a grater. Stop when you have 250g (9oz).

3 Grate the rind from the outside of the orange on the small holes of a grater. Put it in a big bowl.

4 Put the oil and sugar in the bowl with the zest. Beat for a minute with a wooden spoon.

5 Break an egg into a cup. Tip it into the oil and sugar mixture and mix well. Do the same with each of the other eggs.

6 Add the grated pumpkin and mix it in. Sift in the flour, baking powder, bicarbonate of soda and spices. Tip in the chocolate chips.

Move the spoon in the... ...shape of a number 8.

When the cake is cool, peel off the parchment.

7 Fold everything together gently with a spatula or a big metal spoon. Scrape into the tin. Bake for 50 minutes, until risen and firm. Test with a skewer (page 373).

8 Leave in the tin for 10 minutes, then turn the cake onto a wire rack. Leave it upside down to cool completely.

9 For the topping, grate the zest from the orange on the small holes of a grater. Squeeze the juice from half the orange. Put half the zest in a big bowl and add the butter or margarine.

Pumpkin can be hard to cut up. Get someone to help you, or use the same amount of grated carrot or sweet potato instead.

10 Beat until smooth. Sift in the icing sugar. Add 1½ teaspoons of the orange juice and a few drops of red and yellow food dye. Mix until orange and fluffy.

11 Put the cake on a serving plate with the flat side up. Spread the orange frosting around the sides. Put the cake in the fridge.

To make decorations like these, follow the instructions on page 385.

12 Melt the chocolate (see page 380). Stir in the cinnamon, ginger and the remaining orange zest. Pour it on top of the cake – see page 378 for tips on drippy toppings.

Raspberry swirl cake

This recipe is for a vanilla sponge cake, topped with a cloud of whipped cream swirled with crushed meringues and raspberries. You can also make gluten-free raspberry swirl cupcakes, using this topping instead of icing for the cakes on pages 200-201.

1 Heat the oven to 180°C, 350°F or gas mark 4. Grease and line the tin (see page 10).

2 Put the butter and sugar in a large bowl. Beat until you have a smooth mixture.

3 Break the eggs into each a small bowl. Add the vanilla. Beat with a fork. Add the egg to the butter mixture a little at a time, beating well each time.

4 Sift the flour into the bowl. Mix it in very gently, moving the spoon in the shape of a number 8. Then, add the milk and mix it in gently.

5 Pour and scrape the mixture into the cake tin. Smooth the top with the back of a spoon. Bake for 20 minutes, or until it is risen and golden.

When the cakes are cool,
peel off the parchment.

6 Take the cake out of the oven.
Poke the middle gently. If
it is firm and springs back,
it's cooked. If not, bake for 5
minutes more and try again.

7 Leave the cake in its tin for 10
minutes. Then, hold the tin
upside down over a wire rack
and shake. The cake should
pop out. Leave it to cool.

8 Meanwhile, make the topping.
Put the raspberries in a bowl.
Crush them with a fork until
some are squashed and there
is some juice showing.

9 Pour the cream into a big
bowl. Beat it very quickly
with a whisk, until it
becomes thick and stays in
a floppy point when you lift
the whisk.

10 Crumble the meringues into the
cream. Add the raspberries. Mix
them in very gently. Stop when
the mixture still looks swirly.

11 Put the cake on a plate. Spoon
on the meringue mixture. Make
peaks and swirls with the spoon
as you smooth it over the cake.

You could tie a ribbon around your cake,
like this. Take it off before you cut the cake.

Sweetie cake

Ingredients:

15g (½oz) unsalted butter

1 lemon

225g (8oz) softened butter or margarine

300g (11oz) caster sugar

6 medium eggs

350g (12oz) plain flour

1 teaspoon baking powder

½ teaspoon bicarbonate of soda

300ml (½ pint) lemon-flavoured yogurt

For decorating:

225g (8oz) icing sugar

food dye (optional)

sweeties, preferably fruit-flavoured

You will also need a fluted ring-shaped cake tin with a capacity of at least 2.5 litres (5 pints) and a pastry brush. To measure capacity, fill the tin with water then measure it into a jug.

Makes around 20 slices

This recipe is for a ring-shaped cake with a fruity flavour. When the cake is finished, you ice it and fill the middle of the ring with sweeties.

1 Melt the unsalted butter in a small pan over a gentle heat. Brush it all over the inside of the tin. Measure out all the ingredients. Heat the oven to 180°C, 350°F or gas mark 4.

2 Grate the zest from the outside of the lemon using the small holes of a grater. Squeeze the juice from the lemon.

3 Put the zest, butter or margarine and sugar in a big bowl. Beat until fluffy. Break an egg into a cup. Tip it into the bowl. Add 1 teaspoon of the flour. Mix well.

4 Add each of the remaining eggs the same way. Sift in the rest of the flour, the baking powder and the bicarbonate of soda.

5 Start mixing. When the flour is half mixed in, add the yogurt. Fold everything together gently until just mixed.

6 Scrape the mixture into the tin. Bake for 45-50 minutes, or until risen and firm. Then, test with a skewer to see if it's cooked (see page 373).

The top of the cake may crack but this doesn't matter.

7 Put the tin on a wire rack for 15 minutes, then turn the cake out of the tin onto the wire rack. Leave it to cool completely.

8 To make the icing, sift the icing sugar into a bowl. Add 2½ tablespoons of the lemon juice and a few drops of food dye. Mix.

Other shapes

You can use a 20cm (8in) round, deep tin. Grease and line the tin. Halve the quantities. Bake for 30-40 minutes. Cool and ice the cake, then pile the sweeties on top.

9 Spoon the icing over the cake, so it dribbles down the sides. Pour the sweeties into the middle of the ring.

To use a small ring tin (1.5 litre or 2½ pint capacity), halve the ingredients and bake for 30-40 minutes.

Blueberry cheesecake

Ingredients:

175g (6oz) digestive biscuits

75g (3oz) butter

1 tablespoon demerara sugar

1 lemon

350g (12oz) full-fat cream cheese

100g (4oz) caster sugar

3 medium eggs

1 tablespoon cornflour

150ml (¼ pint) whipping cream

150g (5oz) fresh blueberries

For the topping:

4 tablespoons blueberry or
   raspberry jam

150g (5oz) fresh berries

You will need a 20cm (8in) round,
deep tin with a loose base.

Makes 10 slices

This baked cheesecake is made from cream cheese, eggs and double cream. It has a rich, velvety texture, which goes well with juicy blueberries or other berries. It's best eaten chilled.

1 Heat the oven to 150°C, 300°F or gas mark 2. Wipe a little oil over the insides of the tin with a paper towel. Put the biscuits into a clean plastic bag.

2 Seal the top of the bag with an elastic band. Then, roll a rolling pin over the biscuits, to crush them into pieces the size of big breadcrumbs.

3 Put the butter and demerara sugar into a saucepan. Heat gently until the butter has melted. Take the pan off the heat and stir in the crumbs.

4 Spoon the mixture into the tin and spread it out. Press it down with the back of a spoon, to make a firm, flat base. Bake for 15 minutes.

5 Meanwhile, grate the zest from the outside of the lemon on the small holes of a grater. Then, cut the lemon in half and squeeze out the juice.

6 Put the cream cheese, sugar, lemon zest and juice into a large bowl. Stir them together.

You could decorate your cheesecake with fresh mint leaves, if you like.

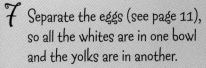

7 Separate the eggs (see page 11), so all the whites are in one bowl and the yolks are in another.

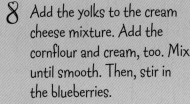

8 Add the yolks to the cream cheese mixture. Add the cornflour and cream, too. Mix until smooth. Then, stir in the blueberries.

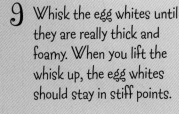

9 Whisk the egg whites until they are really thick and foamy. When you lift the whisk up, the egg whites should stay in stiff points.

10 Add the egg whites to the mixture. Gently fold them in with a metal spoon. Then, pour the mixture over the base. Bake for 50 minutes.

11 Turn off the oven. Leave the cheesecake inside for 1 hour. Take the cheesecake out of the tin and leave it to cool. While it is cooling, make the topping.

12 Put the jam in a pan with 2 teaspoons of water. Heat gently until the jam melts. Spoon it over the cheescake. Arrange the berries on top.

Strawberry shortcake

Ingredients:

225g (8oz) self-raising flour

1 teaspoon baking powder

50g (2oz) butter or margarine

25g (1oz) caster sugar

1 medium egg

5 tablespoons milk

½ teaspoon vanilla essence

a little milk, for brushing

For the filling:

225g (8oz) strawberries

150ml (¼ pint) double or whipping cream

3 tablespoons plain Greek yogurt

a little icing sugar, for dusting

You will also need a baking tray.

Makes 8 slices

Strawberry shortcake is made with layers of sweet scone sandwiched together with cream and strawberries. Fill the shortcake just before you eat it.

1 Heat the oven to 220°C, 425°F or gas mark 7. Grease the tray (page 10). Sift the flour and baking powder into a large bowl.

2 Cut the butter or margarine into chunks. Put them in the bowl. Rub them into the flour (see page 375). Carry on until the mixture looks like fine breadcrumbs.

3 Add the sugar and stir it in. Then, break the egg into a mug. Add the milk and vanilla, then beat with a fork to mix everything together.

4 Pour the egg mixture into the large bowl. Use a blunt knife to cut through the mixture again and again, until it clings together in a lump. Pat it into a ball.

5 Sprinkle a surface and a rolling pin with flour. Put the ball on the floury surface. Flatten it slightly with your hands.

6 Roll out the dough until it forms a circle around 20cm (8in) across. Lift it onto the baking tray and brush the top with a little milk.

7 Bake for 12-15 minutes, until risen and golden. Meanwhile, rinse and dry the strawberries. Remove the stalks. Cut the strawberries into thick slices.

8 Take the shortcake out of the oven and slide it onto a wire rack to cool. When it's cool, carefully cut it into 2 layers using a serrated knife.

9 Put the top layer on a chopping board. Cut it into 8 wedges. Then, whip the cream (see page 377), and mix in the yogurt.

10 Put the bottom layer on a plate. Spread on half the cream mixture. Put the strawberries on top. Spread on the rest of the cream.

You could decorate the top of the shortcake with half strawberries.

11 Lay the 8 wedges on the top. Sift over some icing sugar. When you eat it, use the 8 wedges as a guide to cut through the bottom layer, too.

Stripey cake

Ingredients:

15g (½oz) unsalted butter

4 tablespoons cocoa powder

1½ tablespoons soft light brown sugar

300ml (½ pint) plain natural yogurt

225g (8oz) softened butter or margarine

300g (11oz) caster sugar

6 medium eggs

350g (12oz) plain flour

1 teaspoon baking powder

½ teaspoon bicarbonate of soda

2 tablespoons vanilla essence

For the decorating:

25g (1oz) white chocolate

25g (1oz) plain chocolate

You will also need a fluted ring tin with a capacity of at least 2.5 litres (5 pints) and a piping gun or bag fitted with a tiny, round nozzle, plus a spare bag. To measure capacity, fill the tin with water, then measure it into a jug.

Makes around 20 slices

This recipe is for a moist, ring-shaped cake with wavy chocolate and vanilla stripes. The stripes are made by putting the cake mix into the tin in an unusual way.

1 Melt the unsalted butter in a small pan over a gentle heat. Brush it all over the inside of the tin. Measure out all the ingredients. Heat the oven to 180°C, 350°F or gas mark 4.

2 Sift the cocoa powder and soft light brown sugar into a bowl. Add 5 tablespoons of the yogurt and mix well.

3 Put the butter or margarine and caster sugar in a big bowl. Beat until fluffy. Break an egg into a cup. Tip it into the bowl. Add 1 teaspoon of the flour. Mix well.

4 Add the other eggs one at a time, in the same way. Then, sift in the rest of the flour with the baking powder and bicarbonate of soda.

5 Fold in gently. When the flour is half mixed in, add the rest of the yogurt and the vanilla. Fold again until mixed. Mix one third of the vanilla mixture into the cocoa mixture.

6 Drop 5 heaped teaspoons of the vanilla mixture into the tin, spaced evenly around the central post. Use the back of the spoon to spread them out, so they join up in a ring.

The rings won't reach to the edge...
...of the tin, but this is fine.

7 Drop 4 teaspoons of chocolate mixture on top, and spread them into a ring too. Try not to mix the chocolate into the vanilla.

Don't worry if the...
...layers look messy.

8 Keep on adding alternate layers of vanilla and chocolate mixture in the same way, until they are both used up.

9 Bake for 55-60 minutes, or until risen and firm. Test with a skewer to see if it's cooked (see page 373).

10 Put the tin on a wire rack for 15 minutes, then turn the cake out of the tin onto the wire rack. Leave to cool completely.

11 Melt the white chocolate (page 380). Spoon it into the piping gun or bag. Pipe a zigzag over the cake. Wash the gun or change the bag. Repeat with the plain chocolate.

Other shapes

You can make this recipe in a 20cm (8in) round, deep tin with a loose base. Grease and line the tin. Halve the quantities. At step 7, drop alternate tablespoonfuls of the mixtures into the middle of the tin, one on top of the other. Don't spread them out. Bake for 30-40 minutes.

Raspberry & almond cake

Ingredients:

4 medium eggs

165g (5½oz) caster sugar

225g (8oz) ground almonds

1 teaspoon baking powder
(gluten-free types are available)

For the filling:

150g (5oz) raspberry jam, either
smooth or with seeds

150g (5oz) fresh raspberries

For the icing:

200g (7oz) icing sugar

a handful of raspberries to
decorate

You will also need a 20cm (8in)
round, deep cake tin.

Makes 10 slices

This light, fluffy cake is filled with fresh raspberries and raspberry jam. The cake is made from ground almonds, so if you use gluten-free baking powder, you can make it wheat- and gluten-free.

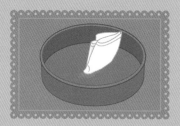

1 Heat the oven to 170°C, 325°F or gas mark 3. Grease and line the tin (page 10).

2 Separate the eggs (see page 11), so the whites are in one bowl and the yolks in another.

3 Add the sugar to the yolks, then use a fork to beat them together until they turn paler. Whisk the egg whites until they make stiff points (see page 11).

Move the spoon in the... ...shape of a number 8.

4 Add the whites to the yolk mixture. Using a metal spoon, gently fold them in. Add the almonds and baking powder. Fold them in.

5 Pour the mixture into the tin. Smooth the top with the back of a spoon. Bake for 35-40 minutes, until firm and golden brown.

Peel off the parchment.

6 Leave the cake in the tin for
20 minutes. Run a knife around
the sides of the tin. Turn the tin
upside down over a wire rack and
shake it so the cake pops out.

7 To cut the cake into 2 layers,
put your hand on top of
the cake to steady it. Cut
very carefully, using a
serrated knife.

8 For the filling, put the jam
in a small bowl. Mix in the
raspberries. Spread the filling
over the bottom half of the
cake. Put the top half back on.

9 Sift the icing sugar into a
bowl. Add 2 tablespoons of
water and stir it in. Spread
the icing over the cake.
Scatter raspberries on top.

Castle cake

Ingredients:

175g (6oz) soft margarine

175g (6oz) caster sugar

3 tablespoons milk

1 teaspoon of vanilla essence

200g (7oz) self-raising flour

3 medium eggs

For decorating:

225g (8oz) icing sugar

food dye

writing icing

small sweets

You will also need a 27 x 18cm (11 x 7in) rectangular cake tin.

Makes 8-10 slices

This spectacular castle-shaped cake is made from a simple sponge. This one is decorated in pink, but you could use other colours such as grey or black.

1 Heat the oven to 180°C, 350°F, gas mark 4. Put the cake tin on some baking parchment. Draw around it. Cut out the shape.

2 Use a paper towel to wipe some cooking oil on the bottom and sides of the tin. Put the parchment shape in the bottom of the tin.

3 Put the margarine and sugar in a large bowl. Mix the milk and vanilla together and pour them in. Then, sift the flour in, too.

4 Break the eggs into a mug and mix them with a fork. Add them to the mixture and stir until it is smooth and creamy.

5 Spoon the mixture into the tin and smooth the top. Bake for 30-35 minutes, until the middle is springy when you press it.

6 After five minutes, run a blunt knife around the cake. Turn it onto a wire rack. Peel off the parchment. Leave to cool.

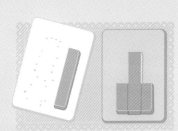

7 Put the cake on a board. Cut it into three strips and cut one strip in half. Move a long strip and the short strips onto another board.

8 Cut the last strip into three equal pieces. Then, cut the pieces into tall triangles, for roofs. Put them on top of the towers.

This cake's roofs were dusted with edible sparkly powder, to make them glitter.

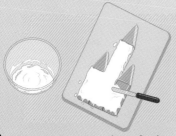

9 To decorate the cake, sift the icing sugar into a bowl. Stir in 3 tablespoons of water to make a smooth mixture. Spread some on the towers.

10 Add a few drops of food colouring to the remaining icing. Spread it over the turrets.

11 Use writing icing to draw doors and windows on the castle. Add lines and dots of writing icing, then press on sweets.

Butterfly cake

Ingredients:

300g (11oz) plain flour

2½ teaspoons baking powder

2½ teaspoons ground cinnamon

½ teaspoon ground mace (optional)

a pinch ground allspice (optional)

150g (5oz) soft dark brown sugar

175ml (6floz) sunflower
  or other vegetable oil

5 medium eggs

2 ripe, medium-sized bananas

1 tablespoon lemon juice

a 400g (14oz) can of crushed
  pineapple

For the frosting:

300g (11oz) full-fat cream cheese

125g (4½oz) icing sugar

For decorating:

coloured butterflies (see page 385)

You will also need a 20cm (8in)
round, deep cake tin.

Makes 12-14 slices

This cake is packed with pineapple and banana, making it really moist and juicy. It's topped with coloured butterflies. Find out how to make them on page 385.

1 Heat the oven to 180°C, 350°F or gas mark 4. Grease and line the tin (see page 10). Take the cream cheese out of the fridge.

2 Sift the flour, baking powder, cinnamon, mace and allspice into a big bowl. Add the sugar and stir it in.

3 Put the oil in a bowl. Break an egg into a cup, then tip it into the oil. Do the same with each of the other eggs. Beat with a fork.

4 Peel the bananas and put them on a plate. Mash them with a fork or potato masher. Stir in the lemon juice. Then add the banana mixture to the oil mixture.

5 Set aside 1½ tablespoons of pineapple from the can. Tip the rest of the contents of the can into the oil mixture. Mix, then pour this into the flour mixture. Mix well. Scrape it into the tin.

When the cake is cool, peel off the parchment.

6 Bake for 55-60 minutes, until risen and springy. Test with a skewer. Leave in the tin for 10 minutes. Turn it onto a wire rack. Leave until completely cold.

Don't beat too hard, or it will go watery.

7 For the frosting, put the cream cheese in a big bowl. Beat until smooth. Sift on the icing sugar. Add the pineapple you set aside. Mix gently.

8 Put the cake on a serving plate. Spread the frosting over the top and sides, making peaks and swirls as you spread it on.

9 Push half a butterfly a little way into the frosting, at an angle. Push the other half in next to it, so it looks as if the butterfly is opening its wings.

Rich chocolate cake

Ingredients:

150g (5oz) plain chocolate

75g (3oz) softened butter

4 medium eggs

100g (4oz) caster sugar

30g (1oz) self-raising flour

For the chocolate glaze:

175g (6oz) plain chocolate

150ml (¼ pint) double cream

1½ tablespoons golden syrup

225g (8oz) fresh berries

You will also need a 20cm (8in) round, deep cake tin and a heatproof bowl that fits snugly into a saucepan.

Makes 12 slices

This dark, moist cake is very rich, so serve it in thin slices. Drizzle it with chocolate glaze and scatter fresh berries on top.

1. Heat the oven to 180°C, 350°F or gas mark 4. Grease and line the tin (see page 10).

2. Fill the saucepan a quarter full of water. Heat gently until the water bubbles. Take the pan off the heat.

Wear oven gloves to lift the bowl in and out of the pan.

3. Break the chocolate into the heatproof bowl. Add the butter. Put the bowl in the pan. Stir the mixture until it melts, then take the bowl out of the pan.

4. Separate the eggs, following the instructions on page 11, so the whites are in one bowl and the yolks are in another.

5. Whisk the egg whites with a whisk until they are really thick and foamy (page 11). When you lift up the whisk, the whites should stand up in stiff points.

6. Add the yolks and sugar to the chocolate mixture. Stir them in. Sift on the flour and stir that in too. Then, add the whisked egg whites.

288

7 Fold in the egg whites gently, moving a metal spoon in the shape of a number 8. Pour the mixture into the tin. Bake for 20 minutes.

8 Take the tin out of the oven. Cover it with kitchen foil to stop the top from burning. Bake for 15-20 minutes more, until the cake is firm.

Peel off the parchment.

9 Leave the cake in the tin for 20 minutes. Run a knife around the sides of the tin. Turn it upside down over a wire rack. Shake it so the cake pops out.

10 For the chocolate glaze, break the chocolate into a small pan. Add the cream and syrup. Heat gently, stirring, until all the ingredients have melted.

11 Spoon the glaze over the cake so it drips down the sides (see page 378). Arrange the fresh berries on top.

Marshmallow & chocolate cake

Ingredients:

150g (5oz) self-raising flour

40g (1½oz) cocoa powder

2 teaspoons baking powder

200g (7oz) softened butter

200g (7oz) soft dark brown sugar

5 medium eggs

2 teaspoons vanilla essence

4 tablespoons milk

For the topping and filling:

240ml (8floz) double or whipping cream

1½ tablespoons icing sugar

1 teaspoon vanilla essence

around 350g (12oz) mini marshmallows

You will also need a 20cm (8in) round, deep cake tin.

Makes 12-16 slices

This delicious chocolate cake is filled and topped with whipped cream and lots of mini marshmallows.

1 Heat the oven to 180°C, 350°F or gas mark 4. Grease and line the tin (page 10). Sift the flour, cocoa and baking powder into a bowl.

2 Put the butter and the sugar in a big bowl. Beat until fluffy.

3 Break an egg into a cup. Tip it into the butter and sugar mixture. Add 1 tablespoon of the flour mixture. Beat well. Do this with each egg.

Move the spoon in the...

...shape of a number 8.

4 Mix in the vanilla and milk. Add the rest of the flour mixture. Fold in gently, using a big spatula or metal spoon.

5 Scrape the mixture into the tin. Level the top with the back of a spoon. Bake for 40-45 minutes. Test with a skewer to see if it's cooked.

When the cake is cold, peel off the parchment.

6 Leave it in the tin for 10 minutes. Remove the tin. Put the cake on a wire rack to cool.

These are multicoloured marshmallows, but you could use ordinary pink and white ones.

Other ideas

You could use ordinary marshmallows instead of mini ones.

Or, replace the whipped cream with chocolate buttercream (page 376) and the marshmallows with malted chocolate balls.

Don't beat too much, or it will go hard.

7 When the cake is cool, put it on a board. Carefully cut it into two layers with a sharp knife. Put the bottom layer on a serving plate.

8 For the topping, pour the cream into a big bowl. Add the icing sugar and vanilla. Whisk very quickly, until it stays in a floppy point when you lift up the whisk.

9 Spread half the cream over the bottom layer of cake. Scatter on some marshmallows. Put the top of the cake back on. Spread the rest of the cream all over the top and sides of the cake.

10 Starting at the bottom of the cake, arrange the mini marshmallows in rows around the sides, pressing them gently into the cream. Arrange more on the top.

White chocolate gateau

Ingredients:

100g (4oz) self-raising flour

40g (1½oz) cocoa powder

1½ teaspoons baking powder

150g (5oz) softened butter or
  margarine

150g (5oz) soft light brown sugar

1 teaspoon vanilla essence

3 tablespoons milk or water

3 large eggs

For the white chocolate mousse:

200g (7oz) white chocolate

300ml (½ pint) whipping cream

You will also need lots of white
chocolate-covered finger biscuits for
decorating, and a round, deep cake
tin, preferably 18cm (7in) across,
but a 20cm (8in) one will do.

Makes 8 slices

This impressive gateau is perfect for celebrations. It
is made with chocolate cake and decorated with white
chocolate mousse and white chocolate finger biscuits.

1 Heat the oven to 180°C, 350°F or gas mark 4. Grease and line
  the tin (see page 10).

Peel off the parchment
when the cake is cool.

2 To make the cake, follow
  steps 2-5 on page 206.
  Scrape the mixture into
  the tin. Level the top. Bake
  for 30-35 minutes until
  risen and springy. Leave in
  the tin for a few minutes.

3 Hold the tin upside down
  over a wire rack. Shake the
  tin, so the cake pops out.
  Leave it to cool.

4 To make the white
  chocolate mousse, follow
  steps 9-11 on page 301.

5 Use a knife to spread
  some white chocolate
  mousse onto the sides
  of cake.

6 Press the white chocolate
  fingers around the sides of
  the cake. Spoon the rest of
  the mousse on top of the
  cake. Put in the fridge for
  at least 1 hour.

You could decorate your gateau with fresh berries and chocolate curls – see page 380.

Other toppings

Sliced peaches or apricots make a good topping for your gateau, too. Or, instead of fruit, decorate the mousse with chocolate hearts and stars (page 384) or butterfly decorations (page 385).

Milk or plain chocolate

Instead of using white chocolate to make the mousse, you could replace it with milk or plain chocolate. Decorate the sides of the gateau with milk or plain chocolate finger biscuits.

Chocolate lime surprise cake

Ingredients:

2 limes

175g (6oz) softened butter or margarine

175g (6oz) caster sugar

3 medium eggs

2 tablespoons cocoa powder

1 teaspoon baking powder

200g (7oz) self-raising flour

5 tablespoons plain natural yogurt

1 pinch chilli flakes (optional)

For the ganache topping:

100g (4oz) plain chocolate

100g (4oz) milk chocolate

150ml (¼ pint) sour cream

You will also need a 20cm (8in) round, deep cake tin.

Makes 8-10 slices

The surprise ingredient in this moist chocolate and lime cake is a pinch of chilli. It adds just a subtle hint of heat, but you can leave it out if you prefer.

1 Heat the oven to 170°C, 325°F or gas mark 3. Grease and line the tin (see page 10).

2 Grate the zest from the outside of the limes, using the small holes of a grater. Cut the limes in half and squeeze out the juice.

3 Put the butter or margarine, sugar and zest in a big bowl. Beat until the mixture is light and fluffy.

4 Break the eggs into a small bowl. Mix with a fork. Put a spoonful in the big bowl. Beat it in well. Add the rest of the egg, a spoonful at a time, beating well each time.

5 Put the cocoa powder in a cup. Stir in 2 tablespoons of warm water to make a smooth paste. Put it in the big bowl and stir it in.

You could decorate your cake with lime zest.

6 Sift in the baking powder and about half the flour. Gently fold the ingredients together with a metal spoon. Then add the yogurt and fold it in.

Move the spoon in the...

...shape of a number 8.

7 Sift in the remaining flour. Add the lime juice and chilli flakes. Stir the ingredients together very gently.

8 Spoon the mixture into the tin. Smooth the top with the back of a spoon. Bake for 1 hour, until the cake is firm and springy.

These little curls of zest were made by scraping a tool called a zester across the surface of a lime.

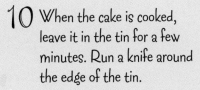

9 Make the ganache following the instructions on page 381.

10 When the cake is cooked, leave it in the tin for a few minutes. Run a knife around the edge of the tin.

11 Hold the tin upside down over a wire rack. Shake it, so the cake pops out. Leave it to cool. Peel off the parchment. Put the cake on a plate and spread on the ganache.

Lemon drizzle cake

Ingredients:

3 lemons

175g (6oz) softened butter
  or margarine

175g (6oz) caster sugar

3 medium eggs

1½ teaspoons baking powder
  (gluten-free types are available)

165g (5½oz) fine cornmeal
  (polenta)

3 tablespoons granulated sugar

You will also need a 20cm (8in)
round cake tin with a loose base.

Makes 8-10 slices

This tangy cake is drizzled with lemon syrup to make it moist and sticky. The recipe contains cornmeal (also called polenta) which gives the cake a lovely, crumbly texture.

You can also adapt this recipe to make a chocolate cake with chocolate icing – follow the instructions on the opposite page. Both cakes are wheat- and gluten-free, and you can make them dairy-free. Read the allergy advice on pages 388 and 392.

1 Heat the oven to 190°C, 375°F or gas mark 5. Line the tin with baking parchment (page 10).

2 Grate the zest from the outside of the lemons, using the small holes on a grater. Put the zest in a large bowl.

3 Cut the lemons in half and squeeze out all the juice. Put the juice in a jug for later.

4 Put the butter or margarine and the caster sugar in the bowl. Beat quickly until the mixture is pale and fluffy.

5 Break an egg into a small bowl. Beat it with a fork. Put it in the large bowl. Mix well. Do the same with the other eggs, too. Beat the mixture well each time.

6 Put the baking powder and cornmeal in the bowl. Add 1 tablespoon of the lemon juice. Mix everything together gently with a metal spoon.

7 Scrape the mixture into the tin and level the top with the back of the spoon. Bake for 40 minutes.

8 While the cake is cooking, put the granulated sugar in the jug with the rest of the lemon juice. Stir to make a grainy syrup.

9 Take the cake out of the oven. Test it with a finger (page 373) to find out if it is cooked.

10 Stir the syrup. Pour it over the cake. Leave the cake in the tin to cool. When it's cold, take it out (see page 373).

Chocolate cake

To make a chocolate cake using the same recipe, you will need 40g (1½oz) cocoa powder and 1 teaspoon of vanilla essence. Leave out the lemons and granulated sugar. Follow the method given on page 190, but using the quantities and tin given here.

This cake is drizzled with syrup, so it has a crunchy, sugary topping.

Chocolate icing

To ice your chocolate cake, you will need 150g (5oz) plain chocolate, 75g (3oz) butter or margarine or margarine and 75g (3oz) icing sugar. For the icing, follow steps 5-7 on page 191.

Light chocolate layer cake

Ingredients:

4 large eggs

125g (4½oz) caster sugar

60g (2½oz) ground almonds

1½ tablespoons cocoa powder

1¼ teaspoons baking powder

For the filling:

300ml (½ pint) double or whipping cream

3 tablespoons jam

To decorate:

around 150g (5oz) fresh fruit, such as raspberries, blueberries and strawberries.

1 tablespoon icing sugar

You will also need three 18cm (7in) round, shallow cake tins.

Makes 8-10 slices

Other ideas

Instead of three 18cm (7in) cake tins, you can use two 20cm (8in) round, shallow tins. Bake for 20-25 minutes. Divide the jam and cream between the two layers.

This light, chocolatey layer cake is filled with jam and cream and topped with fruit. You can easily make it wheat- and gluten-free or dairy-free – see page 392 for suggestions.

1 Heat the oven to 180°C, 350°F or gas mark 4. Grease and line the tins (see page 10).

2 Separate the eggs (see page 11), so the whites are in one bowl and the yolks are in another. Add the sugar to the yolks.

3 Mix the yolks and sugar with a fork. Stir in the ground almonds, cocoa powder and baking powder.

Move the spoon in the shape of a number 8.

4 Beat the egg whites with a whisk until they stand up in floppy points (see page 11).

5 Spoon the egg whites into the egg yolk mixture. Fold them in gently, using a metal spoon. Spoon the mixture into the tins

To decorate your layer cake with chocolate leaves, see page 380.

Instead of berries, you could use sliced peaches, cherries, kiwi fruit or pineapple.

Choose a flavour of jam that goes with the fruit you're using.

6 Bake for 15-20 minutes, until firm and springy. Leave in the tins for 10 minutes. Then, turn them onto a wire rack to cool. When the cakes are cold, whip the cream (page 377).

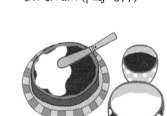

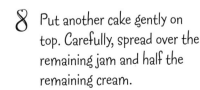

7 Peel off the parchment. Put a cake on a plate. Spread on half the jam and a third of the cream.

8 Put another cake gently on top. Carefully, spread over the remaining jam and half the remaining cream.

9 Put the final cake on top. Spread over the remaining cream. Arrange the fruit on top. Sift over the icing sugar.

White chocolate mousse cake

Ingredients:

125g (4½oz) caster sugar

125g (4½oz) softened butter or margarine

3 medium eggs

2 teaspoons milk

125g (4½oz) self-raising flour

1 teaspoon baking powder

For the chocolate-drizzled strawberries (optional):

150g (5oz) fresh strawberries

50g (2oz) white chocolate

For the white chocolate mousse:

150g (5oz) white chocolate

300ml (½ pint) whipping cream

For the filling (optional)

4 tablespoons strawberry jam

1 tablespoon lemon juice

You will also need two 20cm (8in) round, shallow cake tins and a piping gun or bag fitted with a tiny, round nozzle.

Makes around 12 slices

This soft sponge cake is topped and filled with white chocolate mousse. You can also add a strawberry jam filling and decorate the cake with strawberries, too.

1 Heat the oven to 180°C, 350°F or gas mark 4. Grease and line the tins – see page 10.

2 Put the sugar and butter or margarine in a big bowl. Crack an egg into a cup. Tip it into the bowl. Do the same with the other eggs.

3 Add the milk and mix well. Sift on the flour and baking powder and mix them in gently.

4 Divide the mixture between the tins. Level the tops with the back of a spoon. Bake for 20-25 minutes or until risen and firm.

When the cakes are cool, peel off the parchment.

5 Leave the cakes for a few minutes, then turn them onto a wire rack to cool.

6 To make the chocolate-drizzled strawberries, cover a plate with baking parchment. Arrange the strawberries on it, lying on their sides, so they aren't touching.

7 Melt the chocolate (see page 380). Spoon it into the piping gun or bag.

Instead of using fresh strawberries, you could double the amount of jam and marble it through the topping as well as the filling.

8 Pipe a zigzag line over each strawberry, following the instructions on page 379. Then, put the plate in the fridge.

9 To make the mousse, melt the chocolate (see page 380). Wearing oven gloves, lift the bowl out of the pan. Leave to cool.

10 Pour the cream into a bowl. Whisk it very quickly, until it stays in a floppy point when you lift up the whisk.

Don't beat too much, or the cream will go hard.

Move the spoon... ...in the shape of a number 8.

11 Put a large spoonful of the cream onto the melted chocolate. Fold it in gently, using a big metal spoon. Add the rest of the cream. Fold in gently.

12 To make the filling, mix the jam and lemon juice in a bowl. Spoon in half the mousse. Mix gently. Stop when it looks marbled.

13 Put one cake on a serving plate. Spoon on the filling. Put the other cake on top. Spoon on the remaining mousse. Top with the berries. Refrigerate for 1 hour.

Extremely chocolatey cake

Ingredients:

150g (5oz) self-raising flour
50g (2oz) cocoa powder
2 teaspoons baking powder
200g (7oz) softened butter
200g (7oz) soft brown sugar
1½ teaspoons vanilla essence
4 large eggs

For the ganache:

150g (5oz) plain chocolate
150ml (¼ pint) double cream

You will also need a 20cm (8in) round, deep cake tin and a heatproof bowl that fits snugly into a saucepan.

Makes about 12 slices

This dark, rich chocolate cake is covered with a thick, creamy topping, called ganache. The ganache and the cocoa powder in the sponge give the cake an intense chocolatey taste, so you only need a thin slice.

1 Heat the oven to 180°C, 350°F or gas mark 4. Put the tin onto a piece of baking parchment and draw around it with a pencil. Cut out the circle, just inside the line.

2 Use a paper towel to wipe a little cooking oil over the insides of the tin. Put the parchment into the tin. Sift the flour, cocoa and baking powder into a large bowl.

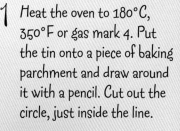

3 Put the butter and sugar in another bowl. Beat until light and fluffy. Add the vanilla and beat the mixture again.

4 Crack one egg into a cup. Add it to the butter mixture with one tablespoon of the flour mixture. Beat well. Then, repeat this step with each of the remaining eggs.

5 Add the rest of the flour mixture. Fold it in gently, moving the spoon in the shape of a number 8. Scrape the mixture into the tin.

Peel off the parchment...

6 Level the top with the back of a spoon. Bake for 40-45 minutes, then test the cake with a skewer to check it is cooked (page 373).

7 Leave the cake in the tin for 5 minutes, then turn the cake onto a wire rack to cool (see page 373).

8 For the ganache, break the chocolate into the heatproof bowl and add the cream. Fill the pan ¼ full with water. Heat the pan gently.

9 When the water bubbles, take the pan off the heat. Wearing oven gloves, put the bowl in the pan. Stir until the chocolate melts. Wearing oven gloves, take the bowl out of the pan.

You can decorate the finished cake with chocolate curls. Find out how to make them on page 380.

10 Leave the ganache to cool for 20 minutes, then put it in the fridge for 30 minutes, or until it's like soft butter. Spread the ganache over the top and sides of the cake.

Chocolate & nut cake

Ingredients:

1 large orange

225g (8oz) plain chocolate

350g (12oz) unsalted almonds, hazelnuts and walnuts, preferably ready-chopped

200g (7oz) caster sugar

25g (1oz) butter

5 large eggs

You will also need a 20cm (8in) round, deep tin with a loose base.

Makes 12 slices

This rich and delicious cake is made from chopped nuts and chocolate, held together with egg whites. Because it contains no flour it's free from wheat and gluten (see the allergy advice on page 388).

1. If you can't get ready-chopped nuts, put whole nuts in a plastic food bag and seal the end. Crush them into small pieces with a rolling pin.

2. Heat the oven to 180°C, 350°F or gas mark 4. Grease and line the tin (page 10). Grate the zest from the orange and squeeze out the juice.

3. Cut the chocolate into very small pieces. Put the chocolate, zest, nuts and sugar into a large bowl.

4. Heat the butter in a pan until it melts. Turn off the heat and add the orange juice. Add the butter mixture to the ingredients in the bowl. Stir everything together.

5. Separate the eggs (page 11). Put the whites into a large, clean bowl. Mix the yolks into the chocolate mixture.

6. Whisk the egg whites until they are really thick and foamy. When you lift up the whisk, they should stay in stiff points.

You could sift icing sugar over your cake using a paper doily as a stencil. See the box below to find out how to do this.

Move the spoon in the...

...shape of a number 8.

7 Add two large spoonfuls of egg white to the chocolate mixture. Use a metal spoon to fold them in gently. Add the rest of the whites and fold them in.

8 Spoon the mixture into the tin. Level the top with the back of a spoon. Bake for 1 hour.

9 Test the cake with a skewer to see if it's cooked (page 373). Leave the cake in the tin for 10 minutes, then turn it onto a wire rack to cool.

Peel off the parchment.

Doily stencil

To make a lacy pattern on top of your cake, you will need a paper doily, 4 cocktail sticks and a little icing sugar. Put the cake on a plate, flat side up. Put the doily over the cake. Push the cocktail sticks through some of the holes at the edge of the doily, a little way into the cake. Sift some icing sugar over the doily, until you have a thin layer. Carefully, take out the cocktail sticks and lift off the doily.

White chocolate cheesecake

Ingredients:

175g (6oz) digestive biscuits
  (gluten-free types are available)
75g (3oz) butter
200g (7oz) white chocolate
400g (14oz) full fat cream cheese
50g (2oz) caster sugar
2 medium eggs
2 teaspoons vanilla essence
10 strawberries, to decorate

For the raspberry sauce:
150g (5oz) raspberries
50g (2oz) icing sugar

You will also need a 20cm (8in)
round cake tin with a loose base
and a heatproof bowl that fits
snugly into a saucepan.

Makes 6-8 slices

This velvety baked cheesecake is made with white chocolate and decorated with sliced strawberries and lots of white chocolate curls. There's a recipe for tangy raspberry sauce to pour over it, too.

1 Leave the cream cheese at room temperature for half an hour. Then, heat the oven to 150°C, 300°F or gas mark 2. Grease the tin (see page 10).

2 Put the biscuits in a clean plastic food bag. Seal the end with an elastic band. Roll a rolling pin over it to crush the biscuits into crumbs.

3 Melt the butter in a saucepan over a low heat. Mix in the biscuit crumbs.

4 Spoon the mixture into the tin. Press it down with the back of a spoon. Put the tin in the fridge to chill.

5 Melt the chocolate, following the instructions on page 380.

6 Put the cream cheese and sugar in a big bowl and mix them together. Put the eggs and vanilla in a small bowl. Beat them with a fork.

7 Add the egg mixture to the cheese mixture a little at a time, beating well each time. Then, stir in the melted chocolate.

8 Pour the mixture into the tin. Level the top with the back of a spoon. Bake for 30 minutes. Turn off the oven and leave the cheesecake in for 30 minutes more.

9 Take the cheesecake out of the oven and leave it on a wire rack to cool. Then, put it in the fridge for at least 2 hours.

10 For the raspberry sauce, put the raspberries in a bowl and sift over the icing sugar. Mash everything together with a fork.

You could make white chocolate curls to top your cheesecake – see page 380.

11 Remove the side of the cake tin, following the instructions on page 373. Then, slide the cake off the base of the tin onto a plate.

12 Remove the green stalks from the strawberries. Cut the strawberries into thin slices, then press them around the edge of the cheesecake.

Breads & scones

Home-made bread

Ingredients:

450g (1lb) strong white
   bread flour

1 teaspoon salt

2 teaspoons easy-blend dried yeast

2 tablespoons olive oil

a little milk, for brushing (optional)

You will also need a baking tray.

Makes 1 loaf or 12 rolls

There's nothing like home-made bread, fresh from the oven. It's not difficult to make: you just need to leave some time for the dough to rise. This recipe shows you how to make one loaf or 12 rolls.

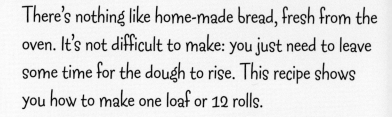

1 Sift the flour and salt into a big bowl. Stir in the yeast. Measure 300ml (½ pint) warm water into a jug. Add the oil. Pour into the bowl.

2 Stir until it comes together. Put the dough on a surface dusted with flour and knead it for 10 minutes (see page 374), or until it is smooth and springy.

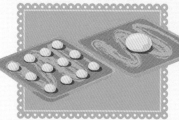

3 If you're in a hurry, skip to step 5. If you're not, put the dough in a bowl, cover with a tea towel and leave in a warm place to rise.

4 Leave for around 1½-2 hours, or until the dough has doubled in size. Put it on a floury surface. Knead it gently, to squash out any air bubbles.

5 Shape it into one big ball or 12 small balls. Grease the baking tray. Put the dough on it. Cover with a tea towel. Leave in a warm place.

6 Wait until the dough doubles in size. This may take 40 minutes to 2 hours. Then, heat the oven to 220°C, 425°F or gas mark 7.

You could decorate the top of your bread with seeds (see below), rolled oats or flour.

7 Brush with milk. If you're making one loaf, bake for 30 minutes. For rolls, bake for 12-15 minutes.

8 The bread is cooked when the crust is brown and it sounds hollow when you tap the bottom. When it's cooked, put it on a wire rack to cool.

Wholemeal bread

This recipe also works if you use strong wholemeal bread flour, or a mixture of half white and half wholemeal bread flour.

Seeded bread

For seeded bread, stir 50g (2oz) poppy seeds, sesame seeds or sunflower seeds into the flour at step 1. Sprinkle an extra tablespoon of seeds over the bread at step 5. Seeds may not be suitable for those with nut allergies.

Other bread ideas

Homemade bread tastes delicious eaten warm, spread with a little butter, jam or lemon curd. You could make your own lemon curd, following the recipe on pages 252-253. If your bread gets a little stale, you could eat it as toast.

Iced fruit loaf

Ingredients:

225g (8oz) strong plain flour

½ teaspoon ground mixed spice

½ teaspoon salt

25g (1oz) butter

1 tablespoon caster sugar

2 teaspoons easy-blend dried yeast

1 medium egg

5 tablespoons milk

100g (4oz) dried mixed fruit

a little milk for brushing

For the icing:

50g (2oz) icing sugar

1 tablespoon lemon juice

50g (2oz) glacé cherries

You will also need a loaf tin measuring around 20.5 x 12.5 x 8cm (8 x 5 x 3½in).

Makes around 12 slices

This sweet bread is packed with dried fruit. When it's cooled, you cover it in icing and then press on lots of chopped glacé cherries. Cut it into slices and eat them while the bread is still warm.

1 Heat the oven to 200°C, 400°F or gas mark 6. Grease and line the tin (see page 10).

2 Sift the flour, mixed spice and salt into a large bowl. Cut the butter into cubes and add them, too.

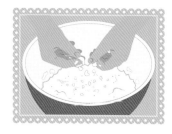

3 Rub in the butter (see page 375) until the mixture looks like small breadcrumbs. Add the egg mixture and the sugar and yeast. Stir until everything comes together.

4 Put the dough on a floured surface. Knead it (see page 374) for 5 minutes, then put it in a bowl.

5 Cover the bowl with plastic food wrap. Leave in a warm place for an hour, or until the dough has doubled in size.

Knead on a floured surface.

6 Turn the dough out of the bowl and sprinkle the dried fruit over it. Knead the fruit into the dough until it is mixed in.

7 Put the dough in the tin and cover the tin with plastic food wrap. Put it in a warm place for 45 minutes to rise.

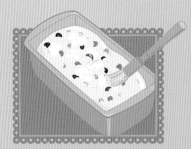

8 Heat the oven to 200°C, 400°F or gas mark 6. Brush the top of the dough with milk. Bake for 30-35 minutes.

Remove the baking parchment.

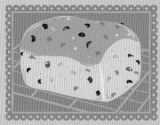

9 Push a skewer into the loaf. If it comes out clean, the loaf is cooked. Take the loaf out of the tin. Put it on a wire rack to cool.

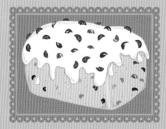

10 Sift the icing sugar into a bowl. Mix in the lemon juice. Spread the icing over the loaf. Cut up the cherries. Press them on top.

Cinnamon bread rolls

Ingredients:

450g (1lb) strong white
   bread flour

2 teaspoons caster sugar

1½ teaspoons salt

2 teaspoons cinnamon

1½ teaspoons easy-blend
   dried yeast

75g (3oz) raisins

275ml (9fl oz) milk

25g (1oz) butter

1 medium egg

You will also need a baking tray.

Makes 16 rolls

These tasty rolls are flavoured with cinnamon and raisins. The bread is not very sweet, so the rolls taste delicious spread with jam or chocolate spread and eaten while they are still warm.

The mixture should be lukewarm, not hot.

1 Sift the flour into a large bowl. Stir in the sugar, salt, cinnamon, yeast and raisins. Make a hollow in the middle.

2 Put the milk and butter into a pan and heat gently until the butter has just melted. Take the pan off the heat.

3 Pour the milk mixture into the hollow in the flour. Stir until it stops sticking to the sides of the bowl.

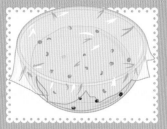

4 Sprinkle a surface with flour. Knead the dough (see page 374) until it is smooth and springy.

5 Dip a paper towel in cooking oil and rub it inside a bowl. Put the dough in the bowl and cover it with food wrap.

6 Leave the dough in a warm place for about 45 minutes, until it has doubled in size.

7 Knead the dough gently for a minute or two, to squeeze out any air bubbles. Then, cut the dough into 16 pieces.

8 Roll each piece of dough to make a sausage around 20cm (8in) long. Tie each one into a knot.

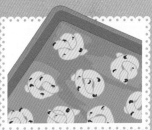

9 Grease the baking tray (page 10) and put the rolls onto it. Heat the oven to 220°C, 425°F or gas mark 7.

10 Rub some plastic food wrap with oil, then cover the rolls. Put them back in a warm place for 20 minutes to rise again.

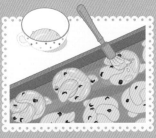

11 Beat the egg in a small bowl. Take the food wrap off the rolls. Brush each roll with some of the beaten egg.

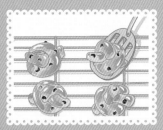

12 Bake for 10-12 minutes until golden-brown. Leave on the tray for 5 minutes, then put them on a wire rack to cool.

315

Contains nuts

Stollen

Ingredients:

1 lemon

50g (2oz) glacé cherries

50g (2oz) almonds

350g (12oz) strong white
   bread flour

1 teaspoon salt

1 teaspoon ground mixed spice

40g (1½oz) caster sugar

2 teaspoons easy-blend dried yeast

100g (4oz) mixture of currants,
   raisins and sultanas

25g (1oz) chopped mixed peel

50g (2oz) butter

200ml (7floz) milk

For the marzipan filling:

1 medium egg

65g (2½oz) caster sugar

65g (2½oz) ground almonds

Makes 8 slices

This fruit bread originated in Germany, where it is traditionally eaten cut into slices as a Christmas treat. Hidden inside the bread is a strip of delicious home-made marzipan.

1 Grate the zest from the outside of the lemon, using the small holes of a grater. Cut the cherries and almonds into small pieces. Put them in a large bowl and add the zest.

2 Put the flour, salt, mixed spice, sugar, yeast, dried fruit and peel into bowl, too. Mix everything together.

3 Put the butter and half the milk in a pan. Heat gently until the butter melts. Take the pan off the heat, then add the rest of the milk.

4 Pour the milk mixture into the bowl. Stir to make a dough.

5 To knead the dough, follow the instructions on page 374. Press the dough into an oblong shape, around 25 x 20cm (10 x 8in).

6 For the filling, break the egg into a bowl. Stir in the sugar and ground almonds. Spread it down the middle of the dough.

7 Fold the two shorter edges over the filling. Then fold over one long edge, then the other.

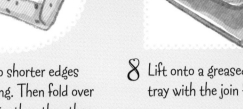

8 Lift onto a greased baking tray with the join facing down.

9 Cover with a clean tea towel. Leave in a warm place for 1-2 hours until it has doubled in size.

10 Heat the oven to 180°C, 350°F or gas mark 4. Remove the tea towel. Cover with baking parchment and bake for 35-40 minutes until lightly browned.

11 Leave on a wire rack to cool. Then, you could sift icing sugar over the top.

Kringle

Ingredients:

8 cardamom pods

2 lemons

350g (12oz) strong white bread flour

⅓ teaspoon salt

25g (1oz) caster sugar

2 teaspoons easy-blend dried yeast

50g (2oz) butter

150ml (¼ pint) milk

1 medium egg

For the cinnamon filling:

50g (2oz) softened butter

50g (2oz) caster sugar

2 teaspoons ground cinnamon

You will also need a baking tray.

Makes 12 slices

This festive Danish bread is flavoured with lemon and cardamom, and filled with cinnamon butter. If you like, you can drizzle the finished bread with icing and scatter on chopped fruit or nuts.

1 Snip open the cardamom pods. Crush the seeds with a rolling pin. Grate the zest from the lemons. Mix the seeds, zest, flour, salt, sugar and yeast in a large bowl.

2 Heat the butter and half the milk in a pan until the butter has melted. Turn off the heat.

3 Beat the egg with the rest of the milk in a jug. Put 1 tablespoonful in a cup for later.

4 Add the egg mixture and the butter mixture to the flour. Stir to make a dough.

5 To knead the dough, press the heels of both hands into it. Push it away from you firmly. Fold it in half and turn it around.

6 Carry on pushing the dough away from you, folding it and turning it around for 10 minutes, until it feels smooth and springy.

If you'd like to top your kringle with glacé icing, you'll find a recipe on page 377.

This kringle was scattered with chopped glacé cherries and pistachios.

It doesn't matter if the edges are wavy.

7 Roll the dough into a sausage about 40cm (16in) long. Flatten it with a rolling pin, so it is about 15cm (6in) wide.

8 For the filling, beat the butter, sugar and cinnamon in a bowl. Spread over the dough, leaving a 2cm (¾in) border around the edge.

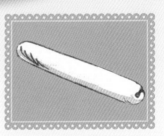

9 Brush water along one long edge. Roll up the dough from the other long edge. Press firmly along the join.

10 Put it onto the baking tray with the join facing down. Shape into a large knot, tucking both ends under. Cover with a clean tea towel.

11 Leave in a warm place for 1-2 hours until it has risen to twice its original size. Heat the oven to 200°C, 400°F or gas mark 6.

12 Take off the towel. Brush the dough with the egg mixture you set aside. Bake for 25-30 minutes until golden. Put onto a wire rack to cool.

Cinnamon buns

These sweet, sticky buns are made using a sweet, rich type of bread dough. To make the buns, the dough is spread with butter and cinnamon sugar, then rolled up into a spiral and cut into pieces.

1   Line the tin with baking parchment (see page 10).

2   Put the flour in a large bowl. Stir in the yeast, caster sugar and salt.

3   Put the milk and 25g (1oz) of the butter in a pan. Put the pan over a low heat, until the butter melts. Turn off the heat.

4   Break the egg into a cup and beat it with a fork. Add the egg and the milk mixture to the flour mixture and stir until it comes together in a ball.

5   Put the dough on a clean surface dusted with flour. Knead it for 10 minutes (see page 374), until it is smooth and springy.

6   If you're in a hurry, skip to step 8. If you're not, put the dough in a clean bowl. Cover it with a clean tea towel and leave it in a warm place to rise.

7   After around 1½-2 hours, the dough should have doubled in size. Put it back on the floury surface. Knead it gently to squeeze out any air bubbles.

8 Put the remaining 25g (1oz) butter in a pan. Heat gently. When the butter melts, take the pan off the heat. Stir in the brown sugar and cinnamon.

9 Roll the dough into a rectangle around 20 x 40cm (8 x 15in). Spread the butter mixture over it, leaving the edges bare. Roll it up from one of the long ends.

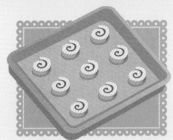

10 Cut across the roll to make 9 pieces. Arrange them in the tin in 3 rows of 3, then cover with a tea towel and leave in a warm place to rise.

11 Wait until the buns have doubled in size. If you followed steps 6-7, it will take around 40 minutes; if not, it will take 1½-2 hours.

12 Heat the oven to 220°C, 425°F or gas mark 7. Take off the tea towel. Bake for 20-25 minutes or until the buns are golden-brown.

13 Leave the buns to cool for 15 minutes. Then, turn the tin upside down over a wire rack and shake so the buns pop out. Turn them over, then brush them with the honey.

You could drizzle some glacé icing over the buns for extra stickiness. See the recipe on page 377.

Tiny pizzas

Ingredients:

For the tomato sauce:

2 cloves of garlic

1 tablespoon olive oil

a 400g (14oz) can chopped tomatoes

2 tablespoons tomato purée

1 pinch caster sugar

½ teaspoon dried oregano

For the pizza bases:

225g (8oz) self-raising flour

½ teaspoon baking powder

150ml (¼ pint) milk

1 tablespoon olive oil

For the toppings:

75g (3oz) cheese such as Cheddar or mozzarella (optional)

toppings such as the ones on the page opposite

You will also need a large baking tray and an 8cm (3in) round cutter.

Makes 10-12

These tiny pizzas have bases shaped from a quick dough made without any yeast. They make a great party snack, or a light lunch or supper.

1 To make the tomato sauce, crush the garlic into a saucepan. Add the oil, tomatoes, tomato purée, sugar, oregano, a pinch of salt and some pepper.

2 Put the pan over a medium heat and cook for 15 minutes, stirring often, until it is really thick. Leave to cool.

3 Heat the oven to 200°C, 400°F or gas mark 6. For the pizza bases, sift the flour and baking powder into a big bowl. Add the milk and olive oil. Mix. Pat the dough into a ball.

4 Sprinkle some flour on a work surface and a rolling pin. Put the dough on the surface and roll it out until it's just thinner than your little finger.

5 Use a paper towel to wipe a teaspoon of cooking oil over the baking tray. Use the cutter to cut lots of circles from the dough. Put them on the tray.

6 Squeeze the scraps of dough together, roll them out again and cut more circles. Keep doing this until the dough is used up.

7 Spread a little tomato sauce over each circle (you will only need about half – save the rest for another day). Then grate or slice the cheese and arrange it over the sauce.

8 Add any other toppings. Bake for 10 minutes, or until the bases are risen and golden and the cheese is bubbling. Then, scatter over any fresh herbs or rocket.

Topping ideas

You could use any combination of these topping ingredients on your pizzas – or add your own favourite ingredients.

- sliced tomatoes
- black olives
- ham
- thinly sliced onion
- sliced red or yellow peppers
- feta or other types of cheese
- fresh basil or other herbs
- pepperoni
- fresh rocket leaves
- sliced mushrooms

Sliced red and yellow peppers with rocket

Mozzarella cheese, sliced tomato and fresh basil leaves

Italian ham (prosciutto) and sliced mushrooms

Feta cheese goes well with red onion and fresh thyme.

This pizza is topped with pepperoni and black olives.

323

Deep-pan pizza

Ingredients:

225g (8oz) strong white
  bread flour

½ teaspoon salt

1 teaspoon easy-blend dried yeast

1 tablespoon olive oil

For the tomato sauce:

2 cloves of garlic

1 tablespoon olive oil

a 400g (14oz) can chopped
  tomatoes

2 tablespoons tomato purée

1 pinch caster sugar

½ teaspoon dried oregano

For the topping:

150g (5oz) ready-grated
  mozzarella cheese

50g (2oz) sliced pepperoni or
  ham cut into small pieces

12 stoned black olives

You will also need a baking tray.

Makes 6 slices

This deep-pan style pizza has a light bread base, topped with a tasty tomato sauce and grated mozzarella. It takes a little while to make the base, but it's delicious. You can put any toppings on your pizza – the ones used here are only suggestions.

1 To make the base, follow steps 1-3 on page 310, but use just 150ml (¼ pint) of water. Put it in a warm place, then make the tomato sauce following steps 1-2 on page 322.

2 When the dough has doubled in size, put it on a floury surface. Knead it gently for about a minute, to squeeze out any air bubbles.

3 Put the dough back into the bowl and leave it in a warm place to rise again for about 40 minutes. Then, heat the oven to 200°C, 400°F or gas mark 6.

4 Using a paper towel, wipe a little oil over the baking tray. Then, sprinkle flour on a surface and a rolling pin. Put the dough on the surface.

You could put other toppings on your pizza - see page 323 for some suggestions.

Spread out the sauce with the back of a spoon.

5 Roll out the dough until it is around 30cm (12in) across. Put it on the baking tray. Spread on the tomato sauce, leaving a gap around the edge.

6 Sprinkle on two-thirds of the cheese. Arrange the pepperoni and olives on top, then sprinkle on the rest of the cheese.

7 Bake for 20 minutes, or until the base is crisp and the cheese is golden-brown and bubbling. Then, cut it into slices with a sharp knife.

Fruit scones

Ingredients:

250g (9oz) plain flour

1 teaspoon bicarbonate of soda

40g (1½oz) butter

200ml (7floz) plain natural yogurt
  or buttermilk

100g (4oz) sultanas

a little milk, for brushing

strawberry jam

whipped or clotted cream

You will also need a baking tray and
a 6-7cm (2½-3in) round cutter.

Makes around 9

These scones are made using yogurt or buttermilk, which gives them a beautifully light texture. You can leave out the sultanas if you prefer plain scones.

1 Heat the oven to 200°C, 400°F or gas mark 6. Grease the baking tray (page 10).

2 Sift the flour and bicarbonate of soda into a big bowl. Cut the butter into chunks and put them in the bowl. Stir, to coat the chunks of butter with flour.

3 Use the tips of your fingers and thumbs to rub the butter into the flour (page 375). Stop when the mixture looks like fine breadcrumbs. Stir in the sultanas.

 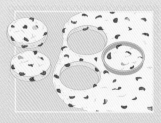 

4 Pour the yogurt or buttermilk into the bowl. Use a blunt knife to cut through the ingredients again and again. Stop when everything clings together in a lump.

5 Dust a clean surface and a rolling pin with flour. Roll out the dough until it is twice as thick as your little finger. Cut out lots of circles.

6 Squeeze the scraps of dough into a ball. Roll them out again. Cut out more circles. Put all the circles on the tray, spacing them out well. Brush the tops with a little milk.

7 Bake for 10 minutes, until golden-brown on top. Lift them onto a wire rack to cool. Then, cut the scones in half and spread them with jam and cream.

Little cheese scones

Ingredients:

40g (1½oz) Cheddar cheese
175g (6oz) self-raising flour
½ teaspoon baking powder
a pinch of salt
25g (1oz) butter
100ml (4floz) milk
a little milk, for glazing

You will also need a baking tray and
some small shaped cutters.

Make around 16

This recipe is for small scones flavoured with Cheddar cheese. They would make a tasty snack to eat at a party or a picnic.

Use the big holes.

1 Heat the oven to 220°C, 425°F or gas mark 7. Grate the cheese. Sift the flour, baking powder and salt into a large bowl.

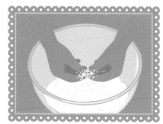

2 Cut the butter into chunks. Put them in the bowl. Rub the butter into the flour (see page 375) until the mixture looks like fine breadcrumbs.

3 Mix in the grated cheese with your hands, then pour in the milk. Use a blunt knife to mix everything together well.

4 Gently press the mixture together with your hands to make a ball of dough. Then, sprinkle flour onto a clean work surface and a rolling pin.

5 Roll out the dough until it is around 1cm (½in) thick. Then, use the cutters to cut out lots of shapes.

6 Squeeze the leftover scraps of dough into a ball and roll them out again. Cut out more shapes, until all the dough is used up.

7 Put the shapes on the baking tray, leaving spaces between them. Brush the tops with a little milk.

8 Bake for 7-8 minutes, until risen and golden. Put them on a wire rack to cool.

Some of these scones had a little plain flour or grated cheese sprinkled onto them, before they were baked.

Eat your scones as they are or cut them in half and spread them with a little butter.

Pastries & tarts

Pear & cranberry pies

These little pies are made using bought shortcrust pastry, but you could make your own following the recipe on pages 340-341 if you prefer.

1. Take the pastry out of the fridge and leave it for 20 minutes. Then, grease the holes of the tin with butter (see page 10).

You don't need the other half of the orange.

2. Grate half the rind from the orange using the small holes on a grater. Cut the orange in half and squeeze the juice from one half.

3. Put the rind and 1 tablespoon of the orange juice in a pan. Add the butter, brown sugar, cranberries and cinnamon.

Just cut tinned pears into small pieces.

Keep stirring all the time.

4. Carefully peel the pears with a vegetable peeler. Cut them into quarters and cut out the cores. Cut the quarters into small pieces.

5. Put the pear pieces in the pan. Cook over a low heat for 10 minutes. Take it off the heat and let it cool. Turn the oven to 190°C, 375°F or gas mark 5.

6. Dust a clean work surface and a rolling pin with flour and roll out the pastry (see page 375) until it is slightly thinner than your little finger.

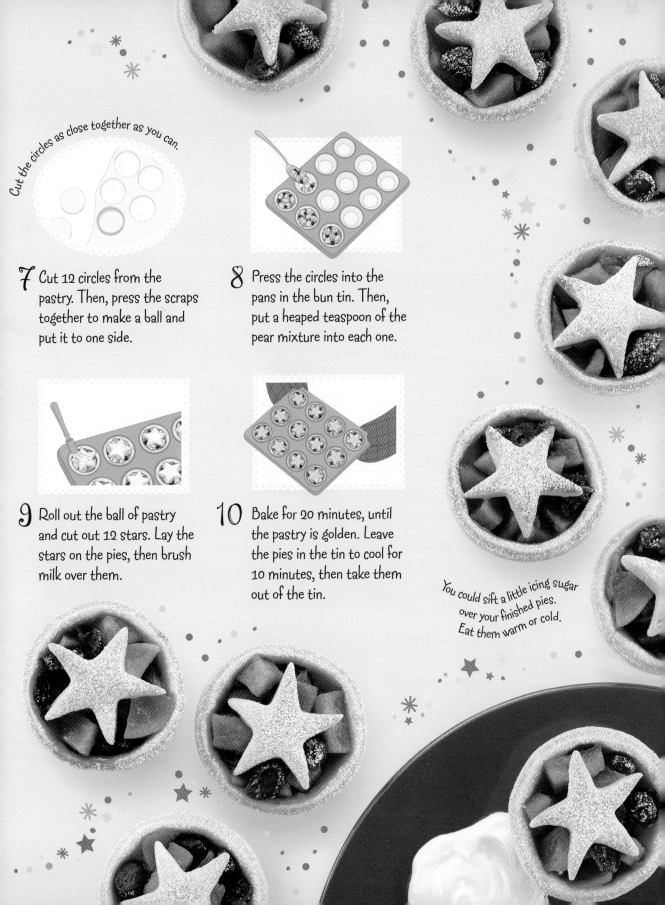

Cut the circles as close together as you can.

7 Cut 12 circles from the pastry. Then, press the scraps together to make a ball and put it to one side.

8 Press the circles into the pans in the bun tin. Then, put a heaped teaspoon of the pear mixture into each one.

9 Roll out the ball of pastry and cut out 12 stars. Lay the stars on the pies, then brush milk over them.

10 Bake for 20 minutes, until the pastry is golden. Leave the pies in the tin to cool for 10 minutes, then take them out of the tin.

You could sift a little icing sugar over your finished pies. Eat them warm or cold.

Cheese twists

Ingredients:

50g (2oz) hard cheese such as Cheddar or Parmesan

100g (4oz) plain flour

50g (2oz) butter

1 medium egg

2 teaspoons poppy seeds (optional – seeds may not be suitable for those with nut allergies)

You will also need a baking tray.

Makes 12-15

These cheesy pastry twists are crisp and delicious eaten while they're still warm from the oven.

1 Line the tray with baking parchment, following the instructions on page 10.

2 Grate the cheese on the medium holes of a grater. Sift the flour into a large bowl. Cut the butter into chunks and stir them into the flour.

3 Rub the butter into the flour, following the instructions on page 375. Stop when the mixture looks like small breadcrumbs.

4 Stir in half the grated cheese. Break the egg into a cup and beat it with a fork. Put two teaspoonfuls of the egg in a cup for later.

5 Stir the rest of the egg into the flour mixture. Squeeze the mixture with your hands until it clings together in a lump.

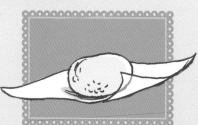

6 Pat it into a flattened ball, wrap it in plastic food wrap and put it in the fridge for 30 minutes. Meanwhile, heat the oven to 190°C, 375°F or gas mark 5.

7 Sprinkle some flour on a work surface and a rolling pin. Unwrap the dough. Roll the pin over the dough once, then turn the dough a quarter of the way around on the work surface.

8 Roll and turn again and again, until the dough is around 20cm (8in) square. Cut off the wavy edges, then cut it into about 12 strips.

9 Squeeze the scraps together, roll them out and make more strips. Brush all the strips with the egg you set aside earlier.

10 Scatter the rest of the cheese over the strips, followed by the poppy seeds. Roll the rolling pin over the strips once, lightly.

11 Hold a strip and twist the ends, like this. Put it on the baking sheet and press the ends down. Do the same with the other strips.

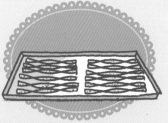

12 Bake for 12 minutes, or until the strips are golden-brown. Leave them on the baking sheet for 5 minutes, then move them to a wire rack to cool.

Feta cheese pies

Ingredients:

1 packet of filo pastry weighing
  around 275g (10oz)

50g (2oz) butter

1 medium egg

250g (9oz) ricotta cheese

200g (7oz) feta cheese

6 sprigs of fresh dill

1 pinch of ground nutmeg
  (optional)

You will also need 2 baking trays.

Makes around 20

Feta is a white, crumbly cheese that's popular in Greece and Turkey. There, people make delicious pies from feta, eggs and herbs wrapped in a thin, crispy pastry known as filo. This recipe shows you how to make a simple version.

1 Take the filo pastry out of the fridge. Leave it in its packet for 20 minutes, to come to room temperature.

2 Put the butter in a small pan. Heat the pan gently, until the butter melts. Break the egg into a bowl, beat it with a fork, add the ricotta cheese and mix.

These pies can be eaten warm or cold.

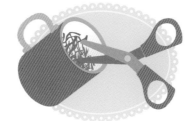

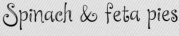

3 Take the feta cheese out of its packet and rinse it under a cold tap. Pat it dry with kitchen paper, then crumble it into the bowl with the eggs and ricotta.

4 Break the hard stalks off the dill. Put the leaves in a mug and snip them into small pieces. Put the chopped dill in the bowl, add the nutmeg and mix everything together.

Spinach & feta pies

For spinach and feta pies, you will also need 75g (3oz) frozen spinach. Defrost the spinach. Then, put it in a sieve over a bowl and push down on it with the back of a spoon to squeeze out the water. Follow steps 1-2. At step 3, use just 175g (6oz) of feta. At step 4 add the spinach along with the dill.

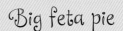

5 Heat the oven to 190°C, 375°F or gas mark 5. Unwrap and unroll the pastry. Cut it into strips around 10cm (4in) wide and 25cm (10in) long. Cover the strips with a damp tea towel.

6 Brush some melted butter over the baking trays. Take a strip of pastry. Put a heaped teaspoonful of the filling at the top right-hand corner.

Big feta pie

For one large pie, follow steps 1-4, then heat the oven to 190°C, 375°F or gas mark 5. Brush the inside of an ovenproof dish with butter. Line it with 1 sheet of filo and brush it with butter. Add 5 more sheets, brushing each one with butter. Spread on half the cheese mixture. Add 6 filo sheets, brushing each with butter. Add the rest of the cheese. Top with the rest of the filo, brushing each sheet with butter. Bake for 20-30 minutes until golden. Cut into slices.

7 Fold the corner down to make a triangle. Keep folding the triangle down the length of the strip, to make a parcel. Put it on a tray. Make more.

8 Brush the parcels with melted butter. Bake for 20 minutes, or until golden and crisp. Leave on the trays for a few minutes, then put them on a wire rack to cool.

Plum puff tarts

Ingredients:

375g (13oz) packet of ready-rolled puff pastry

300g (12oz) red plums

1 thick slice of white bread, preferably stale

50g (2oz) butter

50g (2oz) soft light brown sugar

½ teaspoon ground mixed spice

4 tablespoons apricot jam

You will also need 2 baking trays and a 6½cm (2½in) round cutter.

Makes 14

These golden tarts are made from ready-rolled puff pastry. They are topped with juicy plums, tossed together with sugar, crunchy breadcrumbs and a gentle hint of warming spices.

1 Take the pastry out of the fridge and leave it out for 15-20 minutes. Then, heat the oven to 220°C, 425°F or gas mark 7. Cut the plums in half with a sharp knife.

2 Remove the stones from the plums. Put the plum halves on a chopping board, cut side down. Cut each one into small chunks. Put the chunks in a big bowl.

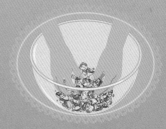

3 Use your fingers to tear and crumble the bread into small crumbs. Put the butter in a frying pan. Heat gently until the butter has just melted. Pour half into a small bowl.

4 Turn up the heat a little. Put the breadcrumbs in the frying pan. Fry them for around 5 minutes, stirring them often, until they are brown and crisp.

5 Remove the pan from the heat and leave it to cool. Then, add the breadcrumbs to the plums, with the sugar and spice. Use your hands to toss everything together.

6 Unroll the pastry. Use the cutter to cut out 14 circles. Put the circles on the baking trays, leaving spaces between them. Prick the middle of each circle twice with a fork.

7 Brush some butter from the bowl around the edge of each circle, to make a border around 1cm (½in) wide. Spoon half a teaspoon of jam into the middle of each circle.

8 Spoon the plum mixture onto the jam. Bake for 12-15 minutes, until golden and risen. Lift them onto a wire rack to cool.

Chocolate tarts

Ingredients:

175g (6oz) plain flour

75g (3oz) butter

For the ganache:

200g (7oz) plain chocolate

100ml (3½floz) double cream

You will also need a 12-hole shallow bun tin and a round or wavy cutter around 7cm (2½in) wide.

Makes 12

These little pastry tarts are filled with a combination of chocolate and cream, known as ganache. You could use plain, milk or white chocolate ganache (see page 381).

1 Sift the flour into a big bowl. Cut the butter into chunks and stir them into the flour.

2 Rub the butter and flour together, following the instructions on page 375. Carry on rubbing until the lumps are the size of small breadcrumbs.

If the mixture feels too dry, add another teaspoon of water.

3 Add 2 tablespoons of cold water. Stir it in using a blunt knife, cutting through the mixture, until everything starts to stick together.

4 Pat the pastry into a ball and press gently to flatten it. Cover it with plastic food wrap and put it in the fridge for 20 minutes. This will make it easier to roll out.

5 Heat the oven to 180°C, 350°F or gas mark 4. Make the ganache, following the instructions on page 381. Then, grease the holes of the bun tin – see page 10.

6 Sprinkle some flour on a clean work surface and a rolling pin. Unwrap the pastry and put it on the floury surface.

7 Roll out the pastry until it is about 30cm (12in) across. Use the cutter to cut out lots of pastry circles.

8 Put one pastry circle over each hole in the bun tin. Push the circles gently into the holes.

9 Roll the scraps into a ball. Roll it out again and cut more circles, until you have filled the tin. Use a fork to prick each pastry circle several times.

10 Bake for 10-12 minutes until golden brown. Take out of the oven and leave in the tin to cool.

11 Spoon ganache into each pastry case. Put the tarts in the fridge for 30 minutes, to set.

341

Mini raspberry swirls

Ingredients:

225g (8oz) ready-made puff pastry cut from a block

a little icing sugar

3 tablespoons smooth raspberry jam – or any other flavour of jam

1 tablespoon caster sugar

You will also need 2 baking trays.

Makes around 40

These crispy little treats are made using bought puff pastry and raspberry jam.

1 Take the pastry out of the fridge and leave it for 20 minutes. Then, line the baking trays, following the instructions on page 10.

2 Dust some icing sugar over a clean work surface and a rolling pin. Roll out the pastry to a square as wide as the rolling pin.

3 Use a sharp knife to trim the edges so that they are straight. Then, cut the pastry down the middle to make two rectangles.

Use a blunt knife.

4 Spread half of the jam on one piece, leaving a thin border around the edges. Then, spread the remaining jam on the other piece.

5 Brush water along one edge of one piece. Then, roll the pastry up tightly from the opposite edge. Do the same with the other piece.

6 Wrap the rolls in plastic food wrap and put them in the fridge to chill for 30 minutes. Meanwhile, heat the oven to 200°C, 400°F or gas mark 6.

7 Unwrap the rolls of pastry and put them on a chopping board. Cut the rolls into slices about as wide as your finger, using a sharp knife.

8 Put the swirls on the baking trays, leaving spaces in between them. Sprinkle half the caster sugar over them.

9 Bake for 10-12 minutes, until the pastry is golden. Then, sprinkle the rest of the caster sugar over the swirls.

10 Leave them on the trays for for 5 minutes, then move onto a wire rack to cool.

You could use any flavour of jam in these swirls — or use chocolate spread instead.

343

Choux buns

Ingredients:

65g (2½oz) plain flour

2 medium eggs

50g (2oz) butter

For the vanilla cream:

200ml (7fl oz) double or
    whipping cream

½ teaspoon vanilla essence

1 tablespoon icing sugar

For the chocolate topping:

100g (4oz) plain chocolate

25g (1oz) butter

You will also need 2 baking trays
and a heatproof bowl that fits
snugly in a saucepan.

Makes around 15

These light and airy buns are made from a type of puffy pastry called choux. They are filled with vanilla cream and have a lovely smooth chocolate topping.

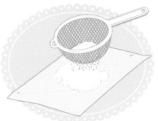

1 Heat the oven to 220°C, 425°F or gas mark 7. Grease the baking trays with butter (page 10). Hold each tray under a cold tap, then shake off the excess water.

2 Sift the flour onto a piece of baking parchment and put it to one side. Then, break the eggs into a small bowl and beat them with a fork.

3 Cut the butter into small pieces and put it in a pan. Add 150ml (¼ pint) cold water. Heat the pan very gently. As soon as the mixture boils, take it off the heat.

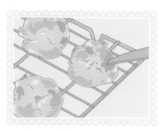

4 Straight away, tip all the flour into the pan. Stir it in for about a minute, until the mixture begins to form a ball in the middle of the pan. Let it cool for 5 minutes.

5 Add a little egg. Stir it in well, then repeat this until you've added all the egg. Then, put teaspoonfuls of pastry onto the baking trays, leaving spaces between them.

6 Bake for 10 minutes, then turn down the heat to 190°C, 375°F or gas mark 5. Bake the buns for 25 minutes more, until puffy and dark golden.

7 Put the buns onto a wire rack to cool. Then, make a hole in the side of each one with a sharp knife to let out any steam.

8 While the buns are cooling, make the vanilla cream following the instructions on page 377. When the buns are cold, cut each one in half.

9 Fill the buns with vanilla cream. For the chocolate topping, fill a pan ¼ full of water. Heat until the water bubbles, then take the pan off the heat.

Wear oven gloves.

10 Break up the chocolate. Put it in the heatproof bowl. Add the butter and 2 tablespoons of water. Put the bowl into the pan. Stir until smooth.

11 Wearing oven gloves, lift the bowl out of the pan. Spoon some chocolate topping onto each bun.

Crispy apple pies

Ingredients:

100g (4oz) filo pastry

1 medium orange

4 eating apples

50g (2oz) dried cranberries

50g (2oz) caster sugar

½ teaspoon cinnamon

50g (2oz) butter

2 teaspoons icing sugar

You will also need a 12-hole deep muffin tin.

Makes 12

These little crispy pies are made using bought filo pastry to bake little, crispy cases. They're filled with apples and cranberries and flavoured with a hint of orange and cinnamon.

1 Heat the oven to 190°C, 375°F or gas mark 5. Take the filo pastry out of the fridge, but leave it in its wrapping. Grate the zest from the outside of the orange.

Use the small holes.

2 Cut the orange in half and squeeze out the juice. Cut the apple into quarters. Peel them, then cut out the cores. Cut the quarters into small chunks.

Put a lid on the pan when you're not stirring.

3 Put the apple, zest and 3 tablespoons of the orange juice in a pan. Heat gently for 20 minutes, stirring often. Stir in the cranberries, sugar and cinnamon.

4 Cook for 5 minutes more. Take the pan off the heat. Unwrap the pastry and cut each sheet into six squares. Cover them with plastic food wrap.

5 Put the butter into a small saucepan. Heat gently until the butter melts. Use a pastry brush to brush a little butter over one of the pastry squares.

Press the pastry gently into the hole.

6 Put the square into a hole in the tin, buttered side up. Brush butter onto another square. Put it over the first one, so the corners overlap. Butter and add a third square.

7 Repeat in all the holes. Bake for 10 minutes. Leave them in the tin for 5 minutes to cool. Then, carefully take the cases out of the tin.

8 Heat the apple mixture again until it bubbles. Then, spoon the mixture into the cases. Sift a little icing sugar over the pies.

Raspberry profiteroles

Ingredients:

2 medium eggs

65g (2½oz) plain flour

50g (2oz) butter

150ml (¼ pint) water

For the raspberry cream:

125g (5oz) fresh raspberries

1 tablespoon caster sugar

150ml (¼ pint) double or
    whipping cream

For the chocolate sauce:

100g (4oz) plain chocolate

2 tablespoons golden syrup

15g (½oz) butter, preferably
    unsalted

You will also need 2 baking trays.

Makes around 15

Profiteroles are filled choux pastry buns, often eaten with chocolate sauce. These buns are stuffed with raspberry cream. Eat them while the sauce is warm.

1 Heat the oven to 200°C, 400°F or gas mark 6. Grease the baking trays with butter (see page 10). Hold them under a cold tap, then shake off the excess water.

2 Sift the flour onto a piece of greaseproof paper. Break the eggs into a small bowl and beat them with a fork.

3 Cut the butter into small pieces. Put them in a pan with 150ml (¼ pint) water. Heat the pan over a low heat. As soon as the mixture boils, take it off the heat.

4 Straight away, tip all the flour into the pan. Stir for about a minute, until the mixture begins to form a ball in the middle of the pan. Let it cool for 5 minutes.

5 Add a little egg. Stir it in well, then repeat this until you've added all the egg. Then, put teaspoonfuls of pastry onto the baking trays, leaving spaces in between them.

6 Bake for 10 minutes, then turn up the heat to 220°C, 425°F or gas mark 7. Bake for another 15-20 minutes, until they are puffy and dark golden.

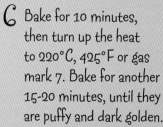

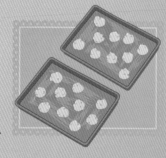

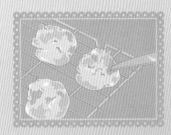

7 Move the buns to a wire rack. Then, make a hole in the side of each one with a sharp knife, to let out any steam.

8 Rinse the raspberries and pat them dry with a paper towel. Put them in a bowl with the sugar. Mash with a fork until they are smooth.

9 Whip the cream, following the instructions on page 377. Add the mashed raspberries and mix them in very gently.

10 When the buns are cold, cut a hole in the side of each one. Fill the hollow inside with raspberry cream. Put the buns in a bowl in the fridge.

11 For the sauce, break up the chocolate. Put it in a pan. Add the syrup, butter and 2 tablespoons of water. Heat gently, stirring all the time. Pour over the profiteroles.

You could pile all the profiteroles in a heap, before pouring on the chocolate sauce.

Little fruit tarts

Ingredients:

175g (6oz) plain flour

75g (3oz) chilled butter

For the filling:

4 tablespoons raspberry jam or
   apricot jam, or lemon curd

For the fruit topping (optional):

around 300g (10oz) fresh berries
   such as raspberries, blueberries
   and strawberries

For the glaze (optional):

4 tablespoons seedless
   raspberry jam or apricot jam

1 tablespoon lemon juice

You will also need a 12-hole
shallow bun tin and a
6½cm (2½in) round or
wavy cutter.

Makes 12

This recipe shows how to make jam tarts topped with fresh berries and a shiny glaze. If you prefer plain jam tarts, you can just leave out the fruit.

1 To make the pastry, follow steps 1-4 on pages 340-341. Heat the oven to 200°C, 400°F or gas mark 6. Use a paper towel to wipe a little softened butter into the holes of the tin.

 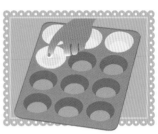

2 Roll out the pastry by following the steps on page 375. Use the cutter to cut out lots of circles from the pastry.

3 Put one circle over each hole in the tin. Dip your finger in some flour and use it to push the circles gently into the holes.

4 Roll the scraps of pastry into a ball, roll it out again and cut more circles, until you have filled the tin.

5 Spoon one teaspoon of jam or curd into each hole. Bake for 10-12 minutes, until the pastry is golden.

6 The jam will be very hot. Leave the tarts in the tin for 10 minutes, then lift them onto a wire rack to cool completely.

7 For the fruit topping, rinse the berries under a running cold tap, then pat them dry with a clean tea towel.

8 Pull the green stalks and leaves out of the strawberries. Cut any large strawberries into pieces.

9 If you'd like to make a glaze for your tarts, put the jam into a small bowl and add the lemon juice. Mix.

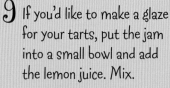

10 Pile all the berries into the tarts, then brush the glaze over the berries.

Large fruit tart

You could make one large tart, using a 20cm (8in) flan dish. Follow the instructions on page 375 to line the dish. Spoon 4 tablespoons of jam into the pastry case. Spread it out with the back of a spoon. Bake for around 20 minutes, until the pastry is golden. Follow steps 7-10 of the main recipe here, to fill your tart with berries and add a glaze.

Mini savoury pastries

Ingredients:

375g (13oz) packet of ready-rolled puff pastry

1 medium red onion

1 tablespoon olive oil

½ teaspoon dried mixed herbs

a pinch of salt

a pinch of ground black pepper

150g (5oz) mozzarella cheese, either in a ball or grated

12 small cherry tomatoes

1 tablespoon milk

You will also need 2 baking trays.

Makes 24

These little savoury pastries are made from bought puff pastry cut into tiny squares and then topped with cheese and tomatoes. They would make a good snack for a party.

1 Heat the oven to 220°C, 425°F or gas mark 7.

2 Take the pastry out of the fridge and leave it for 20 minutes. Then, carefully cut the ends off the onion.

3 Peel the onion and cut it in half. Then, cut each half into two pieces. Very carefully cut each piece into thin slices.

 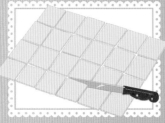 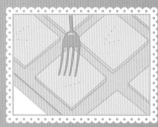

4 Gently heat the olive oil in a frying pan. Then, add the onion and cook for 5 minutes, stirring every now and then.

5 Take the pan off the heat and stir in the herbs, salt and pepper. Unroll the pastry and cut it into 24 squares.

6 Put the squares on the baking trays, leaving spaces between them. Prick the middle of each square twice with a fork.

7 If you're using a ball of mozzarella, cut it into tiny cubes. Then, cut the tomatoes in half.

8 Brush milk around the edge of each square, making a border around 1cm (½in) wide.

9 Spoon some of the onion and herb mixture onto each square, making sure you don't cover the milk border.

10 Put half a tomato on the top of each square, then scatter a little mozzarella on top of each one.

11 Bake for 12-15 minutes, until the edges have risen and gone brown. Leave for 5 minutes before you eat them.

Chocolate profiteroles

These profiteroles are made from chocolate choux pastry. They're filled with tangy raspberry cream and drizzled with melted white chocolate.

1 Heat the oven to 220°C, 425°F or gas mark 7. Grease the baking trays with butter (see page 10). Hold each tray under the cold tap briefly, then shake off the water.

2 Cut a large rectangle of baking parchment. Fold it in half. Unfold it again. Sift the flour and cocoa onto it. Sprinkle on the sugar. Break the eggs into a small bowl and beat them.

3 Cut the butter into small chunks. Put them in a pan with 150ml (¼ pint) water. Heat gently. As soon as it boils, take it off the heat.

4 Right away, fold up the parchment and tip the flour into the pan. Beat quickly for about a minute, until the mixture begins to form a ball in the middle of the pan.

5 Leave to cool for 5 minutes. Then, add a little egg and stir it in. Add the rest of the egg a little at a time, stirring well each time.

6 Put heaped teaspoons of the mixture onto the baking trays, spacing them well apart.

7 Bake for 10 minutes, then turn down the heat to 190°C, 375°F or gas mark 5. Bake for another 10-12 minutes until they are puffy.

8 Use a spatula to move the puffs to a wire rack to cool. Then, make a hole in the side of each one with a sharp knife to let out any steam.

9 For the raspberry cream, put the raspberries in a bowl with the sugar and mash them with a fork.

Don't beat too much, or the cream will go hard.

10 Pour the cream into a big bowl. Beat it quickly with a whisk until it thickens. The cream should stand up in a floppy point when you lift the whisk.

11 Add the raspberries. Mix them in very gently with a metal spoon. Melt the white chocolate (see page 380).

12 The puffs should now be cold. Cut a slit in the side of each one. Spoon in some raspberry cream, then drizzle the white chocolate over them.

Pear & almond tart

Ingredients:

175g (6oz) plain flour

75g (3oz) butter

For the filling:

50g (2oz) softened butter

50g (2oz) caster sugar

50g (2oz) ground almonds

1 medium egg

15g (½oz) self-raising flour

3 small, ripe pears

For the glaze:

2 tablespoons smooth apricot jam

1 tablespoon lemon juice

You will also need a 20cm (8in) round flan dish and some baking beans or a packet of dried beans or peas.

Makes around 8 slices

This large pastry tart is filled with pears and a delicious mixture of ground almonds, sugar and butter. The mixture rises around the fruit as it cooks, to make a dense, almondy layer.

Be very careful when you remove the hot foil and beans.

1 To make the pastry, follow steps 1-4 on pages 340-341. Then, follow steps 1-2 on page 370 to grease the dish, line it with pastry and blind bake it.

2 Put the hot baking tray back into the oven on its own. Reduce the temperature of the oven to 170°C, 325°F or gas mark 3.

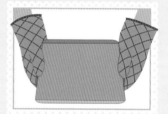

3 For the filling, put the butter and sugar in a large bowl. Beat until light and fluffy. Add a tablespoon of ground almonds and beat it in.

4 Break the egg into a small bowl and beat it with a fork. Add the egg to the mixture in the large bowl, a little at a time, beating well each time.

5 Add the remaining ground almonds and beat them into the mixture. Sift in the flour. Gently stir everything together.

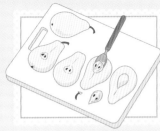

6 Put a pear onto a chopping board. Cut it in half lengthways. Using a small teaspoon, scoop out the core in the middle of each half.

7 Using a vegetable peeler, carefully scrape the peel off the half pears. Put each half flat side down on the chopping board. Score a few shallow slits in the thick end of each piece.

8 Spoon the almond filling into the pastry case. Spread it out using the back of the spoon. Arrange the pears on top, flat side down, with the thin ends in the middle.

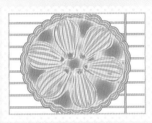

9 Bake for 30-35 minutes, until the pastry case and filling are dark golden. Carefully take the tart out of the oven. Put it on a wire rack to cool.

10 For the glaze, mix the apricot jam and lemon juice in a small bowl. Brush the mixture over the warm tart.

You could use tinned pears instead of fresh pears. You won't need to peel them.

Strawberry tarts

Ingredients:

175g (6oz) plain flour

75g (3oz) butter

For the filling:

300g (10oz) small strawberries

3 tablespoons bought lemon curd
(or, to make your own, you can
follow the recipe given on
pages 252-253)

100ml (4fl oz) double or
whipping cream

For the glaze:

4 tablespoons redcurrant jelly or
smooth raspberry jam

You will also need a 12-hole
shallow bun tin and a 7½cm (3in)
round cutter.

Makes 12

These little tarts are filled with delicious lemon cream and topped with juicy strawberries. You could make them with other fruits. Try raspberries, kiwi fruits or grapes.

1 To make the pastry, follow steps 1-4 on pages 340-341. Take it out of the fridge. Leave it for 10 minutes, then unwrap it. Heat the oven to 200°C, 400°F or gas mark 6.

2 Dust a clean surface and a rolling pin with flour. Roll out the pastry (see page 375) until it is around half as thick as your little finger.

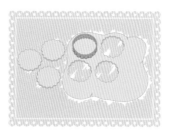

3 Cut circles from the pastry. Squeeze the scraps into a ball and roll it out, then cut more circles. Put a pastry circle in each hole in the bun tray.

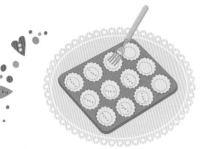  

4 Use a fork to prick each circle several times. Bake for 10-12 minutes until golden. Leave in the tin to cool.

5 Rinse the strawberries, then pat them dry with a clean tea towel. Carefully, cut off the green stalks with a sharp knife.

6 Spoon the lemon curd into a bowl. Add one tablespoon of cream and stir it in. Pour the rest of the cream into another bowl. Use a whisk to whip it (see page 377).

7 Add the lemon curd mixture to the cream and fold it in gently. Put the pastry cases on a wire rack. Spoon 2 teaspoons of filling into each.

8 Place a whole strawberry in the middle of each tart. Cut the rest of the strawberries in half and arrange them around the whole strawberry.

9 Put the jelly or jam in a pan with 2 teaspoons of water. Heat gently until the jelly or jam has melted. Leave it to cool for 2 minutes, then brush it over the tarts.

Butterscotch profiteroles

Ingredients:

65g (2½oz) plain flour

2 medium eggs

50g (2oz) butter

For the filling:

2 oranges

200ml (7floz) double or
   whipping cream

1½ tablespoons icing sugar

For the butterscotch sauce:

25g (1oz) unsalted butter

75g (3oz) dark brown sugar

150ml (¼ pint) double cream

You will also need 2 baking trays.

Makes around 15

These profiteroles are drizzled with butterscotch sauce and filled with whipped cream and fresh orange pieces. Leave out the oranges if you prefer.

1 Heat the oven to 220°C, 425°F or gas mark 7. Grease the baking trays with butter (page 10). Hold them under a cold tap briefly and shake off the water.

2 Cut a big piece of baking parchment. Sift the flour onto it. Break the eggs into a cup and beat them with a fork.

3 Cut the butter into chunks. Put them in a pan with 150ml (¼ pint) cold water. Heat gently. As soon as the mixture boils, take it off the heat. Straight away, tip in all the flour.

4 Quickly beat in the flour. Keep on beating for about a minute, until the mixture starts to come away from the sides of the pan and forms a ball in the middle. Leave it to cool for 5 minutes.

5 Add a little egg to the mixture and beat it in well. Add the egg a little at a time, beating well each time. Put teaspoonfuls of the mixture on the trays, spacing them well apart.

6 Bake for 10 minutes. Turn down the heat to 190°C, 375°F or gas mark 5. Leave the buns in for 10-12 minutes until puffy and dark golden.

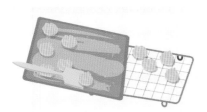

Use the small holes of a grater.

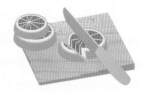

7 Move the buns to a wire rack, to cool. Make a hole in the side of each bun with a sharp knife, to let out any steam.

8 For the filling, grate the zest from the outside of the oranges. Put it in a big bowl.

9 Cut the oranges into slices as thick as your little finger. Cut the skin off the slices, like this. Then, cut the slices into small pieces.

10 Pour the cream into the bowl. Sift in the icing sugar. Whip the cream (see page 377). Fold the orange pieces in gently.

11 Cut the buns in half. Spoon some cream and fruit into the bottom halves. Replace the tops. Put them in the fridge.

Butterscotch sauce

To make the butterscotch sauce, follow the instructions for butterscotch filling on page 377, but add the cream (see ingredients list opposite) instead of the cream cheese. Pour the sauce over the profiteroles.

Contains optional nuts

Mince pies

Ingredients:

For the mincemeat:

1 orange

1 lemon

75g (3oz) seedless grapes

25g (1oz) hazelnuts (optional)

1 apple

150g (5oz) raisins

a pinch each of ground cinnamon, ground nutmeg and ground ginger

For the orange pastry:

1 medium orange

1 medium egg

175g (6oz) plain flour

35g (1¼oz) icing sugar

100g (4oz) butter

You will also need a 12-hole shallow bun tin, a 6½cm (2½in) round cutter, a 5cm (2in) round cutter and a small shaped cutter.

Makes 12

Mince pies have been a Christmas-time treat in Britain for centuries. Mincemeat used to contain real meat as well as fruit, but now it's made from fruits and spices. You can make your own mincemeat following the recipe below, or just buy some to put in these mince pies.

1 For the mincemeat, see the box on the opposite page. For the pastry, grate the zest from the orange on the small holes of a grater. Squeeze the juice from half the orange.

2 Separate the egg and put the yolk into a small bowl. Mix in the zest and 2 teaspoons of the orange juice.

Save the egg white to use later.

3 Put the flour and sugar into a large bowl. Cut the butter into chunks. Rub it into the flour (see page 375), until it looks like fine breadcrumbs.

4 Add the orange mixture. Stir it in until you have a lump of pastry. Wrap it in food wrap and put it in the fridge for 30 minutes. Heat the oven to 190°C, 375°F or gas mark 5.

5 Put the pastry onto a clean surface. Roll over it once. Turn it a quarter of the way around and roll over it again. Carry on until it's as thick as your little finger.

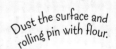

Dust the surface and rolling pin with flour.

Sift a little icing sugar over your finished mince pies.

6 Use the large round cutter to cut out 12 circles. Put one in each hole in the tin. Squeeze the scraps together and roll them out. Use the small round cutter to cut 6 lids.

7 Use the shaped cutter to cut holes in the 6 lids. Then, spoon a heaped teaspoon of mincemeat into each pastry case.

8 Put lids with cut-out shapes onto half the pies. Put the small shapes on the others. Brush the pastry with the egg white you saved.

9 Bake for 20 minutes until golden. Leave in the tin for a few minutes. Then, put them on a wire rack to cool.

Mincemeat

Grate the zest from the orange and lemon on the small holes of a grater. Cut the grapes and nuts into pieces. Grate the apple on the big holes of a grater. Put the zest, grapes, nuts, apple, raisins, cinnamon, nutmeg and ginger in a bowl. Mix well.

Mini éclairs

Ingredients:

40g (1½oz) plain flour

1 medium egg

25g (1oz) butter

For the vanilla cream:

½ teaspoon vanilla essence

1 tablespoon icing sugar

150ml (¼ pint) double or
    whipping cream

For the chocolate icing:

125g (4½oz) icing sugar

3 tablespoons cocoa powder

You will also need a baking tray.

Makes around 8

Other flavours

For raspberry icing,
squash 10 raspberries
through a sieve. Mix the
raspberry juice with 150g
(5oz) sifted icing sugar.

For coffee icing, dissolve
2 teaspoons instant
coffee in 3 teaspoons hot
water. Mix in 150g (5oz)
sifted icing sugar.

Eclairs are long choux buns with cream inside and icing on top. These ones are filled with vanilla cream and topped with chocolate, raspberry or coffee icing.

1 Heat the oven to 220°C, 425°F or gas mark 7. Grease the baking tray with butter (see page 10). Hold the tray under a cold tap briefly, then shake off the water.

2 Cut out a large rectangle of baking parchment. Fold it in half. Unfold it again. Sift the flour onto it. Break the egg into a small bowl and beat it.

3 Cut the butter into small chunks. Put them in a pan with 75ml (3floz) cold water. Heat gently. As soon as it boils, take it off the heat.

4 Right away, fold up the parchment and tip the flour into the pan. Beat quickly for about a minute, until the mixture begins to form a ball in the middle of the pan.

5 Leave to cool for 5 minutes. Then, add a little egg and stir it in. Add the rest of the egg a little at a time, stirring well each time.

6 Put a teaspoon of the mixture onto the baking tray. Put on another teaspoon, touching the first one. Use the back of the spoon to smooth the blobs into a long éclair shape.

7 Spoon the rest of the mixture onto the tray in the same way. Make sure you space the éclairs well apart.

8 Bake for 10 minutes, then turn down the heat to 190°C, 375°F or gas mark 5. Bake for another 5-7 minutes, until they are puffy and golden-brown.

9 Use a spatula to move the éclairs onto a wire rack to cool. Carefully, make a hole in the side of each one with a sharp knife to let out any steam.

Don't beat too much, or the cream will go hard.

10 Pour the cream into a big bowl. Add the vanilla and sift over the icing sugar. Then, whip the cream (see page 377).

11 To make the icing, sift the icing sugar and cocoa into a bowl. Add 3 teaspoons warm water. Mix to make a spreadable paste. Add a little more water if it's too stiff.

12 Cut the éclairs in half. Spoon vanilla cream into the bottom halves, then put the tops back on. Spread on some icing.

Chocolate & raspberry tart

Ingredients:

1 orange

175g (6oz) plain flour

25g (1oz) icing sugar

100g (4oz) butter

1 medium egg

For the filling:

175g (6oz) plain chocolate

2 medium eggs

175ml (6fl oz) double cream

75g (3oz) soft light brown sugar

To decorate:

175g (6oz) fresh raspberries

1 tablespoon icing sugar

orange zest (optional)

fresh mint leaves (optional)

You will also need a 20cm (8in) flan dish, some baking beans or a packet of dried beans or peas, and a heatproof bowl that fits snugly into a saucepan.

Makes around 8 slices

This tart has orange-flavoured pastry and a baked chocolate filling. It's decorated with fresh raspberries. You could scatter on orange zest and mint leaves, too.

Save the rest of the orange juice for later.

1 Grate the zest from the orange on the small holes of a grater. Squeeze the juice from the orange. Put the zest and 2 teaspoons of the juice in a bowl.

2 Follow steps 1-5 on pages 362-363 to make the pastry, heat the oven and roll out the pastry. Keep rolling until the pastry is a little bigger than your flan dish.

3 Follow steps 1-2 on page 370 to line the pastry case and blind bake it.

4 Put the pastry case on a wire rack to cool. Put the hot baking tray back into the oven on its own. Reduce the oven temperature to 160°C, 325°F or gas mark 3.

These strips of orange zest were made using a tool called a zester.

5 For the filling, break up the chocolate and put it in the heatproof bowl. Fill the saucepan ¼ full of water. Heat it until the water bubbles. Take the pan off the heat.

6 Wearing oven gloves, carefully put the bowl in the pan. Leave until the chocolate melts. Then, lift the bowl out of the pan. Let the chocolate cool for 10 minutes.

7 Break the eggs into a large bowl and beat them with a fork. Add the cream, sugar and 1 tablespoon of the remaining orange juice. Mix.

8 Pour the melted chocolate into the large bowl, a little at a time, stirring well each time. Then, pour the mixture into the pastry case.

9 Bake for 30 minutes, until the filling is firm. Take it out of the oven. When it is cool, put the raspberries, zest and mint on top. Sift on the icing sugar.

Tomato tarts

Ingredients:

1 large red onion

a 375g (13oz) packet of ready-rolled puff pastry

2 tablespoons milk

100g (4oz) full-fat cream cheese

1 tablespoon olive oil

225g (8oz) ripe tomatoes

½ teaspoon dried mixed herbs

You will also need a baking tray.

Makes 6

This recipe uses ready-rolled puff pastry as a base for tasty tomato tarts. The instructions opposite show you how to make red pepper tarts, too.

1 Heat the oven to 220°C, 425°F or gas mark 7. Grease the baking tray (see page 10). Take the pastry out of the fridge.

2 Cut the onion into thin slices. Put the olive oil and onion in a pan over a gentle heat. Cook for 10 minutes, stirring every now and then, until the onion is soft.

3 While the onions are cooking, unwrap and unroll the pastry and put it on the baking tray. Cut the pastry into 6 pieces.

4 Mix 1 tablespoon of the milk into the cream cheese. Spread the cheese over the pastry, leaving a 2cm (1in) border at the edge. Brush the remaining milk onto the border.

5 If the tomatoes are big, cut them into slices. If they are small (cherry) tomatoes, cut them in half. Arrange them over the cream cheese. Don't cover the milky border.

6 When the onions are cooked, stir in the herbs and a pinch each of salt and pepper. Spoon the onions over the tomatoes.

7 Bake for around 15-20 minutes, until the pastry is risen and golden brown. Leave the tarts on the baking sheet for 3 minutes to cool a little.

Red pepper tarts

For red pepper tarts, you will need 2 red peppers instead of the tomatoes. To prepare the peppers, cut off the tops, cut the peppers in half, pull out the seeds and white pith and cut the peppers into slices as thick as a pencil. At step 2, cook the onions for 5 minutes, add the peppers and cook for 5 more minutes.

You could scatter some fresh herbs over the finished tarts.

Quiche

Ingredients:

175g (6oz) plain flour

75g (3oz) butter

For the filling:

6 rashers of bacon

1 onion

1 tablespoon sunflower oil or other cooking oil

100g (4oz) hard cheese such as Cheddar or Gruyère

2 medium eggs

150ml (¼ pint) milk

You will also need a 20cm (8in) round flan dish, a baking tray and some baking beans or dried beans or peas.

Makes around 8 slices

Other flavours

For leek and bacon quiche, replace the onion with 1 large leek. Wash and slice the leek. At step 5, cook the leek instead of the onion.

This quiche has a pastry case filled with onion, bacon, cheese and eggs. To make the pastry, you'll need to follow steps 1-4 on pages 340-341.

1 Grease the flan dish (page 10), then line it with pastry following the instructions on page 375. Put the baking tray in the oven. Heat the oven to 200°C, 400°F or gas mark 6. Cut a big square of kitchen foil and press it gently into the pastry case.

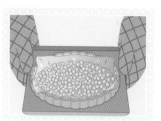 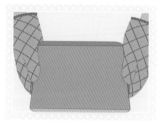

2 Fill the foil with baking beans or dried beans. Lift out the baking tray and put the flan dish on it. Bake for 10 minutes, then take it out again. Very carefully, remove the hot foil and beans.

3 Put the hot baking sheet back in the oven on its own. Turn down the temperature to 170°C, 325°F, gas mark 3. Then, prepare the filling.

4 If there is any rind on the bacon, cut it off with scissors and throw it away. Then, cut the rest of the bacon into small pieces.

5 Peel the onion and cut it in half. Slice it, then cut the slices into small pieces. Put them in a frying pan with the oil. Cook gently for 5 minutes.

6 Put the bacon in the pan. Cook for 5 minutes. Then, turn off the heat and tip the pieces of bacon and onion into a bowl. Let them cool for 5 minutes.

7 Grate the cheese on the large holes on a grater and sprinkle half of it over the bottom of the pastry case. Then, scatter the bacon and onion over the top.

8 Sprinkle on the rest of the cheese. Break the eggs into bowl and beat with a fork. Put the milk in a jug. Mix in the egg and a pinch of pepper.

The top should be golden and the middle set firm.

9 Carefully pour the egg mixture over the filling in the pastry case. Then, carefully lift the hot baking sheet out of the oven and put the quiche onto it.

10 Bake for 25 minutes, then push a knife into the middle. If it isn't firm, bake for 5-10 minutes more. Leave in the dish for 10 minutes before you eat it.

More flavours

For mushroom and onion quiche, leave out the bacon and instead use 150g (5oz) mushrooms. Wipe and slice the mushrooms. At step 6, cook the mushrooms instead of the bacon.

Quiche is equally delicious served warm or chilled.

Baking tips for biscuits & cakes

Hand heat

Some of the recipes tell you to use your hands to mix things. Pat and squeeze the mixture gently. The heat from your hands will help to bring the ingredients together.

Squeezing scraps

When you cut shapes from biscuit dough using cutters, you'll have lots of scraps left. Squeeze them together, roll them out and cut more shapes, until you have used up all the dough.

Cookie cutters

Several of the recipes in this book say to use particular types of cookie cutters, but these are only suggestions. You can make your biscuits with any shape of cookie cutter you like.

1 Put a cutter over the rolled-out dough and press down gently, without twisting.

2 Lift up the cutter. If the dough shape comes too, hold the cutter over your baking tray and poke the shape, so it falls out. Otherwise, use a spatula to lift the shape carefully onto the baking tray.

Rolling out biscuits & cookies

1 Sprinkle a little flour over a clean work surface and a rolling pin. Put the dough on the surface.

2 Roll the rolling pin over the dough, going from the front to the back, then from the back to the front.

3 If you want a wide sheet of dough, turn the dough a quarter of the way around on the work surface. Roll over it again in the same way, to make it wider.

Storing cakes & biscuits

Most cakes and biscuits will keep in an airtight container for a few days. If they contain fresh fruit, cream or cream cheese, it's best to put the container in the fridge.

Adding eggs

When you mix eggs into a cake mixture, you usually have to add them a little at a time. If you add them all at once, the mixture can separate. The recipe will tell you just what to do.

Cake sizes

Always use the size and shape of tin or paper case the recipe says, or your cakes might not turn out right. To find out how to grease and line tins and trays, see page 10.

Muffin tins

Some of the recipes in this section use a 6-hole deep muffin tin, but if you don't have one you can use a 12-hole one instead. Put the cake mix in the holes closest to the middle. Spoon a little water into the other holes, to stop the tin from overheating.

Tiny paper cake cases

There are different sizes of tiny paper cake cases, so the number of cakes given in the recipe is only a guide. Tiny paper cases may flop during cooking. To prevent this, put a second case inside each one before you fill it.

Removing cakes from tins

To remove a cake from a tin with a loose base, undo any clips. Put the tin over a full food can. Press the sides of the tin down. Then, slide the cake off the base of the tin, onto a plate.

To remove a cake from a tin with a fixed base, run a knife around the edge of the tin. Hold the tin upside down over a wire rack and shake. The cake should pop out.

Is it cooked?

At the end of the cooking time, take the cake out of the oven and test it to see if it's cooked.

If the recipe says to test with a skewer, poke a clean skewer into the middle of the cake. Pull it out again. If there is wet cake mix on the skewer, bake the cake for 10 minutes more, then test again.

If the recipe says to test with a finger, poke the middle of the cake quickly with your finger. It should feel firm and springy. If it doesn't, bake for 10 minutes more, then test again.

Using silicone

You can buy individual silicone cake cases in most sizes. These hold their shape on an ordinary, flat baking tray. Silicone cases can stick to cakes, so it's a good idea to grease them first (page 10).

Baking tips for bread & pastry

Raising agents

Most bread is made from a dough made of wheat flour, water and yeast. When yeast becomes warm and moist, it gives off tiny bubbles of gas that make the dough rise. Some bread contains other ingredients to make it rise, such as bicarbonate of soda.

Bread flour

Bread is usually made using a type of flour called strong flour. When it's pushed, squashed and stretched, it becomes stronger and stretchier than normal flour. This is called kneading.

Leaving dough to rise

When you make bread, you need to leave it somewhere warm, such as in a warm kitchen, on a sunny windowsill (with the window closed) or near a radiator. The warmth helps the yeast make the dough rise quickly.

Leftover bread

Bread can go stale and hard quite quickly. To keep it fresh for longer, store it in an airtight container or bag. However, stale bread is ideal for making toast.

Kneading dough

1 When you're making bread, knead by pressing the heels of both hands, or your knuckles, into the dough. Then, push the dough away from you firmly.

2 Fold the dough in half and turn it around. Push the dough away from you again. Then, fold it in half and turn it around again.

3 Carry on pushing the dough away from you , folding it and turning it, until it feels smooth and springy.

Cutting bread

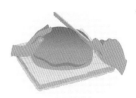

1 To cut a loaf of bread into slices, put it on a chopping board. Take a serrated knife. Hold the bread in one hand and the knife in the other.

2 Move the knife back and forth across the bread in a sawing movement. If the bread is very fresh, it's easier if you don't press down on it, and if you cut thickish slices.

Bought pastry

Some of the recipes in this book use bought pastry. You can buy it frozen or chilled. Some bought pastry comes already rolled out, while some comes in a block. To roll out a block, follow the instructions below for rolling out pastry.

Rolling out pastry

1 Sprinkle some flour on a clean surface and on a rolling pin. Put the pastry on the surface.

2 Roll the rolling pin over the pastry once, then turn the pastry a quarter of the way around on the surface.

3 Roll and turn the pastry again and again in the same way. Carry on until the pastry is the size or thickness you need for the recipe.

Blind baking

When you make a pastry case for a tart or quiche, you need to bake it on its own first. This is called 'blind baking'.

Resting pastry

When you make pastry, or roll it out, you sometimes need to leave it in the fridge for a little while before you cook it. This is called 'resting' the pastry. It stops it from shrinking too much when you put it in the oven.

Rubbing butter into flour

1 Stir the chunks of butter into the flour, to coat them. Pick up some butter and flour with the tips of your fingers and thumbs. Squash and rub them together, letting the mixture drop back into the bowl.

2 Carry on picking up the mixture, rubbing it and letting it fall back into the bowl. The lumps of butter will get smaller. Stop when they are the size of small breadcrumbs.

Lining a dish with pastry

1 First, wipe a little softened butter or oil over the inside of the dish, using a paper towel. Then, roll the pastry around the rolling pin.

2 Lift up the rolling pin and unroll the pastry over the dish. Gently push the pastry into the hollow of the dish.

3 Trim off the edges using scissors, but don't cut too close to the dish. Then, cover the pastry with plastic food wrap and put the dish in the fridge for 20 minutes.

Toppings & fillings

Quantities

The recipes given here make enough to top or fill one 20cm (8in) round cake (apart from the butterscotch filling, which fills 6 macaroons). If you're making a topping or filling to go with a particular recipe in this book, check there for the exact quantities you need.

Vanilla buttercream

You will need 50g (2oz) softened butter or margarine, 100g (4oz) icing sugar, 1 teaspoon vanilla essence and 1 teaspoon milk or water (optional).

1 If you're using butter, put it in a bowl and beat until it's soft and fluffy. If you're using margarine, just put it in a bowl.

2 Sift on half the icing sugar and stir it in. Then, sift on the rest of the icing sugar and add the vanilla and milk or water. Mix well.

Cream cheese frosting

You will need 50g (2oz) icing sugar, 200g (7oz) full-fat cream cheese at room temperature and 1 tablespoon of lemon juice.

Sift the icing sugar into a big bowl. Add the cream cheese and lemon juice and mix gently.

Don't beat too much, or it will go watery.

Chocolate buttercream

You will need 50g (2oz) softened butter or margarine, 75g (3oz) icing sugar, 25g (1oz) cocoa powder, 1 teaspoon vanilla essence and 1 teaspoon milk or water.

Follow the instructions for vanilla buttercream (left) but sift in the cocoa at the same time as the icing sugar.

Citrus buttercream

You will need 1 orange (or 1 lemon or 2 limes), 50g (2oz) softened butter or margarine and 100g (4oz) icing sugar.

Grate the zest from the outside of the fruit on the small holes of a grater. Follow the instructions for vanilla buttercream (left) but at step 2, instead of adding the vanilla and milk or water, add the zest and 2 teaspoons of the juice.

Lime mascarpone

You will need 1 lime, 250g (9oz) mascarpone cheese and 25g (1oz) icing sugar.

Grate the zest from the outside of the lime, using the small holes of a grater. Put the zest and mascarpone in a big bowl. Sift over the icing sugar. Mix well.

Chocolate frosting

You will need 40g (1½oz) butter (preferably unsalted) and 75g (3oz) plain or milk chocolate, broken into pieces.

1 Put the butter in a small pan. Put the pan over a low heat, until the butter melts. Take the pan off the heat.

2 Add the chocolate. Stir until it melts. If you're using the frosting as a cake topping or filling for sandwiching cookies, scrape it into a bowl and refrigerate for 20 minutes.

Whipped cream

1 Pour 150ml (¼ pint) double or whipping cream into a big bowl. Hold the bowl firmly with one hand. Use the other hand to beat the cream with a whisk as hard as you can.

2 Carry on beating until the cream becomes stiff. When you lift the whisk, the cream should stand up in a floppy point.

Don't beat too much, or the cream will go hard.

Vanilla cream

For vanilla cream, follow the instructions for whipped cream (above) but, before you start beating, sift 1 tablespoon of icing sugar into the bowl and add ½ teaspoon vanilla essence.

Glacé icing

You will need 100g (4oz) icing sugar, 2 teaspoons of water and some food dye (optional).

1 Sift the icing sugar into a bowl. Mix in the water until you have a smooth, spreadable paste.

2 Mix in a few drops of food dye, if you like. Or, for more than one shade, divide the icing between separate bowls and mix a different shade into each.

Citrus glacé icing

Follow the instructions for glacé icing (above) but replace the water with orange, lemon or lime juice.

Butterscotch filling

You will need 15g (½oz) butter, 40g (1½oz) soft dark brown sugar and 100g (4oz) full-fat cream cheese.

1 Put the butter and sugar in a pan. Put it over a low heat. Keep stirring until the butter melts and the sugar dissolves.

2 Take the pan off the heat. Add the cream cheese. Beat with a wooden spoon to mix it in. Leave to cool for 5 minutes.

Icing & piping tips

Flat icing

Use a blunt knife or the back of a spoon to spread a fairly thin layer of icing all over a cake or biscuit.

Rough icing

Use a blunt knife to spread a generous layer of icing all over a cake. Then, drag and swirl the knife over the surface, making rough peaks.

Feather icing

You will need glacé icing (page 377), a gun or bag fitted with a small round nozzle and filled with glacé icing in a contrasting shade, and a cocktail stick.

1 Flat ice a cake or biscuit (above). While the icing is still wet, pipe on some lines.

2 Drag the point of the cocktail stick across the lines, to make points. Move the stick along, then drag it across again, to make more points.

Food dye

Ordinary liquid food dye is fine for tinting icing or buttercream in pale shades, but too much can make the icing or buttercream runny. For strong shades, use gel food dye.

Drippy toppings

Spoon on the topping. Spread it to the edge of the cake. Keep spreading, so a little spills over.

Filling a piping gun

First, attach a nozzle. Then, stand the gun nozzle-end down in a mug or glass. Spoon in some frosting. Attach the plunger to the gun.

Filling a piping bag

1 Push a piping nozzle down to the pointed end of the piping bag. If you're using a plastic piping bag, snip the end off first.

2 Stand the bag point-down in a mug or glass. Open up the bag and turn over the top edge. This will help to keep it open while you fill it.

3 Spoon in some frosting. Stop when the bag is half full. Unfold the top edge. Make a twist in the bag just above the frosting.

Piping rosettes & swirls

You will need a filled piping gun or bag fitted with a star- or flower-shaped nozzle.

1 Hold your piping bag or gun so the nozzle is around ½cm (¼in) from the surface of the cake.

2 Squeeze until some icing comes out and touches the cake. Keep the nozzle in the same place and keep squeezing until a small rosette forms.

3 To finish the rosette, stop squeezing and lift the nozzle up and away quickly.

4 For a swirl, follow steps 1-3, then pipe a spiral, starting at the edge of the cake and going in and up, over the rosette. Lift up and away quickly to finish.

Piping lines & dots

You will need some writing icing, or a filled tube, gun or bag fitted with a tiny round nozzle.

1 For a dot, squeeze until a dot of icing comes out. Stop squeezing and lift the nozzle away quickly.

2 For a line, keep squeezing as you move the nozzle along. Stop squeezing and lift the nozzle away quickly.

Piping roses & flat spirals

For roses, you will need a filled piping gun or bag fitted with a snowflake-shaped nozzle. For flat spirals, see step 3.

1 Pipe a spiral, starting in the middle of the cake, and going outwards and around.

2 When you reach the edge of the cake, stop squeezing and move the nozzle away quickly, to finish.

3 For a flat spiral follow steps 1-2, but using a medium star-shaped nozzle instead of a snowflake-shaped one.

Chocolate skills

Melting chocolate

1. For best results, find a heatproof bowl that fits snugly in a saucepan, so that the bottom of the bowl doesn't touch the bottom of the pan – there should be a gap of around 5cm (2in) between them.

2. Fill the pan a quarter with water. Put it over a medium heat. When the water bubbles, take it off the heat.

3. Break up the chocolate. Put it in the bowl. Wearing oven gloves, put the bowl in the pan. Leave for 5 minutes. Stir until the chocolate melts.

Chocolate curls

You will need a bar of chocolate that's at room temperature.

Scrape strips from the side of the bar using a vegetable peeler.

For wider curls, break the bar into strips. Scrape the peeler along the back of the strips.

Types of chocolate

For cooking, you can use chocolate chips or chocolate from a bar.

Chocolate leaves

You will need 100g (4oz) plain chocolate, about 15 fresh mint leaves, a baking tray lined with parchment, a small, new paintbrush and a cocktail stick.

Don't paint the stalks.

Make more than you need, as some may break.

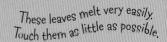

These leaves melt very easily. Touch them as little as possible.

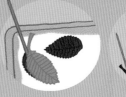

1. Melt the chocolate (see above). Wearing oven gloves, take the bowl out of the pan. Paint the chocolate onto the backs of the mint leaves in a thick layer.

2. Put the leaves on the tray, chocolate side up. Put in the fridge for 45 minutes, or until the chocolate has set.

3. Use the cocktail stick to flip over a leaf. Hold the chocolate down with the stick. Grasp the stalk and gently peel off the mint leaf. Do this with each leaf.

Drizzling melted chocolate

1 Melt 75g (3oz) plain, milk or white chocolate following the instructions on the opposite page.

2 Scoop up some melted chocolate. Hold the spoon over a cake or treat. Tip the spoon, then move it over the cake or treat, leaving a trail of chocolate.

Marbled chocolate topping

You will need 100g (4oz) white chocolate chips and 50g (2oz) plain chocolate chips.

1 While the cake is still hot, sprinkle the white and plain chocolate chips over the cake. Leave them for 5 minutes to melt.

2 Use the back of a teaspoon to swirl the chocolate gently into a marbled pattern. Put the cake in the fridge until the topping has set.

Ganache

Ganache is a creamy, chocolatey filling or topping. You will need 200g (7oz) plain or milk chocolate and 100ml (3½floz) double cream.

1 Melt the chocolate (see opposite). Stir in the cream. Wearing oven gloves, take the bowl out of the pan.

2 Let it cool for 10 minutes, then put it in the fridge for 1 hour. Stir every now and then.

To make white chocolate ganache, replace the plain or milk chocolate with 300g (11oz) white chocolate.

You can also make ganache with sour cream instead of double cream. It will taste slightly sharper.

Chocolate paste

You will need 75g (3oz) plain or milk chocolate, 1½ tablespoons golden syrup and some cocoa powder.

2 Pat the mixture into a ball. Wrap it in plastic food wrap and put it in the fridge for 1 hour. Take it out 10 minutes before you want to use it.

1 Melt the chocolate (see opposite page). Wearing oven gloves, take the bowl out of the pan. Stir in the syrup until the mixture forms a clump in the middle of the pan.

3 Put it on a surface dusted with cocoa powder. Make decorations such as buttons (page 382), or roll it out and cut it into shapes with cutters (page 382).

Decorating ideas

Dyed marzipan or ready-to-roll icing

You will need some bought 'white' marzipan or white ready-to-roll icing and some food dye (for strong shades, use gel food dye).

1 Take a golf-ball-sized blob of marzipan or icing. Make a hollow in the middle. Drop in 3 or 4 drops of food dye.

2 Fold the marzipan or icing over the dye. Keep on folding and squashing until the dye is evenly mixed through.

Sprinkle-covered shapes

You will need some marzipan, chocolate paste or ready-to-roll icing shapes, some sugar sprinkles and 2 teaspoons of icing sugar.

1 Put the icing sugar in a small bowl. Add ⅓ teaspoon of water and mix to a thin, smooth paste.

2 Brush a thin layer of paste over the shapes. Scatter on some sprinkles. Leave to dry.

Buttons and balls

1 Take a little marzipan, ready-to-roll icing or chocolate paste. Use your hands to roll it into a ball.

2 To make a button, put the ball on a surface and flatten it with the back of a spoon.

Rolling out and cutting

1 To roll out marzipan or ready-to-roll icing, dust a surface and a rolling pin with a little icing sugar. For chocolate paste, use cocoa powder.

2 Roll out the marzipan, icing or chocolate paste until it's around 2mm (⅛in) thick. Then, cut out shapes using tiny cookie cutters.

Roses

Roll out some marzipan, chocolate paste or ready-to-roll icing, so it's around 2mm (⅛in) thick.

1 Use a sharp knife to cut a strip 4cm (1½in) long and 1cm (½in) wide. Cut another strip the same length but only half as wide.

2 Put the narrow strip on top of the wide strip, against one of the long edges. Roll up both strips together, with the wide one on the outside. Pinch the base, to make it stick.

Cake ribbons

If you'd like to decorate a cake with ribbon, it's best not to frost the sides of the cake, or the ribbon will get sticky. Put the ribbon around the cake, with the ends at the back. Stick the top end over the bottom end, using sticky tape.

Coloured icing sugar

You will need some icing sugar and a little food dye.

1 Put 1 tablespoon of the sugar on a plate. Mix in a few drops of food dye. Use a spoon to press the mixture through a sieve. Sieve the mixture 3 times.

2 Spread out the sugar and leave it to dry for around 2 hours. When the sugar is dry, press it through a clean sieve one last time.

Stencilled decorations

You will need some icing sugar or cocoa powder and a piece of paper bigger than the cakes or treats you want to decorate.

1 Fold the paper in half. Draw half a heart (or other shape) against the fold. Cut it out. Unfold the paper.

2 Attach a loop of sticky tape to the shape. Put the shape on a cake or treat. Put the paper with the hole in it on another.

3 Sift a little icing sugar or cocoa over the cakes or treats. Carefully remove the stencils.

Cake toppers

You will need some patterned paper, shapes to draw around such as little cookie cutters or coins and 12 cocktail sticks.

1 Put the paper on a surface, patterned side down. Put on the cookie cutters or coins and draw around them so you have 12 shapes.

2 Cut out the shapes. Lay them patterned side down. Put a cocktail stick over each one, so the point of the stick is in the middle of the shape.

3 Stick sticky tape over each cocktail stick, to stick it to the paper shape. Then, push the toppers into your cakes.

4 For cake flags, cut strips of paper. Fold them in half. Spread on glue. Place a cocktail stick along the fold of each strip. Press the two ends of the strip together. Leave to dry.

More decorating ideas

House decorations

You will need a rolling pin, icing sugar and red, blue, brown and white marzipan or ready-to-roll icing.

1 Take a golf-ball-sized blob of icing or marzipan. Shape it into a rough cube. Pat it against a clean, flat surface to make the sides flat.

2 Put the cube down. Pinch and squash two of the sides together into a point to make a roof on top of the cube, like this.

3 Dust a clean surface and a rolling pin with a little icing sugar. Roll out some white marzipan or icing until it is half as thick as a pencil.

4 Cut 2 rectangles. Each one should fit over one side of the roof. They should meet at the middle. Pat gently into place.

Add a chimney, a door and a door handle, too.

See page 382 for tips on dyeing marzipan or ready-to-roll icing.

Chocolate stars & hearts

You will need 40g (1½oz) white chocolate and 40g (1½oz) plain or milk chocolate, a chopping board, some baking parchment, sticky tape and a piping gun or bag fitted with a tiny, round nozzle.

1 Follow steps 1-2 on the opposite page (butterfly decorations), but trace over the star and heart templates (page 386-387) until you have around 20 shapes. Melt the white chocolate (page 380).

If they soften, put them back in the fridge.

2 Spoon the chocolate into the piping gun or bag. Pipe it over half the pencil shapes (see page 379 for tips on piping lines). Wash and dry the nozzle. Attach it to a clean, dry gun or a fresh piping bag.

3 Make the plain chocolate shapes in the same way. Put the board in the fridge for 15 minutes. Then, unstick the parchment. Very carefully, peel off a shape. Push it into the frosting on a cake.

Butterfly decorations

You will need a chopping board, some baking parchment, 75g (3oz) white chocolate, a heatproof bowl that fits snugly into a pan, some food dye and a piping gun or bag fitted with a tiny, round nozzle.

1 Cut some parchment to fit your board. Place the parchment over the butterfly templates on pages 386-387. Trace over them with a pencil.

2 Move the parchment along and trace over them again, until you have around 20 butterflies. Turn over the parchment. Stick it to the board with sticky tape.

3 Melt the chocolate (see page 380). Take the bowl out of the pan. Stir in a few drops of food dye. Don't add too much dye. Spoon the chocolate into the gun or bag.

4 Pipe over the pencil butterflies – see page 379 for tips.

If they soften, put them back in the fridge.

5 Refrigerate for 15 minutes. Unstick the parchment. Peel off the butterflies. Push two matching halves into the frosting on a cake, so it looks as if the butterfly is opening its wings.

Pumpkin decorations

You will need some whole cloves, a cocktail stick and red, yellow and green marzipan or ready-to-roll icing (see page 382 for tips on dyeing marzipan or ready-to-roll icing).

1 Squash and knead some red and yellow marzipan or icing together, to make orange. Roll some into a ball the size of a golf ball.

2 Put the point of the cocktail stick against the bottom of the ball. Tilt the stick up and over, so it makes a groove up the side of the ball, ending in the middle.

3 Make more grooves all the way around. Push your thumb into the middle of the ball, to make a dent.

4 Take a little green marzipan or icing. Roll it into a thin string. Wrap it around the cocktail stick to make a tendril. Push it off the end of the stick.

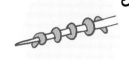

5 Remove the round part of a clove. Put the end of the tendril in the dent of the pumpkin. Use the end of the clove to spear it in place.

You could add eyes, a nose and a mouth, too.

Templates

These templates are for making piped chocolate stars, hearts and butterflies. For full instructions on how to make them, see pages 384-385. For tips on how to pipe lines, see the advice on page 379.

Some of the templates here are shown in two different shades, but this is just to show you which lines to pipe first. Go along the lines shown in the lighter shade first. Then, fill in the darker lines afterwards.

A big heart

A tiny star

Use the smaller shapes for decorating little cakes.

A small butterfly

Little butterflies

A big butterfly

Allergy advice

Some recipes in this book have ingredients marked as optional. Leave them out if you're cooking for someone who's allergic to them. There are suggestions in ingredients lists, boxes and captions for allergy-free ingredients you can use. The list below tells you about ingredients that might be a problem for those who can't eat wheat, gluten, dairy, egg or nuts. It also suggests ways of making recipes allergy-free.

If you're cooking for someone with food allergies, check any packaged ingredients, such as vanilla essence, jam, chocolate, baking powder, icing sugar, cocoa powder or sugar sprinkles, to make sure they don't contain anything unsuitable.

Biscuits & cookies

Tiny pink cookies
Contain wheat, gluten and dairy.

Oat & raisin cookies
Contain wheat, gluten, dairy and egg.

Chocolate-dipped shortbread
Contains wheat, gluten and dairy. For gluten-free shortbread, see page 35.

Sparkly star biscuits
Contain wheat, gluten, dairy and egg.

Stripey biscuits
Contain wheat, gluten and dairy.

Chocolate & cherry cookies
Contain wheat, gluten, dairy and egg.

Bright flower biscuits
Contain wheat, gluten, dairy and egg. To make them dairy-free, use dairy-free margarine and water.

Orange shortbread stars
Contain wheat, gluten and dairy.

Mini chocolate chip cookies
Contain wheat, gluten, dairy and egg.

To make them dairy-free, use dairy-free margarine and dairy-free chocolate.

Chocolate florentines
Contain wheat, gluten, dairy and nuts.

Cinnamon shortbread fingers
Contain wheat, gluten and dairy. A gluten-free version is included.

Crunchy peanut cookies
Contain wheat, gluten, dairy, egg and peanuts.

Chocolate orange cookies
Contain wheat, gluten, dairy and egg. To make them dairy-free, use dairy-free margarine and dairy-free chocolate.

Lebkuchen
Contain wheat, gluten, egg and nuts.

Lemon spiral biscuits
Contain wheat, gluten and dairy.

Iced biscuits & bookies

Daisy biscuits
Contain wheat, gluten and dairy.

Festive cookies
Contain wheat, gluten, dairy and egg. To make them dairy-free, use dairy-free margarine.

Iced lemon biscuits
Contain wheat, gluten, dairy and egg.

Cinnamon cookies
Contain wheat, gluten and dairy.

Lollipop cookies
Contain wheat, gluten, dairy and egg. To make them dairy-free, use dairy-free margarine.

Iced star biscuits
Contain wheat, gluten, dairy and egg.

Little gem biscuits
Contain wheat, gluten and dairy.

Jewelled crown biscuits
Contain wheat, gluten and dairy.

Lemon cinnamon stars
Contain egg and nuts.

Chocolate cobweb cookies
Contain wheat, gluten and dairy.

Ginger snap biscuits
Contain wheat, gluten and dairy.

Little gingerbread houses
Contain wheat, gluten, dairy and egg.

Confetti cookies
Contain wheat, gluten, dairy and egg.

Gingerbread flowers
Contain wheat, gluten, dairy and egg. To make them dairy-free, use dairy-free margarine.

Snowflake biscuits
Contain wheat, gluten and dairy.

Filled biscuits & cookies

Viennese biscuits
Contain wheat, gluten and dairy.

Jam dimple biscuits
Contain wheat, gluten, dairy and coconut. Coconut may not be suitable for those with nut allergies.

Hidden marzipan biscuits
Contain wheat, gluten, dairy, egg and nuts.

Jammy cut-out biscuits
Contain wheat, gluten, dairy, egg and optional nuts.

Soft-centre cookies
Contain wheat, gluten, dairy and egg.

Chocolate peanut bites
Contain wheat, gluten, dairy, egg and peanuts.

Lace biscuits
Contain wheat, gluten, dairy and egg.

Yoyo cookies
Contain wheat, gluten and dairy.

Chocolate orange hearts
Contain wheat, gluten, dairy, egg and nuts.

Linz biscuits
Contain wheat, gluten, dairy, egg and nuts.

Tray cakes & bakes

Coconut cake
Contains wheat, gluten, dairy, egg and coconut. Coconut may not be suitable for those with nut allergies.

Iced fancies
Contain wheat, gluten, dairy and egg.

Swiss roll
Contains wheat, gluten and egg. To keep it dairy-free, avoid the whipped cream, chocolate mousse and buttercream filling suggestions.

Lemon & mango loaf
Contains wheat, gluten, dairy and nuts.

Lemon ricotta cake
Contains wheat, gluten, dairy and egg.

Chocolate roulade
Contains wheat, gluten, dairy, egg and nuts. To make it wheat- and gluten-free, use wheat- and gluten-free baking powder. To make it dairy-free, use the filling from pages 104-105 instead.

Apple & cinnamon cake
Contains wheat, gluten and egg.

Carrot cake
Contains wheat, gluten, dairy, egg and optional nuts. To make it dairy-free, leave out the topping. You could use glacé icing instead (see page 377).

Gingerbread cake
Contains wheat, gluten, dairy and egg.

Chocolate party cake
Contains wheat, gluten, dairy and egg.

Chocolate traybake
Contains dairy and egg. To make it dairy-free, use dairy-free margarine and dairy-free chocolate.

Christmas log
Contains wheat, gluten, dairy, egg and nuts. To make it wheat- and gluten-free, or dairy-free, follow the suggestions given in the 'other ideas' box on page 123.

Honey spice cake
Contains wheat, gluten, dairy, egg and nuts. To make it wheat- and gluten-free, use cornmeal and wheat- and gluten-free baking powder. To make it dairy-free, use dairy-free margarine.

Moist fruit cake

Contains wheat, gluten, dairy, egg and optional nuts. To make it nut-free, leave out the marzipan.

Bars & brownies

Cherry crumble bars

Contain wheat, gluten, dairy, egg and optional seeds. Seeds may not be suitable for those with nut allergies.

Apple flapjacks

Contain gluten, dairy and optional seeds. Seeds may not be suitable for those with nut allergies.

Chocolate fudge brownies

Contain wheat, gluten, dairy, egg and optional nuts.

Cherry chocolate brownies

Contain wheat, gluten, dairy, egg and optional nuts. To make them dairy-free, use dairy-free margarine and dairy-free chocolate.

Chocolate chip brownies

Contain wheat, gluten, dairy, egg and optional nuts.

Chocolate peanut brownies

Contain wheat, gluten, dairy, egg and peanuts. To make them dairy-free, use dairy-free margarine and dairy-free chocolate.

White chocolate brownie bites

Contain wheat, gluten, dairy and egg.

Ice cream & brownie cake

Contains wheat, gluten, dairy and egg.

Meringues & macaroons

Filled meringues

Contain dairy and egg. To make them dairy-free, leave out the raspberry cream.

Multicoloured meringues

Contain egg.

Meringue nests

Contain dairy and egg.

Chocolate swirl meringues

Contain dairy and egg. To make them dairy-free, use dairy-free chocolate.

Mini meringues

Contain dairy and egg. To make them dairy-free, leave out the whipped cream.

Raspberry macaroons

Contain dairy, egg and nuts.

Chocolate macaroons

Contain dairy, egg and nuts.

Macaroon creams

Contain dairy, egg and nuts. To make them dairy-free, use dairy-free margarine in the buttercream.

Butterscotch macaroons

Contain dairy, egg and nuts.

Muffins & whoopie pies

Iced muffins

Contain wheat, gluten, dairy and egg.

Chocolate muffins

Contain wheat, gluten, dairy and egg. To make them dairy-free, use dairy-free chocolate and soya milk.

Spiced apple muffins

Contain wheat, gluten, dairy and egg.

Marbled muffins

Contain wheat, gluten, dairy and egg. To make them dairy-free, use dairy-free chocolate and soya milk.

Lemon & berry muffins

Contain wheat, gluten, dairy and egg.

Banana fudge muffins

Contain wheat, gluten, dairy and egg.

Vanilla whoopie pies

Contain wheat, gluten, dairy and egg.

Chocolate whoopie pies

Contain wheat, gluten, dairy and egg.

Little cakes

Tiny cupcakes

Contain wheat, gluten, dairy and egg. To make them dairy-free, use dairy-free margarine and dairy-free chocolate chips.

Little red velvet cakes

Contain wheat, gluten and dairy.

Chocolate fudge cupcakes
Contain egg.

Maple syrup cupcakes
Contain wheat, gluten, dairy, egg and optional nuts.

Upside-down berry cakes
Contain dairy and egg. To make them dairy-free, use dairy-free margarine.

Butterfly cakes
Contain wheat, gluten, dairy and egg. To make them dairy-free, use dairy-free margarine.

Little coconut cakes
Contain wheat, gluten, dairy, egg and coconut. Coconut may not be suitable for those with nut allergies.

Flower cupcakes
Contain dairy and egg. To make them dairy-free, use dairy-free margarine and soya milk.

Apricot sprinkle cakes
Contain wheat, gluten, dairy, egg and nuts. To make them wheat- and gluten-free, use polenta and wheat- and gluten-free baking powder.

Lemon & lime cupcakes
Contain wheat, gluten, dairy and egg.

Chocolate cupcakes
Contain wheat, gluten, dairy and egg. To make them dairy-free, use dairy-free margarine and water.

Tiny butterfly cakes
Contain wheat, gluten, dairy and egg.

Little chocolate gateaux
Contain wheat, gluten, dairy and egg. The hazelnut version contains nuts.

Tiny citrus cakes
Contain wheat, gluten, dairy and egg. To make them dairy-free, use dairy-free margarine.

Christmas cupcakes
Contain wheat, gluten, dairy and egg.

Little raspberry cakes
Contain egg and nuts.

Orange drizzle cupcakes
Contain dairy and egg. To make them dairy-free, use dairy-free margarine.

Mocha butterfly cakes
Contain wheat, gluten, dairy and egg.

Chocolate orange cakepops
Contain wheat, gluten, dairy and egg.

Mini cheesecakes
Contain wheat, gluten, dairy and egg. To make them wheat- and gluten-free, use wheat- and gluten-free biscuits.

Little pink cakes
Contain wheat, gluten, dairy and egg. To make them dairy-free, use dairy-free margarine.

Little rose cakes
Contain wheat, gluten, dairy and

egg. To make them dairy-free, use dairy-free margarine. Spread on the buttercream rather than piping it.

Party cupcakes
Contain wheat, gluten, dairy and egg. To make them dairy-free, use dairy-free margarine, water and dairy-free chocolate.

Little banana cakes
Contain wheat, gluten, dairy, egg and optional nuts. To make them dairy-free, use dairy-free margarine and leave out the topping.

Vanilla cupcakes
Contain wheat, gluten, dairy and egg. To make them dairy-free, use dairy-free margarine. Spread on the buttercream rather than piping it.

Very chocolatey cupcakes
Contain wheat, gluten, dairy and egg. To make them wheat- and gluten-free, use wheat- and gluten-free baking powder and chocolate.

Mini crispy buns
Contain wheat, gluten, dairy and egg.

Mint choc chip cakes
Contain wheat, gluten, dairy and egg. To make them dairy-free, use dairy-free margarine and dairy-free chocolate.

Fairy cakes
Contain wheat, gluten, dairy and egg. To make them dairy-free, use dairy-free margarine.

Small strawberry sponge cakes
Contain wheat, gluten, dairy and egg.
To make them dairy-free, use dairy-free margarine.

Big cakes

Classic sponge cake
Contains wheat, gluten, dairy and egg.

Quick sponge cake
Contains wheat, gluten, dairy and egg. To make it dairy-free, use dairy-free spread and avoid the creamy and mascarpone fillings.

Lemon layer cake
Contains wheat, gluten, dairy and egg.

Coffee cake
Contains wheat, gluten, dairy, egg and optional nuts. To make it dairy-free, use dairy-free margarine.

Strawberry jam cake
Contains wheat, gluten, dairy and egg. To make it dairy-free, use dairy-free margarine.

Luscious lemon cake
Contains wheat, gluten, dairy and egg.

Chocolate orange cake
Contains wheat, gluten, dairy and egg.

Pink layer cake
Contains wheat, gluten, dairy and egg. To make it dairy-free, replace the whipped cream with vanilla buttercream (page 376) made with dairy-free margarine and water instead of milk.

Vanilla cheesecake
Contains wheat, gluten, dairy and egg. To make it wheat- and gluten-free, use wheat- and gluten-free biscuits.

Sticky chocolate cake
Contains wheat, gluten, dairy and egg.

Pineapple cake
Contains wheat, gluten, dairy and egg.

Pumpkin cake
Contains wheat, gluten, dairy and egg. To make it dairy-free, use dairy-free margarine and dairy-free chocolate.

Raspberry swirl cake
Contains wheat, gluten, dairy and egg.

Sweetie cake
Contains wheat, gluten, dairy and egg.

Blueberry cheesecake
Contains wheat, gluten, dairy and egg. For a wheat- and gluten-free version, use wheat- and gluten-free biscuits.

Strawberry shortcake
Contains wheat, gluten, dairy and egg.

Stripey cake
Contains wheat, gluten, dairy and egg.

Raspberry & almond cake
Contains wheat, gluten, egg and nuts. To make it wheat- and gluten-free, use wheat- and gluten-free baking powder.

Castle cake
Contains wheat, gluten, dairy and egg. To make it dairy-free, use dairy-free margarine and replace the milk with soya milk.

Butterfly cake
Contains wheat, gluten, dairy and egg.

Rich chocolate cake
Contains wheat, gluten, dairy and egg.

Marshmallow & chocolate cake
Contains wheat, gluten, dairy and egg.

White chocolate gateau
Contains wheat, gluten, dairy and egg.

Chocolate lime surprise cake
Contains wheat, gluten, dairy and egg.

Lemon drizzle cake
Contains wheat, gluten, dairy and egg. To make it wheat- and gluten-free, use wheat- and gluten-free baking powder. To make it dairy-free, use dairy-free margarine. To make the chocolate version dairy-free, use dairy-free margarine and dairy-free chocolate.

Light chocolate layer cake
Contains wheat, gluten, dairy, egg and nuts.

White chocolate mousse cake
Contains wheat, gluten, dairy and egg.

Extremely chocolatey cake
Contains wheat, gluten, dairy and egg.

Chocolate & nut cake
Contains wheat, gluten, dairy, egg and nuts. To make it wheat- and gluten-free, use wheat- and gluten-free baking powder.

White chocolate cheesecake
Contains wheat, gluten, dairy and egg. To make it wheat- and gluten-free, use wheat- and gluten-free biscuits.

Breads & scones

Home-made bread
Contains wheat, gluten and optional seeds. Seeds may not be suitable for those with nut allergies.

Iced fruit loaf
Contains wheat, gluten, dairy and egg.

Cinnamon bread rolls
Contain wheat, gluten, dairy and egg.

Stollen
Contains wheat, gluten, dairy, egg and nuts.

Kringle
Contains wheat, gluten, dairy and egg.

Cinnamon buns
Contain wheat, gluten, dairy and egg.

Tiny pizzas
Contain wheat, gluten and dairy.

Deep-pan pizza
Contains wheat, gluten and dairy.

Fruit scones
Contain wheat, gluten and dairy.

Little cheese scones
Contain wheat, gluten and dairy.

Pastries & tarts

Pear & cranberry pies
Contain wheat, gluten and dairy.

Cheese twists
Contain wheat, gluten, dairy, egg and optional seeds. Seeds may not be suitable for those with nut allergies.

Feta cheese pies
Contain wheat, gluten, dairy and egg.

Plum puff tarts
Contain wheat, gluten and dairy.

Chocolate tarts
Contain wheat, gluten and dairy.

Mini raspberry swirls
Contain wheat, gluten and dairy.

Choux buns
Contain wheat, gluten, dairy and egg.

Crispy apple pies
Contain wheat, gluten and dairy.

Raspberry profiteroles
Contain wheat, gluten, dairy and egg.

Little fruit tarts
Contain wheat, gluten, dairy and egg. To make them egg-free, don't use lemon curd.

Mini savoury pastries
Contain wheat, gluten and dairy.

Chocolate profiteroles
Contain wheat, gluten, dairy and egg.

Pear & almond tart
Contains wheat, gluten, dairy, egg and nuts.

Strawberry tarts
Contain wheat, gluten, dairy and egg.

Butterscotch profiteroles
Contain wheat, gluten, dairy and egg.

Mince pies
Contain wheat, gluten, dairy, egg and optional nuts.

Mini éclairs
Contain wheat, gluten, dairy and egg.

Chocolate & raspberry tart
Contains wheat, gluten, dairy and egg.

Tomato tarts
Contain wheat, gluten and dairy.

Quiche
Contains wheat, gluten, dairy and egg.

Index

Senior designer: Helen Lee

Additional design by Nicola Butler, Helen Edmonds, Non Figg, Louise Flutter, Nelupa Hussain, Emma Latham, Stephen Lambert, Nancy Leschnikoff, Antonia Miller, Mike Olley, Kate Rimmer, Pete Taylor & Josephine Thompson

Digital imaging by Emma Julings, John Russell & Nick Wakeford

With thanks to Lucy Bowman, Rachel Firth, Rebecca Gilpin, Sarah Khan, Sue Meredith, Leonie Pratt & Will Severs